Future of Social Work Research

Selected Papers
National Conference on the Future of Social Work Research
(1978 : San Antonio, Tex.)   October 15–18, 1978,
San Antonio, Texas

DAVID FANSHEL, *DSW, Editor*
Professor, Columbia University
School of Social Work
New York, New York

NATIONAL ASSOCIATION OF SOCIAL WORKERS, INC.
1425 H Street, N.W., Washington, D.C. 20005

International Standard Book No.: 0–87101–084–4

Library of Congress Catalog Card No.: 79–92733

NASW Catalog No.: CBQ–084–C

Printed in the U.S.A.

Designed by The Wenk Organization

Contents

Contributors

Positions are those held at the time of the conference (October 1978)

DAVID FANSHEL, DSW (EDITOR)
  Professor, Columbia University School of Social Work, New York, New York
SCOTT BRIAR, DSW
  Dean and Professor, School of Social Work, University of Washington, Seattle
CLAUDIA J. COULTON, PH.D.
  *Assistant Professor, School of Applied Social Sciences, Case Western
  Reserve University, Cleveland, Ohio*
ROSE DOBROF, DSW
  *Professor, School of Social Work, and Director, Brookdale Center on Aging,
  Hunter College of the City University of New York, New York*
RONALD A. FELDMAN, PH.D.
  *Professor, George Warren Brown School of Social Work, Washington
  University, St. Louis, Missouri*
ROBERT B. HILL, PH.D.
  Director of Research, National Urban League, Washington, D.C.
WYATT C. JONES, PH.D.
  *Professor of Social Research, Florence Heller Graduate School of
  Advanced Studies in Social Welfare, Brandeis University, Waltham,
  Massachusetts, and Research Sociologist, Veterans Administration
  Medical Center, Brockton, Massachusetts*
HAROLD LEWIS, DSW
  *Dean and Professor, Hunter College School of Social Work, Hunter College
  of the City University of New York, New York*
ABRAHAM MONK, PH.D.
  *Brookdale Professor of Gerontology, Columbia University School of Social Work,
  New York, New York*
WILLIAM J. REID, DSW
  *George Herbert Jones Professor of Social Work, School of Social Service
  Administration, University of Chicago, Chicago, Illinois*
JACK ROTHMAN, PH.D.
  Professor, School of Social Work, University of Michigan, Ann Arbor
FREDRICK W. SEIDL, PH.D.
  *Associate Director and Associate Professor, School of Social Work,
  University of Wisconsin–Madison*
EDWIN J. THOMAS, PH.D.
  *Professor of Social Work and of Psychology, School of Social Work,
  University of Michigan, Ann Arbor*
PETER J. TROPMAN, MSSW
  *Administrator, Division of Policy and Budget, Department of Health and Social
  Services, Madison, Wisconsin*

Foreword

THE NATIONAL ASSOCIATION of Social Workers inherited a concern for research, both in its origin in 1955 from seven professional associations and in its mission. The high value placed on research had been reflected in the traditions of all seven predecessor organizations. The particular identification with the research needs of the profession had come from a dedicated group of social work researchers organized as the Social Work Research Group and was continued in an NASW Research Council. From many of the conferences held by this group over several decades came a series of NASW monographs dealing with problems of research methodology and research focused on substantive interests of the profession. These publications constitute an important part of social work's research-oriented literature.

During the "cultural revolution" of the 1960s and the early 1970s, this spark of concern in NASW was kept alive by periodic emanations from the Publications Department. With the financial, organizational, and program maturity of NASW in the 1970s came increased capacity to execute the professional association's basic responsibility to stimulate and develop social work research. The Conference on the Future of Social Work Research, with great indebtedness to the wisdom of Dr. Juan Ramos and the National Institute of Mental Health, is the landmark for the NASW effort.

The conference, which provided the impetus for this publication, was held in San Antonio, Texas, October 15–18, 1978. It was organized to bring practitioners and researchers together to consider the current state of research being carried out under social work auspices. The organizers of the conference were particularly interested in the quality of the contribution of research to practice and the future course of social work's research effort.

Those involved in the initiation and planning of the conference as well as the writers of papers and attendees shared the view that the research productivity of social work deserved a high priority in the association's program efforts and concerns. It was further agreed that the long separation between "researchers" and "practitioners" was a continual barrier to professional progress, and a joining of forces in a collaborative spirit was needed to further developments in this area.

The increasing expansion of service programs and the demands of legislators and other concerned citizens for evidence that such programs are indeed helpful to users pose a challenge to the profession. Aside from the matter of accountability, however, the conference has stressed the need to use empirical investigations to help shape service programs. Decisions about how to better serve client populations should be informed by operations of monitoring agencies in the course of service delivery rather than treating programs as static phenomena.

It is our hope that the aspirations for a new flowering of practice-oriented research reflected in these pages will soon come to fruition. The role of NASW as a catalytic agent for such research, one of its most important missions, is indispensable to achieving this goal.

CHAUNCEY A. ALEXANDER
Executive Director
NASW

Washington, D.C.
October 1, 1979

Preface

WE ARE PLEASED to be able to make these articles available. They were commissioned by the National Association of Social Workers for the National Conference on the Future of Social Work Research, which was convened in San Antonio, Texas in mid-October 1978. This important professional meeting was the outgrowth of a concern that the research underpinnings of professional social work were not yet secure and required scrutiny. The need for a more adequate understanding of recent trends had been keenly felt by both researchers and practitioners, and this concern was shared by the National Institute of Mental Health of the U.S. Department of Health, Education, and Welfare, which provided generous funding in support of the conference.

By publishing these articles, NASW is following through on its commitment to research as an essential ingredient of professional life. There was a strong feeling among the participants at the San Antonio conference that much needed to be done to expand the production of research that would help build the profession's knowledge base and improve the delivery of social services.

The articles were written by the authors after general consultation with the editor about the major content areas that would be covered. All the writers have had quite substantial experience in social work research, although their interests and backgrounds are quite varied. Collectively, the articles serve to highlight strengths and weaknesses in the research domains covered and point the way to more productive emphases and developments for the future.

One cannot speak too highly of the labors of the NASW staff, who did much of the spadework in the organization of the San Antonio conference. Elizabeth A. Keith provided stalwart service in her NASW staff assignment as project manager. She executed her responsibilities with consummate skill and considerable investment of her creative energies. Jessie Reed, also of the NASW staff, provided superb backup support in the management of the project.

Major support for undertaking the conference came from Chauncey A. Alexander, executive director, and Leonard W. Stern, associate executive director. Their initiative and follow-through provided the main impetus for obtaining the NIMH grant.

The idea of a conference on the future of social work research grew out of Chauncey Alexander's concept that the professional association should develop a national social work research communication center to act as a clearinghouse, catalyst, and developer for social work research. A serendipitous discussion between Mr. Alexander and Dr. Juan Ramos of NIMH brought about the result.

The initial planning for the conference began in the editorial committee of *Social Work Research and Abstracts* under the leadership of William J. Reid, editor-in-chief. The committee was in a particularly advantageous position to gain perspectives on the different trends characterizing social work research, since its function required review of research articles being submitted to the journal. The ranks of the committee were augmented to create a conference planning task force. The success in carrying through the project owes much to the work of this group. Membership of the task force included Alexander J. Allen (National Urban League), Scott Briar (University of Washington), Lela Costin (University of Illinois), Ina J. Javellas (Oklahoma State Department of Mental Health), Dorothy H. Miller (Scientific Analysis Corporation), William J. Reid (University of Chicago), Jack Rothman (University of Michigan), Armando J. Sanchez (San Jose State University), Frederick W. Seidl (University of Wisconsin–Madison), and the editor, David Fanshel (Columbia University).

A special contribution was made at the conference by individuals who agreed to chair the six discussion groups, each of which met for five sessions. These individuals were Lewis W. Carr (Howard University), Glenn S. Allison (NASW), Roger R. Miller (Smith College), Sidney E. Zimbalist (University of Illinois), Delores A. Taylor (United Way of Greater Milwaukee), and Katherine M. Wood

(Rutgers University). Their assistance was invaluable.

I should like to thank Beatrice N. Saunders, director of publications of NASW, for her thoughtful advice in the preparation of this volume. There is by now an army of writers and editors in the profession who are indebted to Mrs. Saunders for the benefits they have received from her talents, energy, and publishing wisdom. It is painful to consider where we would be without her. A note of appreciation is also due Rick Langstaff for his editing labors and Ellen Bilofsky for her liaison work.

The National Institute of Mental Health funded the project. Dr. Juan Ramos of NIMH was most helpful in recognizing the value of such a landmark conference and supporting the planning activity that went into its creation.

DAVID FANSHEL

New York City
October 1, 1979

PART 1

Trends and Future Perspectives

The Future of Social Work Research: Strategies for the Coming Years

DAVID FANSHEL

EVERY PROFESSION must systematically carry out high-quality research about its practices if its performance in the service of clientele is to remain effective and up to date. A sustained and creditable program of research is also essential to a profession's self-respect and to its ability to maintain the positive regard of outsiders whose opinions help support and legitimize the profession's endeavors. No profession can afford any equivocation on the importance of research.

These sentiments were shared by many of the participants in the National Conference on the Future of Social Work Research. As Specht pointed out a few years ago, the alternative course for social work is deprofessionalization. His message had a sense of urgency:

> Research should be the major area of knowledge around which all others are built. Schools preparing people to teach, administer, plan, and evaluate social welfare programs should insist that their curricula be founded firmly on knowledge and

facts. Compassion and commitment in social welfare should be directed by well-defined competence, as it has not been in social work.[1]

What is the state of the research enterprise in social work? This was a dominant concern of the conference. During the preceding two decades, a number of trends had emerged that gave a mixed picture of the nature and quality of social work research. There was a sense, for example, that distinct advances in research productivity had been achieved since the early 1950s. A substantial cadre of social work researchers had emerged, and some of the published literature demonstrated a high degree of methodological sophistication. The appearance of two new research journals also contributed to the sense of growth.

Other trends were less promising. Members of the profession had frequently expressed concern about the drying up of some sites in which research had formerly been carried out. This loss appeared to limit opportunities for graduates of doctoral programs who sought to launch research careers. At the same time, the increased technical sophistication of many researchers appeared to be offset by a growing estrangement from research of a large number of social work practitioners who found recent research publications incomprehensible and irrelevant.

All these developments contributed to the timeliness of the National Conference on the Future of Social Work Research, which was held in San Antonio, Texas, on October 15–18, 1978. The conference was sponsored by the National Association of Social Workers (NASW), which received major support for the gathering through a contract with the National Institute of Mental Health. The papers for the conference, including the articles that appear in this volume, were written by invitation of the coordinating committee of the conference. The papers were distributed in advance to the almost two hundred people who attended the meetings in San Antonio. The participants formed six task groups, each of which met for five working sessions to discuss issues raised by the papers, by the coordinating committee, and by the participants.

This article summarizes some of the key issues discussed at the conference, which can be identified as follows:

1. Important changes have taken place in the location and sponsorship of social work research, with universities, private management firms, and departments of state and local governments replacing agencies in these roles.

2. Social work research is growing in its methodological rigor and sophistication, and the new methodologies are enabling the investigators to study an increasingly wide variety of phenomena in greater depth than before.

3. The tendency of social work researchers to emphasize clients' problems and deficits instead of their strengths often reduces the usefulness and validity of research findings.

4. Partly as a consequence of the increasingly technical nature of the social work research, practitioners are finding the published results irrelevant to their needs, but many conference participants were hopeful that an emphasis on practice-relevant research, along with certain changes in social work education, could reduce the rift between research producers and research consumers.

5. Computerized information systems are increasing in importance as research and management tools.

6. Social work's long period of absorption in several unflattering studies of the effectiveness of casework has given the profession some perspective on the usefulness and meaning of evaluation.

7. Decades of experience in conducting empirical studies have greatly expanded the profession's knowledge of what makes one research project succeed and another fail.

8. NASW has the potential to contribute to the profession's research enterprise by assuming a more active role in the pursuit of research grants.

It should be noted that this list and the elaboration of it that follows reflect the writer's sense of what emerged from the conference as recurrent and important points of view. They are hardly objective, however, and are no doubt influenced by personal perspectives developed in over twenty-five years of engagement in social work research.

Shifting Sites of Research

The view that the principal location of research activity is shifting away from agencies is an impressionistic one, but it was referred to repeatedly at the conference. It may appear overstated to some readers, and significant exceptions to the trend can be identified. One exception—the national census carried out, in 1960 and 1970, by the Family Service Association of America of clients served by its member agencies—is an example of the use of survey technology on an impressive scale. The published results increased the profession's understanding of important service delivery issues.[2] Nonetheless, as funds to support services have become difficult to obtain, the social service agency that is willing to invest even modest portions of its budget in research has increasingly become a rarity. This trend threatens to undermine the research productivity of the profession, particularly in the area of practice research. A similar decline in research activity has taken place in community planning agencies, which, from the years just after World War II through the 1960s, had been important sponsors of social work research. The discernible decline in research investments by these organizations occurred at a time when many community planning agencies faced extinction.

This decline in the importance of agency-based research is partly responsible for the cloudy picture facing those who wish to develop careers in social work research. Just as new doctoral graduates in physics, astronomy, philosophy, and other sciences and humanities have been finding the employment market grim in recent years, new DSWs and Ph.D.s in social work have begun to find that there are few job outlets for their investigative skills in social welfare organizations. Although the recent doctoral graduate is still likely to find employment possibilities in social work research, there is no plenitude of jobs and no certainty that investment in doctoral training will lead to paid work in research.[3]

University and Government Sponsorship. Although research activity has decreased significantly in direct service agencies, national social welfare organizations, and such organizations as community councils, federations of agencies, and community interest groups, university-based research has grown continually for several decades and has produced a large body of scholarly work in the form of books, monographs, and articles as well as unpublished doctoral dissertations. This development can be explained by a number of factors. Universities expect their professional schools to meet academic standards in building faculty, and an increasingly important criterion for appointment and tenure is whether a candidate has engaged in scholarly research of good quality and whether this is reflected by publication in refereed journals and other forums.

At the same time, the university environment, with its intellectuals from diverse disciplines, offers a context in which scholarliness is valued and stimulated. In university committees, social work professors find themselves interacting with faculty from the pure and applied sciences, particularly with professors from the behavioral and social sciences. Doctoral candidates in social work must defend their dissertations before committees that often include faculty from other academic disciplines. The relationships between social work faculty and scholars from other disciplines often grow close and in some instances lead to interdisciplinary collaboration. Such on-campus experiences provide new frames of reference for the scholarly tasks facing social work and reinforce an emphasis on scientific principles in the pursuit of knowledge.

A third reason for the growth of social work research on university campuses is that federal and state funding agencies favor research that originates at such sites. Peer review panels established to scrutinize applications for research funds have heavy representation from academic settings, and there is a tendency to look with more favor on research proposals that reflect the language and concepts of the scientific community.

Like the universities, state and local governments are gaining importance as sponsors of social work research. The direct involvement of these levels of government is primarily in research dealing with human services funded through Title XX and other federal programs. Almost all state departments of social services maintain research departments, although the quality of the efforts varies from state to state. The contribution from this source to the literature of the profession has been more modest in quality and quantity than might have been expected, but the increased activity in this area portends a higher yield of published materials. Tropman's article in this volume describing an ambitious research effort by a state department of human services suggests what the future may hold.

Research by Private Management Firms.
The influence of private management firms in research dealing with the delivery of social services has become more visible in recent years. These organizations have found it profitable to take advantage of the federal government's change in emphasis from funding research on the basis of unsolicited grant applications to contracting for research. These firms employ scholars from the social sciences and other academic fields, especially persons trained in economics, operations research, and sociology, and the firms' staffs have become knowledgeable about the human services in recent years. As these organizations gained finesse in grantsmanship, they garnered an appreciable share of the funding available for research in the social services and related areas.

Conference participants felt they understood the appeal that proposals submitted by private management firms have for federal agencies. The firms package proposals quickly and carry out studies in the relatively short periods called for in federal requests for proposals. Despite this, conference participants expressed some misgivings about the research conducted by these private firms:

• The final reports produced by the firms are often shallow documents, and it is often clear that they have been mass produced. Much of this research is lackluster and not good enough to be published in professional or academic journals.

• The employees who produce the research reports for the private firms lack depth in the service fields they study. Their recommendations frequently have a superficial foundation in management science, but in actuality they promote neither sound service administration nor humane and effective practice.

In fairness, it must be noted that conference participants also pointed out the uneven performance of social work scholars in carrying through research projects under federal and state grants. Protracted delays in the completion of studies and even failures to complete investigations have been known to occur. Conference participants also conceded that not all studies carried out under social work auspices have led to findings that were published in the appropriate journals. Further, some of the final reports are as hackneyed as those produced by the "production mills." Nevertheless, a fairly large number of good quality research enterprises have been carried out under social work auspices, and many have been published as books and articles, thus entering the mainstream of professional communication.

Conference participants agreed that certain nonprofit organizations have earned the admiration of scholars for their research in the human services. The Poverty Research Institute at the University of Wisconsin, for example, has demonstrated what a massive concentration of well-trained scholars can produce. The field experiments to study income maintenance are only one part of the institute's large program of research.[4] The collective performance of the institute's interdisciplinary staff, which includes social work scholars, has been remarkable. A high level of productivity has also been demonstrated by such nonprofit organizations as the Urban Institute in Washington, D.C., and various interdisciplinary groups with strong interests in social policy issues have carried out research projects in the human services with considerable skill.

Social Work Responsibility. The shift in the locus of research activity from service agencies to universities, management firms, research institutes, and "think tanks" has been accompanied by other changes that will affect the social services in a variety of ways. In the simpler, earlier days of several decades ago, one could know something about most of the social work studies taking place across the country; recently research of relevance to the social services has spread out and become something of a large, if not vast, undertaking. The research is more interdisciplinary in character and reflects a concern with broad issues of social welfare.

Conference participants were unified in the view that the profession needs to struggle vigorously to retain its own research capacity and to increase the competence of its researchers and practitioner-researchers. It is important for social workers to study practice methods in areas in which the profession

has responsibility and to guard against the tendency to assign to other groups the task of validating practice approaches. It is necessary to resist a division of responsibilities in which social work would be assigned the doing while other professions and disciplines took on the intellectual tasks.

Quest for Research Methodologies

In recent years, improvement in the methodological rigor of social work research has been appreciable, and conference participants frequently cited published works that reflected growing sophistication in measurement techniques, in the use of research design, and in procedures of data analysis. This has come about because doctoral programs in graduate schools of social work and scholars trained in various academic disciplines helped create a pool of researchers with skills in such areas as the construction and testing of instruments, the use of laboratory techniques for experimentation, and the use of multivariate analyses of time-ordered data. The complexity of most of the phenomena of interest to social work made it necessary for social work education to give a high priority to the promotion of skill in research methodology. Gradually, social work researchers developed flexibility in using a range of methodologies to study social work methods and institutions. Thus, for example, qualitative or "naturalistic" approaches to describing agency clientele and service delivery situations came to be accepted as a way of illuminating professional practice.[5]

Maas observed that the quantity and quality of social work scholarship varies considerably from one field of practice to another.[6] Some fields, such as child welfare, show a high degree of research productivity; other practice fields have been relatively barren, producing only a meager amount of creditable empirical research. This uneven development appears to be related to federal funding policies, which favor targeted subject areas. Certain fields have greater attraction for social work researchers, and this also tends to create uneven development.

Methodological Variety. No single methodological approach to the conduct of social work research is adequate; the needs of the profession dictate that a pluralism prevail. Scholars' willingness to live with differences in investigative procedures and styles will create the best yield for social work. Sociologists prefer survey methods; anthropologists are inclined to use naturalistic field methods with a heavy emphasis on participant observation; and psychologists are strongly committed to experimental methods. Social work, however, has had no need to develop a special identification with any particular approach. The profession's research experience has been characterized by diversity and multiple communities of investigators. An investigator is often able to study any problem of interest to social workers with a number of available design options: descriptive cross-sectional surveys, longitudinal investigations of developmental processes, laboratory experiments, field experiments, single-subject research, naturalistic field research, or historical studies and social policy analyses using published materials.

With schools of social work based in universities that have a variety of academic disciplines, the possibilities for interdisciplinary learning and collaboration are numerous. Such collaboration can be highly productive. The writer's personal experience in teaming with the linguist Labov on the Columbia University campus and spending eleven years using linguistic methods to analyze the social work interview can be cited as a most rewarding experience.[7]

Community of Scholarship. In addition to maintaining a diversity of investigative procedures, the profession also needs to strengthen the sense that social work research originates from a community of scholars. A scientific ethos would protect the researchers against the biases that surround social welfare problems and the programs designed to ameliorate them. Whether the researcher is executing a laboratory experiment to test the manner in which social workers evaluate the behavior of their clients, carrying out a survey of how natural parents perceive agencies that provide foster care services to their children, or living in a ghetto community to obtain firsthand knowledge of the natural support systems that enable poor people to survive, the rules of the scientific method should always obtain.[8]

Each investigative mode makes its own demands. The laboratory researcher has to be concerned with the verisimilitude of the experiment.[9] The survey researcher encourages respondents to reveal their true feelings by wording questions in an unbiased manner and by creating a neutral interviewing environment.[10] The field investigator strives to make sense out of copious notes from field observations and to insure that what the final report claims to see in a community is really there for other observers to report.[11] The reader of such research has the right to remain skeptical if the researcher has not adequately explained how the methodology controlled for bias.

Coping Strengths

Despite advances in its methodological rigor and sophistication, social work research is often compromised by a cognitive stance that comes all too easily to a profession intent on perceiving needs and helping—the tendency of social workers to view clients from a perspective that focuses exclusively on problems and deficits and that neglects strengths and adaptive capabilities. This view, which is presented in this volume by Hill, drew considerable support from participants at the conference. Minority clients in particular appear to be subject to such stigmatization, and there is concern that this is true both of practice as carried out in social agencies and of research as conducted by social work investigators.

A possible corrective to this myopic view of the world would be to conduct research about people who are not clients of social agencies. Many poor families—white and minority—live on the edge of disaster. Although they are poor, are housed in mean circumstances, and often lack basic amenities, they somehow remain intact, their children do not enter foster care, and the youngsters manage to stay clear of serious criminal involvement. Why do some families survive and others succumb in the face of massive adversity?

Shifting the focus of research from the weaknesses of clients to the strengths of survivors poses a challenge. Nonclient populations may be more difficult to study, and obtaining useful information about them is likely to require a special quality of inventiveness on the part of investigators. Gaining access to the average family in a black ghetto or barrio is only one aspect of the problem; one also has to win the confidence of the persons involved. Lewis, Liebow, and others have shown that creative and dedicated investigators using the field methods of anthropology can secure a high measure of cooperation from subjects whose lifestyles and conditions are vastly different from those of the investigator.[12]

Gulf between Practitioners and Researchers

Since university-based graduate schools of social work have assumed increased importance in the production of research for social work practice, their relationship to the social agencies that deliver social services bears examination. The gulf between the teachers in the schools and the agency practitioners who serve clientele is often talked about. The situation can be contrasted with the collaboration between hospitals and medical schools: that partnership makes possible a natural tie-in between research scholars and those who provide professional services; the functions are often carried out by the same individuals. At present, formidable institutional boundaries often stand in the way of collaboration between researchers and practitioners.

A persistent complaint is that agencies are reluctant to open their doors to scholars eager to gain access to clientele and staff to study social work processes and outcomes. A countervailing theme from practitioners concerns the irrelevancy for practice of much of university-stimulated research. Both contentions underscore the need to repair and solidify the relationship between schools and agencies.

Researchers are challenged to produce knowledge useful in the delivery of service. They are further asked to respect the complexity of the tasks facing the service practitioner and to be realistic about the limitations of research methodologies in capturing that complexity. Researchers are seen as too often showing arrogance in their approach to practitioners, overestimating their own wisdom and productivity, and oversimplifying the challenges facing their co-professionals seeking to render effective services. Because they are not directly involved in the tasks of service delivery, researchers are prone to misperceive the challenges posed by clients, to disregard environmental constraints that limit solutions, and to misread the phenomena they are studying, such as the subtle psychosocial factors that cause clients to resist various offers of assistance.

Researchers have their own views about problems impeding collaboration. They report that practitioners are so embedded in their individual case situations that larger perspectives about clientele and their problems often elude them. Practitioners are said to show little appreciation for the insights offered by aggregated information and to profess firm knowledge of the basic essentials required for effective service delivery without demonstrating any scholarly underpinnings to support this knowledge. According to researchers, practitioners tend to perceive experiments to test the basic assumptions of practice as threatening, and they often show in their reactions to the results of research that such approaches to building knowledge are outside their frame of reference. In short, practitioners are asked to change basic attitudes.

A number of participants in the Conference on the Future of Social Work Research urged close collaboration between researchers and practitioners as a way of overcoming these barriers. They suggested experiments in which scholar-practitioners would be invited to participate in the life of the agency, become involved in service delivery tasks, and help develop a number of plans for research enterprises that researchers and practitioners would jointly conceive and carry out. Leading practitioners of the agency might, in turn, participate in classroom teaching and other academic assignments. Given the long-standing nature of the gulf between researchers and practitioners in social work, some conference attendees expressed doubt that such experiments could be promul-

gated on a large scale or that they would be successful even if the initial barriers were overcome. This skepticism was not universally shared, however.

Research in Search of a Readership. The absence of collaboration between researchers and practitioners was not the only part of the service-research gap that drew the attention of conference participants. The tendency of social workers not to utilize research as a guide to practice or even to read research articles was a frequent subject of discussion. This avoidance of essential intellectual work was established a decade ago in research by Rosenblatt, who reported that only 9 percent of the social workers who responded to his study said that they read research articles.[13] A more recent study by Austin indicated that this situation has not improved.[14]

The increased statistical sophistication of the published research may have exacerbated the problem in recent years, but some conference participants also expressed the view that practitioners have become less literate—that their ability to read technical research has declined. The responsibility for some of this incapacity can be laid at the doors of the graduate schools of social work. In recent years, the graduate schools have required fewer research courses of students, and most practice courses include little research content. It is ironic that at the same time professors are becoming more technically proficient researchers, their students are learning less and less about research.

Several conference participants described exceptions to the trend in the graduate schools of downgrading and isolating research. There were reports, for example, that faculty members who normally taught practice courses had begun to teach research courses and that research faculty have occasionally taught practice courses. Many conference participants strongly favored doing away with the artificial division between practice and research in graduate social work education. Such an approach has parallels in the structure of other university disciplines and would require that each faculty member demonstrate capability in a reasonably broad repertoire of research methodologies as well as interest and skill in substantive areas of social work practice or social welfare policy.

Conference participants expressed hope that the development of two new research journals in fall 1977—*Social Work Research and Abstracts*, the successor to *Abstracts for Social Workers*, and the *Journal of Social Service Research*—would result not just in a richer research literature for the profession, but also in increased consumption of research by practitioners. At present, however, the new journals' lists of subscribers remain modest, and most practitioners never get to see the journals. The task of securing appropriate articles also poses some problems. An ample supply of high-quality manuscripts is not yet guaranteed for the new publications, and the journals' sponsors must actively seek out articles.

A fundamental issue in the production and reporting of research concerns the recurrent question: For what audience is the research produced? The degree to which the new journals meet the needs of direct service practitioners, who constitute by far the largest group in the profession, may well determine their ability to attract wide readerships.

Researching Practice as Process. One type of research that practitioners tend to view as highly useful to the performance of professional tasks is the investigation of the transactions that routinely take place between social work practitioners, their clients, and relevant social institutions. These studies can usually be subsumed under the rubric "process research," and the practice arena is replete with opportunities for such research. Although the recurrent events of service delivery are experienced as routine occurrences, it has long been recognized that these events need to be comprehended more fully, particularly if the profession is to identify the skills required for competent professional performance. The following are some examples of practice phenomena that need such investigation:

1. Intake interviews, the initial encounters between potential recipients of service and those who provide them, are crucial in determining the course of cases. They are also highly dynamic events in which complex interactions take place. Creative and careful analyses of "openings" are required to determine why some encounters lead to good working relationships between the parties involved—the practitioners and clients—and others are marked by failure. Related questions that need investigation are: What professional techniques are associated with continuance of clients in service contacts? How does the agency environment that surrounds the encounter affect the participants? What are the predictors of early termination of contact?

2. Referrals should be examined for answers to the following questions: What helps clients make use of agencies other than the ones they have come to or are already connected with? How does a social worker in one service system obtain needed services for a client in another? What does the process look like when it is done well? What does it look like when the effort to make a connection for the client fails?

3. Contracting needs to be understood more fully: If a client is ready to continue with an agency, how are goals of treat-

ment established between the parties? What does contracting look like when it is skillfully carried out by the practitioner? What does an unskillful performance look like? How can the skills of contracting be sharpened?

4. The subject of caseloads also offers many opportunities for research: How is a caseload fashioned for a social worker? What is a manageable number of cases in each field of practice? What skills are required of the practitioner to render adequate service in the context of a given caseload—to give selective attention to emergency situations while other cases are on the back burner? What characteristics of caseloads are associated with the staff burn-out syndrome?

These and other generic activities of social workers can be studied in the context of process research using a variety of techniques. For example, an investigator can analyze transcripts of audiotapes of intake interviews to study how social workers orient new clients to the available services. Similarly, techniques of participant observation can be used to understand institutional programs carried out under social work auspices.

Since process studies attempt to portray practice as it is actually performed, they can produce, as a by-product of the research, an excellent yield of teaching materials for schools of social work and agency training programs. Such materials can also serve as source documents for the generation of practice theory, which can subsequently be tested in more focused descriptive studies as well as through the conduct of controlled experiments.

Computerized Information Systems

The tendency to foster cooperation between researchers and practitioners is one of the more surprising benefits of computerized information systems. Until recently, most social service systems have been administered with only the most primitive capacity for gathering and organizing information about the clientele and the services rendered. Legislative bodies and private funding sources have been especially frustrated in their efforts to obtain the information necessary to determine accountability, improve managerial efficiency, and expedite social planning. Although computers have been available for several decades, their use in management information systems for social services is a relatively recent phenomenon. It appears, however, that the time has come to exploit the new technology. As Reid said, the yield of useful data from this source is promising.[15]

Social services take place in time, and each resembles a longitudinal investigation. Clients gain access to the system as members of entering cohorts, stay connected with those rendering service for various lengths of time, and terminate their relationships when cases are closed. Time-series data can be gathered routinely at the opening encounters of clients and agency personnel, at some point further along the continuum of service delivery, and at closing. Agencies can also gather follow-up data through routine periodic contacts with clients.[16]

The gathering of social service data through computerized information systems requires collaboration between practitioners and researchers if the yield of useful knowledge is to be maximized. Routinely gathered service information has as much claim to being called data as that provided by a social survey of households or data obtained through a field experiment. Consultation with researchers about data elements to be included in such undertakings helps the practitioner take into account the variables in previous studies which have been completed in that area of practice. The researcher can also collaborate with the practitioner in simplifying the wording of data elements, constructing codes, testing practitioners' understanding of the data system, and assaying its reliability and validity. Developing plans for extracting useful knowledge about the service system and its clientele is also a likely area for collaboration.

A continuous flow of information from direct service practitioners makes possible a relatively new kind of research enterprise. Changes in the demographic characteristics of new clients can be monitored. Routinely accumulating information about the types of problems different categories of clients bring to agencies and the expectations clients have of services can help in planning programs. Gathering and organizing administrative service data provide a picture of the number of interviews with clients, referrals to other agencies, and similar phenomena.

The routine nature of data collection in computerized systems assures a continuous updating of information. The analysis of such data can also become a routine procedure through the creation of software programs that produce reports containing simple frequency distributions, cross-tabulations, and other forms of aggregated information. The data files of individual agencies can thus be analyzed periodically without a researcher on the premises, and larger units, such as federations of agencies, county units, and statewide public departments, can have their data files accessed and reported on without a single word being typed by a secretary.[17]

Evaluations of Social Work

During the past two decades social work has undergone an interesting, if somewhat painful, experience in having its efforts subjected to systematic evaluation. A number of creatively contrived field studies have shown that untreated groups fare as well as clients who have received social work treatment.[18] The full picture of this type of evaluative research is more mixed than some recognize, however, and challenges to the bleak view of social work effectiveness have also appeared in the literature.[19]

As was evident at the conference, the profession has acquired a degree of wisdom about evaluations of effectiveness, which can be summarized as follows:

1. It is foolish and unseemly to become excessively defensive in the face of adverse findings. Given the severe nature of the problems targeted for intervention, it may well be unreal to expect more promising outcomes.

2. The social work profession may have matured so that it will no longer blithely claim a capacity to transform people or eliminate problems which are rooted in pernicious social circumstances. Such assertions are based more in fancy than in reality. The claim that social casework could make a major impact on problems of economic dependency led to the 1962 Amendments to the Social Security Act, but resulted in the profession looking foolish and winding up with egg on its collective face.

3. Social work need not respond to every invitation to evaluate its efforts. Some contemplated enterprises rest on patently absurd foundations—for example, that school failures of poor and minority children can be overcome through personal counseling, although the school as a social institution is not subject to change; that persons who are not motivated to seek help for their problems can be recruited and treated with the same effectiveness as clients who come on their own volition; and that the politics surrounding a field of practice do

not affect a decision about participation in an evaluation.

4. The evaluation of effectiveness remains an important professional obligation. The public that supports and makes use of the social services has the right to know that programs are under continuous scrutiny by researchers. This insures that ineffective approaches to human problems can be modified or abandoned and that new avenues of assistance will be sought when necessary. Not wishing to become involved in foolhardy evaluative ventures does not obviate the need to be accountable on appropriate occasions.

5. The issue of effectiveness has perhaps been used in a tyrannizing way and overemphasized at the expense of research that would illuminate the treatment processes used by practitioners. Evaluative studies are not the only investigations that are useful to the profession. This is particularly true of new fields of service in which interventive procedures are being improvised and are not yet based on extensive experience.

6. Research that enables professionals to "engineer their product"—help shape the modes of intervention—may be highly useful and ought to be promoted.

Some Lessons in Research

The experience of conducting empirical studies has also enriched the profession's wisdom about how to undertake successful research. The following are some of the lessons that received attention during discussions at the San Antonio conference:

1. Smaller may be better. Large grants of money do not always insure a useful research product. Some enterprises have been so grandiosely conceived and made so elaborate that their published reports have never seen the light of day. They collected masses of data, and the re-

searchers attempted some analysis, but closure by way of published material eluded the investigators. By contrast, modest undertakings have often been productive and useful. Some investigators have even done the outlandish—they have produced creditable scholarly work without funding. Such individuals have discovered that it does not always require a research grant to scrutinize practice, to collect relatively simple data, and to do analysis. It may free some scholars not to have to tailor their research to the constraints of requests for proposals, to the advice of teams that visit the research site, or to the conventions of mainstream research organizations.

2. Replicating promising studies may be a more efficient way to accumulate knowledge than to undertake new ventures. This type of research is too often overlooked by social work researchers. Some of the most promising studies, such as those reported in Reid and Shyne's *Brief and Extended Casework* and Thomas and McLeod's *In-Service Training and Reduced Caseloads*, have never been replicated.[20]

3. Studies clustered around core areas of interest often produce a higher yield of knowledge than unrelated studies. For example, in the late 1950s a group of scholars collaborating under the leadership of Bieri at the Columbia University School of Social Work produced important studies on the nature of the clinical judgments exercised by social workers.[21] Other clusters of studies carried out under the leadership of Reid and Rosen were similarly productive.[22]

4. The social agency should appear more frequently as a variable. Just as the hospital is a likely site for the investigator of medical practice, the classroom for the educational researcher, and the courtroom for the student of legal practice, so the social agency is an important phe-

nomenon for those studying social work practice. Studies of agencies, public and private, have been rare, however.[23] Since most social workers tend to work in agencies rather than in private practices, this gap in the research literature is a serious one. Field investigations using techniques of participant observation should be able to illuminate the ethos of the social agency in ways that can help program managers humanize service delivery systems.

5. Social work institutions and practices are long overdue for inspection; many of the processes and procedures developed by the social work profession have not been adequately studied. The system of supervision, for example, is taken quite seriously and it is an object of controversy. Yet, in a recent textbook on the subject, Kadushin observes that "the literature of social work supervision is notable for the general absence of empirical research."[24] A similar state of affairs exists in the practice of social work consultation. As Kadushin notes,

> One of the striking features of the literature of evaluation consultation is the very limited number of studies involving social workers as consultees and the almost complete absence of control studies of social work consultants identified as such.[25]

Even as fundamental a phenomenon as the "interview" has begun to be studied only recently.[26]

6. Enhancing professional skills is the ultimate quest of research, and studies that would help social workers to perform their jobs with greater skill, whether in direct practice, planning, or policy work, would be valued by many in the profession. Yet such research is scarce and apparently not easy to carry out. The work of the psychologists Truax and Carkhuff in identifying accurate empathy, nonpossessive warmth, and therapeutic genuineness as important ingredients in effective counseling and therapy has not

had its parallel in social work research. The notable exceptions have been the achievements of Thomas, Fischer, Gambrill, and others who have used behavioral or eclectic approaches to the performance of practice tasks and have clarified the nature of behaviors regarded as skillful.[27]

NASW and the Research Mission

Many of those absorbed in social work research speak with a sense of nostalgia of earlier years in which the research constituency within the profession had its own organizational entity. It was first called the Social Work Research Group, and upon the founding of NASW, it was called the Social Work Research Section. In 1964 it became the Research Council. It has been alleged that since the dissolution of the Research Council, NASW has lacked a mechanism to promote research within the profession. Past organizational arrangements made it possible to garner a more adequate share of staff services from the association; to engage in more program activity, such as the convening of working conferences; and to promote the special interests of working researchers.

The desire to make the research mission of the profession a widely shared one, an aspiration frequently voiced at the conference, makes it questionable that a return to a specialized membership unit within the association can be contemplated. Such a move would only reinforce the insularity of social work researchers.

Nevertheless, the association can undertake a variety of actions supportive of social work research. There is sentiment for the formation of a research clearinghouse within NASW. This might contribute to the association's capacity to assemble information and enable interested members to know about projects being funded in their fields. The association could further become instrumental in bringing together scholars and practitioners working in the same area of interest.

NASW also has the potential to play a more active role in the process of assigning research grants. Many participants in the conference agreed that the profession should make a more effective and meaningful contribution in several areas of the grant process:

1. Some of the research priorities specified by granting agencies in recent years would likely have been improved if the social work profession had played a greater part in the process of problem formulation. Social workers need to develop clarity about their own research agendas and use this as a framework for attempting to influence the grant programs that support research and demonstration projects. The thinking of the profession is likely to be welcomed by the granting agencies; too often in the recent past the profession's views have simply not been forthcoming.

2. Social work as a profession has not been adequately represented on the advisory panels of some of the federal granting programs, and many in the profession fear that the absence of such representation may influence the decisions on grant applications from social work sources. It is not a matter of viewing the predilections of other professions and academic disciplines as less worthy of consideration in the competition for grants; nor is there any expectation that the standards for research enterprises be lowered for social work projects. In the politics of grantsmanship, however, different points of view about research and practice need to be represented on the panels. As a matter of professional self-interest, NASW should submit the names of leading practitioners and researchers as

nominees for review panels with the same frequency as do other professional groups and academic disciplines.

3. NASW should support legislation to sustain and increase the extramural research programs of funding agencies. Although in the past private foundations funded important studies of interest to social work and to the larger purposes of social welfare, the importance of these sources has diminished over the years compared to the federal government's investment in social research. Although contributions of the Department of Health, Education, and Welfare and other departments to research funding has become substantial, it has been subject to the ebb and flow of congressional dispositions. Federal financing of social research is subject to the same kinds of political pressures and lobbying by diverse groups as are nonresearch programs. It has become increasingly important to engage in advocacy to insure continued public investment in research and demonstration projects. Budget-cutting drives affect both services and research, and representatives of the association can make a valuable contribution by appearing before public legislative bodies to argue the cause of research.

Conclusion

The volume and quality of research carried out to support the activities of the social work profession and the purposes of social welfare are the collective responsibility of the profession and not just of a small band of researchers. The profession needs to face up to the changes in the places in which research is being carried out, to the growing sophistication of some research, and to the problems practitioners are having in identifying with the research effort. Certain messages emerged clearly from the Conference on the Future of Social Work Research:

1. Social work should end the artificial division between research and practice.

2. The profession should set its own research priorities instead of depending on funding sources to do this.

3. Research should be made increasingly useful to the practitioner.

4. The evaluation of social work services should continue, but research enterprises should also contribute to the understanding of practice issues.

5. Social work researchers should continue to increase their methodological flexibility and become more creative and even adventuresome in fashioning procedures suitable to the phenomena they are studying.

6. Nonclient populations should be studied for clues to the coping methods used by human beings to survive in the face of adversity.

7. NASW must organize a consciousness of the critical nature of research among its members, develop organizational supports to facilitate research activities by its members, and lobby for a larger public investment in social welfare.

Although much of the discussion at the conference related to the concerns of direct practice and hence was cast in micro terms, participants demonstrated great interest in research that dealt with larger societal issues. Several of the papers related to specific fields of practice, such as Coulton's overview of research about health services, Monk and Dobrof's contribution on services to the aged, and Feldman's analysis of research on youth-related issues. In each of these studies, the writer attempted to see the problems of serving a specialized client population in terms of a larger social framework. Issues of social policy were not seen as invariably separate from those of prac-

tice. The bodies of knowledge generated both from the societal perspective and from the narrowly focused concerns of service delivery were seen as potentially reinforcing one another.

NOTES AND REFERENCES

1. Harry Specht, "The Deprofessionalization of Social Work," Social Work, 17 (March 1972), p. 15.

2. Dorothy Fahs Beck, Patterns of Use of Family Agency Services (New York: Family Service Association of America, 1962); and Beck and Mary Ann Jones, Progress on Family Problems: A Nationwide Study of Clients' and Counselors' Views on Family Agency Services (New York: Family Service Association of America, 1973).

3. A survey of NASW membership in 1976 revealed that 1.13 percent of the male respondents and 0.89 percent of the females identified themselves as researchers. See David Fanshel, "Status Differentials: Men and Women in Social Work," Social Work, 21 (November 1976), p. 449.

4. David Krenshaw et al., The New Jersey Income Maintenance Experiment (3 vols.; New York: Academic Press, 1976 and 1977).

5. John E. Mayer and Noel Timms, The Client Speaks (New York: Atherton Press, 1970). See also David Fanshel and Freda Moss, Playback: A Marriage in Jeopardy Examined (New York: Columbia University Press, 1971).

6. Henry S. Maas, ed., Social Service Research: Reviews of Studies (Washington, D.C.: National Association of Social Workers, 1978), p. 7.

7. William Labov and David Fanshel, Therapeutic Discourse: Psychotherapy as Conversation (New York: Academic Press, 1977).

8. See, for example, Ben A. Orcutt, "A Study of Anchoring Effects in Clinical Judgment," Social Service Review, 38 (December 1964), pp. 408–417; Shirley Jenkins and Elaine Norman, Beyond Placement: Mothers View Foster Care (New York: Columbia University Press, 1975); and Carol B. Stack, All

Our Kin: Strategies for Survival in a Black Community (New York: Harper & Row, 1974).

9. Edwin J. Thomas, "The Experimental Interview: A Technique for Studying Casework Performance," *Social Work*, 5 (July 1960), pp. 52–58.

10. Herbert H. Hyman, *Survey Designs and Analysis: Principles, Cases and Procedures* (Glencoe, Ill.: Free Press, 1955).

11. Leonard Schatzman and Anselm L. Strauss, *Field Research: Strategies for a Natural Sociology* (Englewood Cliffs, N.J.: Prentice-Hall, 1973).

12. Oscar Lewis, *La Vida: A Puerto Rican Family in the Culture of Poverty, San Juan and New York* (New York: Random House, 1966); and Elliot Liebow, *Tally's Corner: A Study of Negro Street Men* (Boston: Little, Brown & Co., 1967).

13. Aaron Rosenblatt, "The Practitioner's Use and Evaluation of Research," *Social Work*, 13 (January 1968), p. 55.

14. David M. Austin, "Research and Social Work: Educational Paradoxes and Possibilities," *Journal of Social Service Research*, 2 (Winter 1978), pp. 159–176.

15. William J. Reid, "The Social Agency as a Research Machine," *Journal of Social Service Research*, (Fall 1978), pp. 11–23.

16. *See*, for example, Dorothy Fahs Beck and Mary Ann Jones, *How to Conduct a Client Follow-Up Study* (enlarged ed.; New York: Family Service Association of America, 1977).

17. *See*, for example, David Fanshel and John Grundy, *CWIS and CCRS Report Series* (New York: Columbia University School of Social Work, 1978).

18. Joel Fischer, ed., *The Effectiveness of Social Casework* (Springfield, Ill.: Charles C Thomas, 1976).

19. Dorothy Fahs Beck, "Research Findings on the Outcomes of Marital Counseling," *Social Casework*, 56 (March 1975), pp. 153–181.

20. William J. Reid and Ann W. Shyne, *Brief and Extended Casework* (New York: Columbia University Press, 1969); and Edwin J. Thomas and Donna L. McLeod, *In-Service Training and Reduced Caseloads: Experiments in a State Department of Welfare* (New York: Russell Sage Foundation, 1970).

21. James Bieri et al., *Clinical and Social Judgment: The Discrimination of Behavioral Information* (New York: John Wiley & Sons, 1966).

22. *See*, for example, William J. Reid and Laura Epstein, *Task-Centered Casework* (New York: Columbia University Press, 1972); Aaron Rosen and Dina Lieberman, "The Experimental Evaluation of Interview Performance of Social Workers," *Social Service Review*, 46 (September 1972), pp. 395–412; and Elisabeth Mutschler and Rosen, "Influence of Content Relevant and Irrelevant Client Verbalizations on Interview Affect," *Journal of Social Service Research*, 1 (Fall 1977), pp. 51–61.

23. For an important exception to the scarcity of studies on agencies, *see* Peter M. Blau, "Orientation toward Clients in a Public Welfare Agency," *Administrative Science Quarterly*, 5 (December 1970), pp. 341–361.

24. Alfred Kadushin, *Supervision in Social Work* (New York: Columbia University Press, 1976), p. 18.

25. Alfred Kadushin, *Consultation in Social Work* (New York: Columbia University Press, 1977), p. 188.

26. *See* Rosen and Lieberman, op. cit. *See also* Labov and Fanshel, op. cit.

27. *See*, for example, Edwin J. Thomas, *Marital Communication and Decision Making* (New York: Free Press, 1977); Joel Fischer, *Effective Casework Practice: An Eclectic Approach* (New York: McGraw-Hill Book Co., 1976); and Eileen D. Gambrill, *Behavior Modification: Handbook of Assessment, Intervention and Evaluation* (San Francisco: Jossey-Bass, 1977).

Toward a Planned Approach in Social Work Research

HAROLD LEWIS

MODERN RESEARCHERS often display the same kind of behavior that distinguished the food-sharing hominids from the great apes.[1] We social work researchers carry our questions, techniques, and husbanded data from place to place, project to project, agency to agency, in our heads, brief cases, computer printouts or in rough drafts of unfinished reports. We communicate by means of a special language, exchanging information about the past and future and regulating our relations to each other. To some extent, social work researchers view the acquisition of knowledge as a corporate responsibility. We define our home base in method, substantive field, and professional association, and while moving independently over the surrounding territory, we somehow manage to join up again, to touch base. We devote more time than most of our nonresearch colleagues to the acquisition of systematic knowledge, and this intellectual fare is

the equivalent of a high-protein diet. More than others, we subject this food for thought to considerable preparation by reducing, manipulating, and processing it, testing and critically debating its validity and reliability as a dish worth ingesting. We are constantly generating new kinds of equipment and technologies in our quest for this food, and we establish long-term bonds among ourselves, including accepting shared responsibilities for maintaining our funding sources, for inducting novices into our culture, and for restricting access to our family circle. We even go so far as to postpone the ingestion of our acquisitions until we find ourselves in home territory among our research kin, where we feel secure in sharing fully what we have learned with others who can truly appreciate our achievements.

All these behaviors and attitudes certainly distinguish us from the great apes. The corollary of this observation is the query, Are we ready to move forward to the next stage in the development of our species? Are we willing to consider a systematic approach to the future development of our professional endeavor? Ought we to have a research policy, as it were, for social work?[2]

Policy inevitably suggests planning, and planning for the acquisition of new knowledge suggests control, direction, and command of a process that most social work researchers perceive as essentially creative, serendipitous, and rich in unanticipated consequences. Policies and plans are usually the by-products of labor by committees, and one researcher's perceptions of such labor and its results in commercial research strikes a chord familiar to social work researchers:

> The best person to decide what research shall be done is the man who is doing the research. The next best is the head of the department. After that, you leave the field of the best persons and meet increasingly worse groups. The first of these is the research director who is probably wrong more than half the time, then comes a committee which is wrong most of the time. Finally, there is a committee of company vice-presidents, which is wrong all the time.[3]

The concern, of course, is that the creative process not be governed by plan, that research not be seen mechanistically even though it must remain subject to the market economy of satisfaction and rewards in the pursuit of longed-for truths.

Social work researchers, like their counterparts in other fields, are reluctant to reject policies and plans at the input, the funding end, since resources are finite. Allocations based on the priorities of the funding source are likely to reflect that source's notions about cost-benefit ratios, but we researchers still do everything possible to insure that the funding source understands how we see the nature of our labors. Practical consid-

erations have taught us to protest when we see allocations used to distort what we judge to be a sensible pattern of priorities, even though these protests are rarely carried to the point where we refuse to participate in studies that involve such distortions.

With these cautions noted, it may prove useful to explore the dimensions of a research policy for social work, stopping short of formulating a policy. Such an exploration, however, must be governed by certain obvious assumptions, which nevertheless need to be made explicit.

In speaking of research and its future, this article is primarily addressing those descriptive and analytical methods of knowing that can systematically add to knowledge. Research is hardly the source of all knowledge. Nor is research-produced knowledge always the most important knowledge for use in a practice. Research contributes to science, the professions, and the humanities, but is not synonymous with them. Knowledge resulting from research is necessarily tentative; it is subject to further clarification as methods of coming to know improve.

Research methods, which are descriptive and analytical, change over time by refinement, attrition, and accrual and by technical innovations. No consideration of research is complete if it ignores the discoveries and inventions that will help shape the future. Nor can it ignore the uneven development of method and those occasions when hardware outstrips substantive software.

This discussion of research must also concern itself with the future of the research worker, whose competence and prevalence will seriously influence the character and scope of research produced. Changes in the complement of intellect and the ingenuity devoted to research are undoubtedly influenced by societal commitments as well as the natural abilities of the available intellectual talents. All such contingencies directly affect the social work profession's capacity to carry out research.

Finally, the social work profession is aware of research as a service, a commodity of considerable cost, and an area of practice that is most demanding of those who would gain support for or work in a research project. Not unlike other forms of professional service, research practice is influenced by market conditions, policy preferences, and such contextual restraints as facilities, local traditions, timeliness, and feasibility. This discussion of research policies must be sensitive to these influences as well.

Policy

The development of a research policy for social work is contingent on a number of factors.[4] Those responsible for funding and doing research must agree that there is a need for such a policy. This agreement can only occur if philosophical differences leave room for such agreement, if the belief in the importance of research to the solution of problems confronting the profession is strong enough, and if there is acceptance of the possibility that research in social work can be carried out in a rational, planned way. If these conditions are met, an additional requirement is agreement on criteria for determining the structure and size of the enterprise responsible for developing a research policy. Once the research policy organization for the profession is established, it becomes necessary to specify the core functions of that organization. Such functions would include the responsibility (1) to coordinate, integrate, balance, and blend, (2) to stimulate, promote, develop, intensify, and improve, (3) to channel, decide, control, and super-

vise, (4) to devise plans and programs, (5) to improve prospective and current planning for all types of research, and (6) to work to promote the utilization of research results as part of the general policies of the profession.[5]

Aid to social work research has hitherto been inadequate. This is largely a reflection of the widespread perception of social work as a partisan activity. Although the funding for social work research has been limited, it is not difficult to cite instances of its misapplication or misdirection. Support has often been given not for well-founded economic, scientific, or professional reasons or on the basis of well-conceived plans, but for political or other partisan reasons. Predictably, research conducted under such circumstances has often been ineffective or wasteful. Unless the profession can have a systematic impact in the area of research policy, there is little chance of changing this inefficient and discouraging pattern.

Attributes of Social Work Research

Despite contrasting philosophical preferences, social work professionals agree on certain attributes of social work research. The points of agreement are strong enough to support a collective belief that research can make a significant contribution and to undergird an ideology that would justify a unified research policy for the profession.

Although policy choices and service decisions in social work are influenced by knowledge developed in the behavioral and social sciences and although social work research shares the methods of other behavioral and social sciences, social work research is nonetheless unique in its need to be sensitive to what is learned from and needed for the formulation of social work policies and the provision of direct services. Knowledge shared with other disciplines may inform practice in a general way and help to point the practitioner in a particular direction, but it is practice knowledge alone that is concerned with the how and that specifies the activity likely to benefit those in need of social services.

Social work research is consequently intentional—it seeks knowledge that will be put to use on behalf of those needing social work services. Whether one views research products as contributing to a practice science as distinct from a theoretical science or to a technological science as distinct from a pure science, or finds such distinctions of no import, social work professionals share the expectation that these products will provide guidance for policy and practice decisions.[6]

The outcomes sought in social work research are most useful when they inform principles of practice and generate rules for action. Principles of practice link propositions that can be or have been tested by research with ethical imperatives that operationalize professional values.[7] Rules that direct and command practice may or may not be justified by such principles. When they are so justified, practice is more likely to be principled.

Rational Planning

The question of whether it is possible to carry out a collective research effort in a planned, rational fashion is moot. The difficulties to be overcome if such intelligence is to be applied to the profession's research are considerable. An examination of the difficulties encountered by efforts to arrive at rational plans for developing research personnel, for funding research, and for promoting the utilization

of research findings will illustrate the complexities involved.

Personnel. A major goal of research policy is to achieve the maximum effect with an economy of means. Since means include personnel as a major item of cost, the recruitment, education, and placement of research workers is an important element in a policy on research. In the past, the profession has responded to the question of whether the number of social worker researchers should be increased with a chorus of "yes" reflecting a knee-jerk reaction to the blockbuster question. Ought not the profession's concern be to increase the few researchers who evidence originality? If we seek this latter objective, is it still appropriate to retain the approach of increasing our numbers, perhaps in hopes of creating a critical mass? Even though there is no shortage of problems to work on, the profession would have real difficulty knowing what use to make of an increased number of researchers. Experience provides evidence for the view that opportunities to engage in research are less widespread than those with the ability to do so; this is true even of our current limited numbers. Increasing the number of researchers might aggravate this situation. Researchers value diversity in subject matter for study and in methods for probing the secrets of phenomena. Would diversity in research talents be helped or endangered if the profession had a manpower policy for research and sought to implement it? These and similar manpower issues are most often resolved by market conditions—supply and demand, rewards and deprivations—not by rational planning.[8]

Funding. In 1900 there was no grantsmanship. There was little public and foundation funding for social work research or research careers in social work. Russell Sage underwrote the first Pittsburgh Survey, but Edith Abbott did not have a Fulbright when she journeyed to London at the turn of the century to study statistics. Nor did Isaac Rubinow have a Silberman Foundation Grant when he did his pioneering work in social security, and Mary Richmond was not a recipient of National Institute of Mental Health Career Teacher Award when she taught her first research class at the Philadelphia Training School for Social Work in 1909. The profession has come a long way from those days in generating support for social work research, but its approach to decisions about allocations remains seriously uninformed.

For example, the profession does not know to what extent its funding of research ought to be contingent on the association of the research effort with service programs in which social work is practiced. The profession has evolved the full complement of research departments, divisions, institutes, centers, and programs, and it has sponsored individual, group, and institutional research efforts, yet it has little solid knowledge of how well these organizational forms achieve particular research objectives. The profession has mingled public and private, tax and nontax monies and has supported large and miniscule fact-gathering studies. Yet there are no differentiating criteria regarding auspices and scope. The preferences of the funding sources provide the major, and possibly the sole, criteria for allocating resources, and too little is known about the impact of these criteria to evaluate their overall influence on the accrual of knowledge. The profession learned long ago that charitable monies do not necessarily go where the need is greatest.[9] Would it find similar constraints operating in the funding agendas that support social work research? Even if the profession could agree on a rational plan for the organization and support of research, could it then agree on what level of support should be provided and in what order of priority?

These and similar questions are currently responded to with arguments intended to persuade rather than enlighten. Unlike choices affecting personnel, the control and direction of funding are influenced far more by campaigns to educate or persuade than by market. Who should give how much to whom for how long? is obviously the sort of question all funding sources probably ask themselves when they make decisions. Unhappily, it is not the sort of question being asked for the whole research enterprise in social work. Some may prefer that it not be asked. Often the best way for all to arrive at a desired destination is to allow each to go a separate way. Social work research has tried this route, and it proved neither efficient nor effective.

Utilization. Whereas the market motivates personnel choices and persuasion shapes funding decisions, neither market nor persuasion significantly influences the utilization of research findings. The utilization of research findings in social work depends on social change; one cannot accomplish the first without implementing the second. Neither providence nor the pursuit of ideal goals by reasonable people can be expected to motivate agencies and programs to utilize the findings of research. It is possible to cite research findings that have accelerated social forces already in motion; other findings have highlighted and exacerbated the instabilities in social relationships that result from the lag between what society knows it should do and what it is doing to meet common human needs; but substantial change in the practice of social work, such as results when thousands of human wills act together to achieve their ends, is rarely the result of the utilization of research findings.

The criticisms of the researchers of the early survey movement—that their studies lacked methodological rigor and that their reports shed more heat than light on issues of professional concern—helped turn social work researchers away from the action focus of that movement. Instead, researchers set about developing counting boards, carrying out studies of limited scope, designing in-house statistical bookkeeping procedures, and pursuing the golden fleece—an infallible means for studying practice in a way that would prove it was worthwhile. Social work researchers have inevitably moved to accountability and evaluation studies, to priority determination and need studies, and away from what science is mostly about. Science is primarily concerned with the new, not with the expected. Original discovery is the central thrust of science, not proof. Only relatively recently, in the work of some of our more creative colleagues, has this thrust toward the new become evident. In subordinating reform to rigor, social work researchers have left behind an important insight about utilization that the reformers understood far better than anyone today. They thought that social research, to be utilized in seeking social change, must be conceived as a form of social action and a form of advocacy service. They denied the power of social science, in isolation, to change society and argued that in its essential methodologies the science of society either engaged with the society it sought to understand and change or paid the price of sterility by disengaging in order to achieve that incredibly elusive phenomenon in social research called objectivity.

Those researchers understood that doubt is akin to objectivity, that doubt inhibits action, and that when one seeks to know, one minimizes certainties and maximizes doubt. From this perspective, they could appreciate why social activists tended to approach social researchers with caution. As researchers intent on influencing policy and guiding practice, these reformers became activists.

Apparently, the inhibiting possibilities in the mind-set of those concerned with knowing, as distinct from the certainties of those intent on doing, have not been fully comprehended. Recently, Aaron concluded his analysis of policy and program efforts in the war on poverty and discrimination with the observation that formal evaluation and program analysis have evidenced profoundly conservative tendencies.[10] Evaluations of service delivery, which have consistently reported that social work practice produces no significant differences, have had a similar conservative tendency. Thus, it is not surprising that Aaron and others report that activists in both practice and policy realms decide on what they want to do and seek funding on the basis of these preferences, rather than let their actions be determined by research findings.[11] What is surprising is that at this late date, scholarly efforts seeking to understand the relationship of research to practice report these conclusions as though they represent new discoveries.

Certain researchers have devised ways of overcoming these frustrating aspects of the relationship between research and practice. Their efforts encourage the social work researcher to include the intentions and options of the policymaker and practitioner as essential elements in the research design. This approach creates a context in which the implications of findings can be acted on, in which the research itself initiates the intended change. Otherwise, research in the realms of social policy and social work practice ceases to be a form of social action and serves as a justification for social inaction.

It has been suggested that to be certain is to be wrong at the top of one's voice.

Still, to act, one must maximize certainty and minimize doubt. Although this stance facilitates action, it also fosters error. Professions which require that their practitioners act in situations that are uncertain need to provide these practitioners with relative certainties. Otherwise they risk practitioners becoming nonparticipating observers in the helping transaction. It is this fundamental need for guiding formulations that promote individualized responses to unique situations and yet provide sufficient certainty as to the range of acceptable actions which generates the form and structure of a practice or technological science as distinct from a theoretical science. It is for this reason, more than any other, that practice principles and rules, not laws of nature or human nature, are what social work research seeks.

Merging Research and Practice

American society favors scientific efforts to achieve control over nature and is suspicious of efforts to achieve control over human nature. It favors a noninterventionist conception of research involving humans, a preference that promotes descriptive rather than experimental designs. If social work research has displayed its own share of this societal preference, it should not surprise anyone. It should caution against uncritical acceptance of explanations that attribute the nonexperimental bias in social work research to the complexity of the subject matter, to the difficulty in achieving objectivity and maintaining controls, to the primitive nature of social work's research technology, or to any of the other handy explanations usually given for the profession's methodological inclinations.

In contrast to its caution about attempts to control human attitudes and behavior by research, the social work profession enthusiastically embraces efforts to control attitudes and behavior in which the control is viewed as treatment. One need only claim to be seeking to enhance a person's well-being to justify practices that obviously and deliberately set out to achieve control. The proliferation of new helping modalities is viewed not as a dangerous expansion of tools for the control of human nature, but as evidence of a new freedom to try novel approaches to shaping human behavior.

If the knowing were conceptualized as a form of doing, if research was wedded inseparably to practice, the profession's need to change attitudes and behavior in order to study them might no longer hinder its scientific efforts. Some have appreciated this possibility and used the problem-solving paradigm as the model for treatment, suggesting that from this congruence of scientific focus and useful treatment can arise a scientific practice.[12] Others have applied the methodologies of the behavioral sciences as treatment procedures, contending that the concurrent benefits of building knowledge and helpful doing are demonstrable.[13] Still others have used impromptu drama to conceptualize the treatment process. They have described the professional act as an artful performance, arguing that treatment can be more readily understood when viewed in this light.[14] Here too the methods of knowing and doing are seen as inseparable.

Such melding of knowing and doing hardly eliminates the fundamental tension that persists between the doubts of knowing and the certainties of doing. Moreover, scientific and artful approaches to treatment are both subject to the suspicions that prevail in the wider society when the demands of practice appear to be subordinated to the methods of study. If one structures practice in accordance with the rigors of science, the cry goes out to beware of the betrayal of ethics, to be suspicious of the consequences. When one structures research in accordance with the art of practice, the warning heard is that blind and uninformed doing, mysticism, is being substituted for what should be an intervention based in science.[15]

When the author served as a member of the Social Work Research Group in 1948, one of the major concerns involved the utilization of findings and of tested methodologies. Out of the committee's discussions developed the first *Abstracts for Social Workers*. The committee's thinking was that utilization was largely a question of communication. To some degree that perception remains; it has helped stimulate new journals and an expanded *Abstracts*. This preoccupation with communication also influenced the committee's thinking about the research curriculum, and Mencher's volume in the Boehm study favored an accreditation standard that stressed the ability to read and apply the findings of research more than skill in performing research.[16]

The analysis thus far in this article suggests an alternate view of the central issue in relation to research utilization, a view that has more basic implications for both method and education. It is not a failure in communication that hinders the use of research findings. It is in the design of the research, including its implementation and the form in which its findings are developed, that one must locate the principal impediments to utilization. Thus the entire research process, not simply the terminal requirement that findings be communicated effectively, needs to be considered. Yet, as noted earlier, neither the market nor persuasion is likely to bring about such a comprehensive approach. Unhappily, the approach to promoting the use of social work research is not based on a planned systematic study of the problem, although similar problems have been studied in depth in relation to other professions.[17] By their very nature, surveys of readers' reactions to research literature inevitably locate the problem of utilization in the realm of communication.

Thus, with respect to the illustrative cases of personnel, funding, and utilization, rational planning has not played a significant role in shaping developments. That such planning is needed seems obvious.

Structure for Research Policy

If the first two prerequisites for a research policy can be met—that there is agreement on the need for such a policy and that useful research can be carried out in a rational, planned way—the next consideration is the structure needed to carry the research policy effort. Assuming that the functions listed earlier are those that would be undertaken by whatever organizational structure is found suitable, what factors then ought to determine the choice of structure?

Ideally, structure should be shaped by function. From the list of functions noted, it is clear that the organization would have to provide the opportunity for collective effort—for a blending of a variety of interests in achieving policy choices. Moreover, it should allow for the monitoring of the implementation of its policies and for the use of feedback to modify or wholly alter policies and to respond to new developments not previously identified or anticipated.

Persons associated with the policy organization should be selected primarily for their ability to consider the whole progress of social work research, not merely their own part in it, and to relate social work research not only to contemporary situations, but to its past and future as well. Collectively, the policy group must understand the relationship of social work research to society as a whole and be sensitive to the economic, social, material, and technical conditions likely to advance its development. It is not by oversight that the collective depth and breadth of substantive knowledge which such a body would assemble are not emphasized here. What needs to be studied should be determined by studying what is being done with what results; it should not be determined by a priori decisions. The policy organization should aim to increase the profession's ability to explain social work phenomena and to influence their development. It should avoid responding faddishly to crises that occur in subject areas favored by the policy organization's members.

Above all, the structure must allow for wider participation in policy formulation, both by the profession and by the community such policies will affect. It should reject an internalist's view of social work research. The natural tendency is to think in terms of how the researcher's work will influence others and to play down or ignore others' influence on the development of the research. Policies formulated with an internalist's perspective are far less likely to be implemented than those whose evolution reflects the perspective of the wider community.

Whether the auspices of the policy organization should be public or voluntary; whether membership should reflect geographic, functional, and similar considerations; and how the organization should be staffed, conduct its business, and assure ethical performance are important considerations, but they are secondary to those discussed here—the relevance of research to practice, the need for rational planning, the feasibility of such planning, the need for a research policy organization, and the functions such an organization would perform.

Only with agreement on these primary considerations do the secondary questions present problems, and once there is agreement to go ahead with the formation of a research policy organization, solutions to the secondary problems will come more easily because convictions will reinforce efforts to achieve them.

In discussing the future problems of science, Kapitsa made an interesting comparison:

> If we compare the weight of that part of the body of an animal occupied with spiritual creative work—the head—with his extremities occupying themselves with physical labour, then we receive an interesting result. Let us take the ichthyosaurus, an animal with a tiny head and gigantic body. Such an animal had no future. The future belonged to man whose head weighed approximately 5–10 percent of his whole body. We perceive here that nature dedicated much more to the spiritual as compared with the physical part of man than many states do at the present time.[18]

The analogy is not inappropriate in describing the distribution of resources for social work research relative to the resources devoted to services whose effectiveness largely depend on such research. Unhappily, in the narrower field of social work research itself, the same maldistribution of resources may also be operating, to the detriment of all concerned.

NOTES AND REFERENCES

1. For the basis of the opening analogy, see Isaac Glynn, "Food Sharing of Proto-Human Hominids," Scientific American, April 1978, pp. 90–108.

2. For a discussion of the dangers if the answer is in the affirmative, see Lewis Thomas, The Lives of a Cell (Middlesex, England: Penguin Books, 1974), pp. 115–120. See also Harvey Brooks, "The Problems of Research Priorities," Daedalus, 107 (Spring 1978), pp. 171–190.

3. Paul Feyerabend, *Against Method* (London: Verso Edition, 1978), pp. 23–28.

4. Stephen Dedijer, "Research Policy—From Romance to Reality," in Maurice Goldsmith and Allan Mackay, eds., *The Science of Science* (Middlesex, England: Pelican Books, 1956), p. 265.

5. Ibid., p. 276.

6. *See*, for example, Herbert A. Simon, *Administrative Behavior: A Study of Decision-Making Processes in Administrative Organizations* (Glencoe, Ill.: Free Press, 1957), pp. 248–253; Mario Burge, "Technology as Applied Science," *Technology and Culture*, 7 (Summer 1966), pp. 329–347; and Scott Buchanan, *The Doctrine of Signatures: A Defense of Theory in Medicine* (London: Kegan Paul, Trench, Trubner & Co., 1938).

7. Harold Lewis, "A Program Responsive to New Knowledge and Values," in Edward J. Mullen and James R. Dumpson, eds., *Evaluation of Social Intervention* (San Francisco: Jossey-Bass, 1972), pp. 78–86.

8. For a discussion of the terms "market," "persuasion," and "plan" as they are used in this essay, *see* Charles E. Lindblom, *Politics and Markets* (New York: Basic Books, 1978).

9. *See* Selsker Gunn and Philip Platt, *Voluntary Health Agencies: An Interpretative Study* (New York: Ronald Press, 1945).

10. Henry Aaron, *Politics and Professors: The Great Society in Perspective* (Washington, D.C.: The Brookings Institution, 1978), p. 33.

11. Ibid., p. 9.

12. Louis J. Lehrman, "The Scientific Nature of the Social Caseworker in Professional Process," in Eleanor E. Cockerill, ed., *Social Work Practice in the Field of Tuberculosis* (Philadelphia: University of Pennsylvania Press, 1954), p. 162.

13. Edwin J. Thomas, "The BESDAS Model for Effective Practice," *Social Work Research and Abstracts*, 13 (Summer 1977), pp. 12–16.

14. Harold Lewis, "The Functional Approach to Social Work Practice—A Restatement of Assumptions and Principles," *Journal of Social Work Process*, 15 (1966), pp. 115–133.

15. For a discussion of a policy developed from the perspective of the wider community, *see* Peter Barton Hutt, "Public Criticism of Health Science Policy," *Daedalus*, 107 (Spring 1978), pp. 157–169.

16. Samuel Mencher, *The Research Method in Social Work Education*, "Social Work Curriculum Study," Vol. 9 (New York: Council on Social Work Education, 1959), pp. 19–26.

17. Human Interaction Research Institute in collaboration with the National Institute of Mental Health, *Putting Knowledge to Use: A Distillation of the Literature Regarding Knowledge, Transfer and Change* (Rockville, Md.: National Institute of Mental Health, 1976). For a current sampling of utilization efforts, *see* David Fields, "The Network of Consultants on Knowledge Transfer," *Evaluation*, special issue (1978), pp. 36–40. The entire issue focuses on elements of the utilization process.

18. Peter Kapitsa, "The Future Problems of Science," in Goldsmith and Mackay, eds., op. cit., pp. 127–128.

PART 2

Research Technology

Toward the Integration of Practice and Research

SCOTT BRIAR

THE RELATIONSHIP BETWEEN practice and research in social work has always been an uneasy one. More often than not, it has been unbalanced and one-sided. Researchers have frequently complained that practitioners ignore their obviously pertinent and important findings. In fact, researchers have worried so much about the problem that they have written papers and held conferences on the subject. Practitioners, for their part, sometimes go for days, months, and, in some cases, years without even a moment's thought about social work research, let alone about whether or how to use it in their work. Such differences in interest hardly provide a sound base for a close and mutually satisfying relationship. To a marriage counselor, the prognosis for such a relationship would be "guarded."

Such differences have been aggravated by the widespread belief among social workers that the same person cannot be both a good researcher and a good prac-titioner. The personal qualities believed to make a good researcher are seen as handicaps for a practitioner, and the reverse also has been said to be true. The stereotypes are familiar. Researchers are supposedly intellectual, rational, unfeeling creatures who lack the sensitivity to understand the subtle nuances that are of primary concern to practitioners. Practitioners are purported to be intuitive, sensitive, creative persons more akin to artists than scientists; they emphasize the importance of seeing clients as whole persons who should not be subjected to the categorization and atomization that research allegedly requires. It is easy, of course, to show that these stereotypes are invalid, but such beliefs, although less prevalent than they once were, continue to influence the relationship between practice and research in social work.

The purpose of this article is to assess the current status of the research-practice relationship, to consider how differences between the two might be reduced, and to identify which developments would foster the integration of practice and research in social work. A good place to begin, and an instructive case study, is the practice-effectiveness movement that has emerged in recent years and attracted the attention of practitioners as well as researchers. What has happened to that movement, where is it headed, and what are the implications for the practice-research relationship in social work?

The Practice-Effectiveness Movement

The widespread preoccupation with evaluating the effectiveness of casework interventions is still a relatively recent development. During the early 1970s, shortly after this topic burst on the scene, the activities surrounding it consisted mainly of passionate polemics: charges of ineffectiveness were answered by ringing defenses of the faith, and pious exhortations to do better were offered at forums and in journals. Although the vital importance of the issue remains, some of the heat surrounding the evaluation of practice effectiveness appears to have diminished. Exhortations about the need for evaluation research have given way to a large and growing body of literature on the subject. This literature has become so extensive and specialized that it is impossible to keep up with more than selected parts of it, and it is so technical that practitioners find it increasingly difficult to use. The pursuit of effectiveness has thus become a serious, institutionalized activity. Although this is clearly desirable, some of the side effects on the practice-research relationship have been less than desirable.

For example, the increasingly sophisticated elaboration of evaluation technology has been accompanied by a new specialization—the evaluation expert. It is possible now for practitioners to transfer to these new experts the responsibility for assessing social work effectiveness. Such transfers of responsibility will become increasingly common if the efforts that practitioners do make to evaluate their own effectiveness are regarded by the experts as crude, unsophisticated, and therefore not worthy of respect. Such an outcome would be unfortunate, since the effectiveness issue has aroused among many practitioners an interest in evaluating their own effectiveness. Because this interest has positive implications for the future of practice-research relationships, it is important that it be supported, not discouraged.

Despite the substantial elaboration of knowledge that has occurred since the subject of evaluating practice effectiveness first surfaced, some of the issues that were identified then continue to command the profession's attention. One such issue is the difficulty of defining practice goals and objectives and of reducing their vagueness. It is now clear that practice effectiveness should be assessed only against those objectives that the practitioner is attempting to achieve; it makes no sense to assess effectiveness by measuring outcomes along dimensions that were not included among the practitioner's objectives. A corollary to this point is that conclusions about effectiveness should not be drawn unless the evaluation includes measures for the outcomes that were sought by the practitioner. Although this principle seems rather obvious now, many studies of effectiveness have not adhered to it, sometimes because the investigators had no way of knowing whether what they were measuring had any connection with the practitioner's objectives.

Some said that this problem was a result of the lack of adequate tools for measurement; when better measures were developed, it was suggested, this problem would be solved. It now seems clear that a more basic problem has been the inability or reluctance of many practitioners to formulate intervention objectives in terms that are sufficiently specific and unambiguous to permit systematic measurement. If intervention objectives are specified in such terms, measures for them usually can be devised. (This is not to imply that there are no measurement problems. There are, and much work needs to be invested in the development of more valid and reliable measurement techniques.) It is also clear now that social workers can learn to formulate their objectives in measurable terms; this has been demonstrated repeatedly. Setting measurable objectives is not always easy, but it can be done.

The continued resistance among practitioners to formulating their objectives and interventions in measurable terms appears to be largely philosophical and conceptual. Social workers have long been attracted to abstract concepts, such as identity, self-realization, ego strength, psychological integration, coping, and homeostasis, to list only a few. In fact, it appears to be a general principle in social work never to use a specifically descriptive term if a more abstract one is available. The nearer terms get to operational or behavioral specificity, the more some social workers turn away from them.

This preference for abstract over empirical terms parallels the strong belief among many social workers that abstract theory is at least as valid a way of knowing something as is empirically verified knowledge. That is, some social workers argue that theory is a viable alternative to empirical research as a means of gaining knowledge about practice effectiveness. One source of this difficulty is that to some social workers the word "empirical" is erroneously interpreted as a synonym for "quantitative" and an antonym to "qualitative." Such misunderstandings create unnecessary obstacles to a closer relationship between practice and research. In any event, many social workers have not yet fully accepted the notion that even the most vague objectives imply specific manifestations in behavior, thinking, or feeling that will be evident when and if the objective has been reached. If, for example, a client achieves a higher degree of self-realization, then the client will act, feel, or think in specific, predictably different ways than before that new state was achieved. These conceptual differences continue to be obstacles to the integration of research and practice, although there are indications that the prevalence of such obstacles is diminishing.

A second set of issues recognized early in the practice-effectiveness movement was methodological. Specifically, the question was, By what research designs can effectiveness most appropriately be assessed? It turns out that practitioners were correctly skeptical about the appropriateness of factorial group-comparison designs for assessing the effectiveness of practice technologies that are individualized and different for each client. It is now recognized that such designs—which are powerful, indispensable tools—are mostly and perhaps only appropriate for those refined situations in which what is being tested is the efficacy of well-defined, replicable interventions applied to clients for whom there are common objectives.[1] The refinement required to make appropriate use of factorial designs probably can be achieved only after considerable preparatory research.

Fortunately, the last ten years have seen the emergence and rapid elaboration of single-subject research designs, which are well-suited to the individualized nature of direct service in social work.[2]

Equally important, these methodologies often lend themselves better than others to developmental research, which is research conducted for the purpose of inventing, refining, and testing new, more effective intervention technologies.[3] Thus, the necessary methodological tools are now available to support vigorous and productive efforts to advance practice effectiveness empirically and systematically. In other words, the tools to support an empirical model of practice are available.

Although the examples given here tend to be drawn from direct service practice, this is a consequence of using the preoccupation with casework effectiveness as an example, but the relevance of these comments is not limited to direct service practice. Single-subject designs, for example, provide another strategy for evaluating programs, and such designs can be used to study the effectiveness of alternative policies, although the application of these methods to policy research has yet to be developed. The potential is clearly there, however.

A third issue identified when the question of effectiveness arose was the lack of institutional and organizational support for a major effort to increase effectiveness through systematic assessment and research. Here less progress has been made. Many social agencies still give little more than lip service to systematic research on effectiveness. Practitioners who want to engage in effectiveness research are not encouraged or supported; as a result, they discontinue their efforts. This is not to say that social welfare agencies have been untouched by the concern with effectiveness. On the contrary, they have been affected profoundly. But their responses have been directed mainly toward the development of increasingly complex and sophisticated systems for establishing managerial accountability. These administrative information systems typically address, at best, no more than formative evaluation questions and rarely attempt the assessment of outcome effectiveness. Since substantial investments have been made in administrative accountability systems and since there is little, if any, evidence that they increase outcome effectiveness, questions have been raised about their cost-effectiveness. Some ambitious management information systems have been abandoned, in part at least, because of their high cost.

The considerable effort devoted to accountability systems stands in dramatic contrast to the negligible investment in developmental research, a difference that is all the more remarkable since it is probably only through some form of developmental research that more effective means of providing service are likely to be discovered. The difference between evaluation research and developmental research is not trivial or semantic. Evaluation research asks whether a particular intervention or program was effective in relation to particular outcome objectives. Developmental research asks what would be the most effective intervention or program to achieve certain objectives. The difference is substantial. The concept of developmental research is a familiar one in other fields—space exploration is one example—but it has yet to be applied and supported to any significant extent in social work and social welfare. In choosing not to move in this direction, social agencies have failed to exploit a significant opportunity to achieve a greater integration between research and practice.

Having sketched what has happened to some of the problems that were identified when the effectiveness issue first emerged, it also is appropriate, before turning to consider the future, to ask what changes have occurred in the state of knowledge about the effectiveness of social work practice.

Perhaps the most important thing to be said is that it no longer is possible to answer the question, Is casework effective? with a single statement, no matter how carefully it is qualified. The reason is that social casework is no longer seen as one monolithic method. Social caseworkers use a great variety of intervention methods and techniques. One has to ask, therefore, about the current state of knowledge about the effectiveness of intervention in specific areas. The encouraging answer to that question is that intervention techniques of demonstrated, empirically tested effectiveness have been developed in a number of areas, such as parent effectiveness, assertiveness training, and reduction of depression, to mention only a few. In areas in which little or no developmental research has been conducted, such as family therapy, the profession knows hardly any more now than it did when the question of their effectiveness was first raised. In still other areas, such as marital counseling, despite a fair amount of research activity, the profession has yet to identify methods of clearly demonstrated, superior effectiveness.

The Practitioner-Scientist

In turning now to a brief consideration of how future social work research might foster a closer relationship between practice and research, it must first be acknowledged that the examination of the effectiveness issue in the first part of this paper was more than an example. In an applied, pragmatic profession such as social work, effectiveness is always a fundamental question. It is not the only question, but other important research questions—such as the analyses of policy alternatives and problems of implementation and service delivery—must also address, eventually, the question of out-

come effectiveness, whether of a policy, a program, or one service delivery system compared to another. Further, some of the distinctions drawn between micro and macro research, especially with regard to outcome effectiveness, are exaggerated and misleading. For example, a question about the effects of a particular social policy is, empirically, a question about the effects of a specific set of social arrangements on the behaviors of the persons subjected to them—and that is a micro question. The point is that policy and organizational research can and should be conducted at the micro or, if one prefers, clinical level.

A most important trend for the future of the practice-research relationship is already under way, and that is the reduction of the sharp separation between research and practice activities. In progress now are significant efforts to merge practice and research activities. The concept of the practitioner-scientist is one symbol of that trend.[4] This concept means not only that the same person can both practice and conduct research, but also that he or she can engage in practice and research simultaneously as a set of integrated activities. The concept makes possible an empirically based model of practice, a possibility that was inconceivable only a few years ago. The practitioner-scientist concept was not actually feasible until the research tools became available to permit rigorous research on a small scale in ways that can be incorporated into the routine of practice.

One of the principal benefits of the practitioner-scientist model is that it provides a way to expand substantially, with comparatively small increases in resources, the amount and variety of developmental research on effectiveness. Such research does not require large-scale projects. Individual practitioner-scientists, with appropriate workloads and modest support resources, can make significant contributions that can be utilized directly and immediately by other practitioners. The feasibility of this model has been demonstrated in programs of social work education that are training students for this role.[5]

Thus far, the model of the practitioner-scientist has been more fully developed in clinical practice, but it can be extended to other areas of practice. As mentioned earlier, micro research on the impact of social policies is an example of a context in which the extension of the practitioner-scientist concept would be desirable. It may well be that most policy research should still be conducted in the library or through large-scale surveys and social experiments, but it is clear that micro policy analysis also would be useful. For example, we need micro studies and experiments on the impact of deinstitutionalization on individuals; such studies would compare the effects of different patterns of deinstitutionalization.

To realize fully the potential inherent in these developments, a number of changes have to be made to support and encourage them. Two of the most important changes deserve mention here. First, social work educators will have to integrate their instruction in research and practice, in the field as well as in class, so that research becomes an integral part of practice methods and procedures. For example, at the University of Washington in Seattle, the School of Social Work has combined research and practice instruction beyond the introductory research course into one course for all direct service students. This fusion is also carried into the field where the student carries clinical research cases. This shift also means that educators need to break down the sharp distinctions between research and other faculty, a distinction that is not maintained to this extent in other disciplines at the graduate level. The integration of practice and research must go beyond rhetoric to living models that exemplify the combination.

The second major change that will have to be made is to create the organizational and institutional supports practitioners need to perform as practitioner-scientists. For example, many of the social work students at the University of Washington have responded enthusiastically to the possibility of incorporating research into their practice and have learned to do so effectively with benefits for the quality of their practice in addition to whatever research products they produce. Some of these students have been followed over time, however, and it has been found that their capacity to sustain these efforts diminishes, not because they lack interest or commitment, but because they lack the necessary supports in the organizations where they practice. Here and there, however, a few graduates have been able to find or construct the necessary conditions and supports to be practitioner-scientists. The organizational changes required to support such developments could be encouraged by the National Association of Social Workers, which has effectively influenced other conditions of practice in social agencies.

A Place for Traditional Research

It would be erroneous to give the impression that fostering the practitioner-scientist and developmental research are the only avenues for bringing practice and research closer together. Traditional research activities remain important, but they need to be directed more explicitly to solving the problems that confront practitioners, rather than to the pursuit of theories that interest the researcher.

There is the danger, of course, that if researchers devote their attention entirely to finding solutions to practice problems, they will become concerned only with technological matters and thereby not address larger questions and issues. That danger can be avoided by developing collaborative efforts between universities and social agencies in which, although the immediate focus is on problem-solving, the university participants would be expected to examine problems in a broader perspective as well. This pattern is followed in some other professions, but has yet to be developed extensively in social work.

Finally, priority should be given to one specific focus for future research, a focus that spans both macro-policy and micro-practice concerns, namely, research on social intervention. Such research would investigate the effects specific social conditions, social environments, and social arrangements have on persons, families, and communities. That is the essence of social policy, and it also is central to the historic mission of social casework. It remains an area in which social work and social work research can make a unique and highly significant contribution.[6]

If the social work profession can make some of the changes identified here, and if it can exploit the directions for development that have emerged in recent years, then the future is bright for a closer and more productive relationship between research and practice, with enormous benefits for the profession and, above all, for those we seek to serve.

NOTES AND REFERENCES

1. For a well-known example, *see* Gordon Paul, *Insight versus Desensitization in Psychotherapy: An Experiment in Anxiety Reduction* (Stanford, Calif.: Stanford University Press, 1966).

2. Rona Levy and Srinika Jayaratne, *The Clinical-Research Model of Intervention* (New York: Columbia University Press, 1978).

3. For an elaboration of the concept of developmental research for social work, *see* Edwin Thomas, "Uses of Research Methods in Interpersonal Practice," in Norman A. Polansky, ed., *Social Work Research* (Chicago: University of Chicago Press, 1975), pp. 254–283.

4. Scott Briar, "Incorporating Research into Education for Clinical Practice in Social Work: Toward a Clinical Science in Social Work," in Allen Rubin and Aaron Rosenblatt, eds., *Sourcebook on Research Utilization* (New York: Council on Social Work Education, 1979), pp. 132–140.

5. Cheryl A. Richey, "The Integrated Educational Unit: An Approach to Combining Methods, Research, and Field Instruction." Paper presented at the Annual Program Meeting of the Council on Social Work Education, Phoenix, Ariz., March 1977.

6. For an excellent presentation of a social intervention focus for direct practice, *see* James K. Whittaker, *Social Treatment* (Chicago: Aldine Publishing Co., 1974). *See also* Scott Briar, "Toward Autonomous Social Diagnosis," *Bulletin of the Menninger Clinic*, 40 (September 1976), pp. 593–601.

Research Strategies for Improving Individualized Services

WILLIAM J. REID

ALTHOUGH OPINIONS about its accomplishments vary, there is agreement that social work should strive continually to improve its services. This goal better describes the profession's obligations than the goal of providing effective service. Social work may not be expected to resolve the many difficult problems thrust upon it, but it is expected to make progress toward finding the means to alleviate them.

A commitment to improve service may require more than a demonstration that a service works. A program can be made more effective and more efficient; it can be extended to new populations, and so on. Although social work has other objectives, the goal of improving its services is central to its mission.

This purpose has been pursued through various means, including the development of practice theory, program innovations, supervision, professional education, and research. Of such means

of shaping service, social work research has been among the least influential. Its actual contribution to bringing about improvements in practice can hardly be underestimated. Only a modest amount of research germane to this purpose has been conducted; the little that has been done has been of uneven quality and poorly utilized.

That research has not played a larger role runs counter to social work's presumed commitment to establishing a scientific base and has long been a source of concern to many in the profession, particularly to its researchers. In theory, research should make a vital contribution to improving services by generating knowledge to guide their development and implementation. It should provide evidence to verify the occurrence of supposed improvements. In the absence of such evidence, there is little basis for asserting that program innovations, professional education, and other devices are in fact enhancing the quality of service. Without research, the very idea of demonstrable progress is open to question.

Because the pathways from scientific effort to service excellence are tortuous, it is unrealistic to expect that research will soon become a dominant factor in the modification of practice. Nevertheless, much can be done to augment the contribution of research to methods of helping. This article examines different research strategies for improving face-to-face social work practice with individuals, families, and groups. This examination is limited to selected strategies that have been assumed to be important or that seem to show particular promise. Although none of the strategies can be considered in the detail that each deserves, the article is intended to provide a useful comparative overview of a range of research approaches and some worthwhile suggestions about how these approaches might be modified or combined to advance the cause of practice.

Focus of Strategies

Most of the research produced by the social sciences and the related helping professions has some bearing on the improvement of individualized social work. The concern here, however, is with social work research strategies that are specifically related to the development of practice. The focus of these strategies is the study of practice itself; their purpose is to discover what forms or models of intervention used in what way by whom produce what effects with what types of problems or persons. A given study may reflect only part of this strategic focus, but any such study is concerned in one way or another with what is done to affect people's lives.

These strategies produce what Fischer calls "intervention knowledge," the kind

of knowledge most essential to the improvement of practice.[1] For this purpose, it is not enough to learn from the social sciences or other sources "what makes people tick"; one must learn what to do when the ticking goes awry. Intervention knowledge cannot be derived or inferred from basic knowledge about people. It must be developed through study of the relations among the targets, participants, processes, and outcomes of intervention.

An examination of research strategies for improving practice is incomplete if it attends simply to the production of knowledge. To affect practice, knowledge must obviously be utilized by practitioners. Because different research strategies present different advantages and problems for those who use the results, any strategy needs to be assessed for the impact it has on the provision of service. Although this essay emphasizes research over utilization, the strategies considered make sense only when they are viewed as part of a research and utilization system.

Group Field Experiments

Although few in number, group field experiments have traditionally assumed a first order of importance in research on social work practice. Their results have provoked far more discussion about the merits of social work services than any other form of practice research.[2] Typically, group field experiments have been used to assess outcomes of social work programs by comparing treated against untreated or lesser treated groups or, less frequently, by comparing groups receiving competitive forms of treatment.

Despite the considerable investment made in these studies, their contribution to the improvement of service has been limited. Because most of these experiments have failed to demonstrate that the interventions tested were effective, they have provided little guidance for the development of practice.[3] Although it is of value to learn that certain types of service are not effective, that information does not help to design services that are.

It is unlikely that further experimentation of this kind will produce much that is useful in building better practice models. In relation to this purpose, conventional field experiments present two critical weaknesses. First, they are usually conducted as one-shot program evaluations without preparatory testing and development of either service or research methods. Such work is necessary to specify and perfect the service model to be tested and to construct sensitive measures closely attuned to expected inputs and outcomes. Without it, the experiment may turn out to be an overblown pilot study with negative findings the rule rather than the exception. It may then be prematurely concluded that the service approach has little to offer or that its effectiveness cannot be properly assessed. Second, because researchers are usually limited to roles of evaluators of service models developed by others, they usually have little to say about how the interventions tested are carried out, and they at times have only a cloudy idea of the nature of the interventions. A lack of control or understanding of the independent variables of the study makes it impossible for the researcher to design and implement a coherent experiment.

Although the field experiment, as it has commonly been used, offers little promise for improving practice, there is still a need for the testing of service models within the context of agency programs. Only through in-program testing can one determine that supposed improvements in practice methods are working. Field experiments can provide a means for this testing, but a different approach to their

use is needed. Preparatory testing of both the service and the research methods is crucial. As a rule, a major field experiment should be conducted only after pilot testing affords a reasonable expectation that the service model works and that the means to test it adequately have been developed. Responsibility for the design and implementation of an evaluation should ideally be in the hands of a person—a practitioner-researcher perhaps—who can direct both research and service components. If this structure is not possible, the alternative would be a team consisting of a practitioner and a researcher who work closely together and who share responsibility for the conduct of the experiment.

If field experiments are to be used to best advantage in the improvement of service, more sophisticated designs need to be employed—designs that do more than make simple comparisons between treated and nontreated or minimally treated groups. More informative for modifying practice are designs that incorporate multiple comparisons—for example, between treatment approaches or between different client or problem types—and that, in addition, use control groups to rule out extraneous and nonspecific factors which might contribute to client change. The greater costs of such designs may be more than compensated for by the greater utility of their findings.

Field experiments usually involve tests of entire service programs, which tend to be lengthy, changeable, complex, and difficult to study. As a result, research findings are often difficult to interpret, even with the best designs. Moreover, the typical field experiment lasts years and costs sums in the six figures.

There is, consequently, a need for experimental designs that can be used in short-run testing of specific program elements or methods. To illustrate, suppose an investigator wished to determine the efficacy of a set of procedures developed by Weissman for linking clients to community resources in a short-term counseling program.[4] A possible design would be to assign clients randomly to two conditions: in one condition, the special linking procedures would be used; in the other, clients would simply be steered to the relevant resources. Other aspects of the cases could be allowed to vary normally. Measurement would concentrate on the linking procedures—on their characteristics and immediate effects—rather than on the nature and outcome of the counseling service as a whole. In fact, the experiment might be confined to the first two interviews, during which the linking procedures would either be used or not depending on the condition to which the case was assigned. Following this period, the procedures could be used in the control cases. Such highly focused micro experiments could provide needed information on the immediate effects of specific interventions—a type of knowledge that is impossible to obtain from evaluation of total programs.[5] Moreover, such experiments are relatively economical, raise no great ethical or practical programs in the use of controls, and can be completed within a relatively brief time. Although it is necessary that the intervention tested be capable of producing at least some measurable short-term effects, a large variety of interventions have this property.

If it is kept firmly in mind that the purpose of control groups in experiments is to rule out the role of extraneous factors (maturation, contemporaneous events, and so on) in producing changes associated with treatment and not to satisfy some canon of science, then one may find that control groups may not always be necessary to obtain persuasive evidence on the effects of treatment. A quasi-experimental design, without a control group, may suffice if extraneous factors have little or no influence and if evidence can be obtained on their operation. This point is elaborated and illustrated in the context of single-subject designs.

Whatever design is used, it is essential that the service interventions tested be adequately described if the results of field experiments are to contribute to the development of practice. Most field experiments in social work have been particularly deficient in this respect. It is not enough to describe an experimental intervention in terms of what was intended or what practitioners presumably were doing; one must collect data on what was done. Although data supplied by the practitioner in the form of written recordings, logs, and checklists may be useful for certain purposes, they are seldom sufficient to produce an accurate and discriminating account of service. More objective, detailed data obtained through human or mechanical observation are needed. If the treatment under study involves communication between practitioners and clients, descriptions of the practitioners' interventions should be based on analysis of tape recordings of their communications. This is almost a minimum requirement. An experiment without an accurate delineation of the independent variable hardly qualifies as an experiment.

Single-Subject Experiments

In recent years, conventional modes of testing the effects of practice through group field experiments have been challenged by proponents of the single-subject design.[6] The term is used to refer to time-series designs with either single subjects or small sets of subjects, as in multiple-baseline designs. Of particular interest are single-subject designs that can achieve adequate control over extraneous variance through such devices as reversing or withdrawing treatment or staggering its application across subjects or problems.

This methodology unquestionably offers considerable promise as a means of improving practice. Because both treatment and measurement can be tailored to fit individual cases, it is possible to maximize the power of the former and the precision of the latter. Concentrating on one or a few cases enables the investigator to collect an abundance of precise data; the time-series character of the data makes possible a more thorough and exact picture of change in the target problems and of the influence produced by intervention. One can claim that the intervention tested affected a particular individual in a certain way. This kind of knowledge is impossible to obtain in a group experiment, in which one can say that experimental clients, on the average, differed from controls but cannot say which particular experimental clients were benefited or harmed.

Single-subject experiments are also much more feasible than comparable group experiments. It is simpler to recruit, and usually less costly to study, one or a few subjects than many. Moreover, it is possible to carry out a respectable and informative single-subject study without creating a major stir in a service program and having to contend with the waves of disruption that inevitably result. There are still other advantages. In single-subject methodology, responsibility for an experiment is normally in the hands of a practitioner-researcher, thus eliminating the divided leadership that, as noted, has bedeviled conventional field experiments. Finally, reports of single-case studies are easier to digest, particularly by practitioners, and hence the results may be more readily utilized.

The use of single-subject designs has been limited almost exclusively to test of behavioral treatment methods and within that context have been joined to methods of data collection (for example, repeated observation of behavior) and analysis (such as graphing frequencies of behavior over time) that are characteristic of research on behavior modification. The basic design principles can be extended to other forms of intervention if certain conditions are met. Thus, if the effects of treatment are to be measured by observing what happens when the treatment is withdrawn (or reversed), the treatment must be one whose immediate effects are either short-lived or can be readily undone. Many, if not most forms of social work intervention are thought to lack this property, however. For example, once insight is achieved in psychoanalytically based approaches, it is expected to endure; similarly, persons supposedly securing jobs through an after-care vocational counseling program would not be expected to leave if the program were temporarily suspended.

Multiple-baseline designs appear to have a wider range of application since they do not assume that treatment and its effects can be turned on and off like a light switch. In multiple-baseline approaches, the effects of treatment are demonstrated through staggering its application. Perhaps the form with the broadest application is the across-subjects multiple baseline, in which several clients begin treatment at different points in time under the hypothesis that patterns of change in each will show a positive acceleration after treatment is begun. For this design to be feasible, however, the treatment to be tested must be able to generate measurable effects rather quickly; otherwise, the waiting or baseline period before the last client is treated might become excessively long. Many varieties of social treatment meet this requirement. Those that do are potential subjects for multiple-baseline designs, and the methodology need not be that used in behavioral research.

Suppose, for example, that one wished to test the effectiveness of a weekend marathon group that uses methods of Gestalt therapy to treat depression. Three depressed clients would be selected as a sample and their levels of depression measured by a standardized test. The first client waits a week, is measured again, enters a group, and is measured a third time immediately after the experience. This procedure is repeated for the remaining clients with the exception that the second client waits two weeks before having the group experience and the third client waits three weeks. Thus, each client enters treatment at different points with his or her own baseline. If the depression score of each shows improvement over this baseline during the weekend marathon, one has evidence that the group treatment produced the change, since it would otherwise be difficult to explain the coincidence between the group experience and the lessening of depression. The design could be strengthened by introducing brief placebo sessions of friendly listening between baseline tests, and each client could be followed up after the group experience to obtain data on the durability of any changes. If evidence on the effectiveness of the intervention appeared to be inconclusive from this three-client test, or if one were not content with a sample this small, one or more replications with additional sets of clients could be done.

Single-subject designs without controls in the forms of reversing, withdrawing, or staggering treatment can also produce persuasive evidence of treatment effectiveness, but certain conditions need to be met. It is usually necessary (1) to prove through time-series data that the condition treated was relatively stable before intervention, (2) to explicate the specific steps by which the intervention brought about change and to clarify the logic of the process, (3) to demonstrate that the predicted change occurs when the intervention was used, and (4) to show that other factors which might plausibly have caused the change were searched for but not located. Thus, it might be shown through a series of test scores that a child has been doing poorly in arithmetic for some time. A program consisting of structured homework assignments is instituted, and evidence is provided that the child successfully completes the homework assignments. If his test scores then improve and no other factors that might account for the improvement appear to be present, it is reasonable to conclude that the program was at least in part responsible. As the example illustrates, it may be possible to use baseline data already collected or to obtain retrospective baseline data. It is also possible to accumulate a series of such cases with varying baseline periods to create a facsimile of a multiple-baseline design.

The ability to predict specific changes following the use of a method can provide persuasive evidence that the method is the causative agent. For example, in the changing-criterion design, one predicts that an intervention will lead to the client's attainment of a goal; if the goal is achieved, the intervention is reapplied with the prediction that a more demanding goal will be attained.[7] If a series of such predictions can be confirmed, usual design controls may not be necessary to determine the effectiveness of the method. The same principles apply to the quasi-experimental group designs discussed earlier. In both single-subject and group experiments, there are many ways of approximating the central function of conventional designs in outcome research—to minimize risks of error in attributing a change in the client to the interventions of the practitioner.

The most serious drawback of the single-subject design is usually thought to be its limited generalizability, but this aspect is more complicated than it may seem. It is possible to generalize with greater precision from single-subject than group designs because the critical variables can be more carefully delineated in the former. Moreover, a single-subject strategy is well suited to the use of replication with planned variations as a means of demonstrating that a method is effective in a variety of cases.

Nonetheless, in single-subject research there is a greater chance that the cases studied may be atypical of the general run of cases to which one wishes to generalize. This likelihood is further increased by the interaction of selection and reporting factors. A method may work well in a published case, but there may be no way of knowing if the client, through some selection process, is unusual in respect to motivation, cooperativeness, supportiveness of environment, and so on. One also does not know how many failures of the method lie buried in the experimenter's files. Solutions include random selection of research subjects from defined populations and the reporting of consecutive cases, including aborted efforts, in which a method was tested.

Single-subject methodology can be used not only in studies undertaken to generate knowledge for the field, but also by practitioners who wish to test the efficacy of the methods they use or to guide practice in individual cases. Used in this way, the methodology becomes a form of operations research analogous to the use of data from information systems to inform agency practice. In such applications, the generalizability of results may not be of great concern, but feasibility usually is. Practitioners need training in the use of such methods and, above all, the time to use them. The pressures of carrying oversized case loads could keep the idea of practitioners' systematically testing their own methods locked in the realm of fantasy. Nevertheless, the idea has considerable merit and should be pursued.

If such single-subject studies are to be useful, research techniques must be applied within a scientific framework, one that values accurate data over ideology. The collection of baseline data, diagnostic tests, systematic recording of client progress, and other research techniques can be used to guide practice in the case at hand. If their use is guided by fixed beliefs about the causes and cures of the client's difficulties, however, they can become a form of scientific tokenism.

Research and Development Programs

Traditionally, social work research has been directed at the production of knowledge; its main product has been the research report, which has been utilized or ignored. In recent years, a rather different function for research has emerged in what has been called developmental research or research and development.[8]

In a research and development undertaking, research is used in a systematic way to devise and build practice models. Its main product is not a report, but rather a service approach, as set forth for use by practitioners in guidelines, manuals, and the like. The strategy calls for a continuing program in which research and practice are mutually informative. A preliminary practice model may be devised from existing research, theory, clinical trial and error, or other sources. The model or elements of it are subjected to a series of tests in which data are collected on the operations of the model and its apparent outcomes. Data from each test are used to revise the model prior to subsequent testing; in this way, the model can be progressively improved in the light of research data. Different and not necessarily mutually exclusive patterns may be followed. One may begin by testing and perfecting a single practice method; a second method is then added and tested to determine if it improves on the effects that have been attained by the original method. This synthetic approach has been advocated by McFall and his associates and is illustrated in their efforts to develop an intervention model that makes use of different forms of behavioral rehearsal.[9] Methods may be developed and tested separately; those proving to be effective may then be combined. In another approach, one may begin with a package of interventions and, through subsequent varying and testing of components, attempt to replace those that do not contribute to the effectiveness of the package and to maximize the role of those that do. Development may take the form of testing a model with different and perhaps progressively more challenging clinical problems. The starting point may be a laboratory analog of an intervention. The analog is first developed and tested under highly controlled conditions and then applied to actual clinical situations.

Conventional forms of experimental designs, such as small-scale field experiments and single-subject studies, may be employed in the development process. One type of design that may be used in the preliminary testing of a model is somewhat unconventional, however, and thus merits special comment. The design is an experiment in the sense that an intervention is attempted and studied, but design controls are not used and treatment effects are not tested. For these reasons, it may be thought of as an exploratory experiment. This type of experiment may serve a variety of purposes in the process of inventing models, in-

cluding assessing the feasibility of treatment procedures, determining the adequacy of instructions to practitioners, developing and testing instruments, and identifying factors that need to be taken into account in further work on the model. This last function, although the most vaguely stated, is probably the most important. Preliminary models designed for the complex situations that typically occur in social work can provide only rough and incomplete sketches of the realities that will be encountered. If the model is ultimately to be successful, the range and substance of these events need to be mapped and incorporated into the service design. The exploratory experiment serves this mapping function.

An exploratory experiment was conducted with a previously untested model of task-centered intervention aimed at reuniting foster children with their natural parents.[10] Since the model was an attempt to apply short-term, focused interventions with crisis-ridden, multiproblem families, one question concerned the effects of emergencies that might preclude concentrated work on stipulated problems. The exploratory test with eleven families provided considerable information about the nature and effect of emergencies—for example, that emergencies occurred in almost all cases, but seemed to be provoked largely by interpersonal difficulties and could generally be handled in one or two interviews without abandoning focus on contracted problems. Such findings helped guide the next round of model development. Although tentative, they provided empirically grounded directions in an unknown area. Unlike the results of most exploratory research, these findings were immediately applied rather than relegated to use simply in generating hypotheses for further study.

Since its purpose is to create new and superior practice technologies, a research and development strategy offers a direct route between research activity and the improvement of service. The self-corrective powers of research can be used in a systematic and efficient way in constructing models. Research designs and instruments for testing models can be developed progressively to provide an optimum fit to the requirements of the model. This bypasses some intransigent obstacles to the utilization of research. To utilize the fruits of research and development, practitioners need not digest and apply research reports; rather, they can apply the products resulting from the research. This strategy seems to be a major step forward. Thomas puts the point strongly:

> Developmental research may be the single most appropriate model of research for social work because it consists of methods directed explicitly toward the analysis, development, and evaluation of the very technical means by which social work objectives are achieved.[11]

Although research and development approaches need to be pursued vigorously, they are still inchoate. Little is known or has been articulated about the best types of project designs to use at different stages of model development, what is the best sequence for these designs, and how results can best be used to inform model development. The author's experience over the past eight years in research and development projects relating to task-centered practice indicates that the most significant improvements in that approach have come not from the findings of particular projects, but rather from the analyses of innovative work in individual cases drawn from the projects. Without research instruments to capture them, these innovations might have gone undetected. Research has thus played an important role in these developmental projects, but not quite the one that might have been expected.

Research and development can help create service models but cannot insure that they will be used or used appropriately in service programs. For this reason, it makes sense to conceive of research, development, and utilization strategies. This expansion of the term highlights the importance of utilization, but does nothing to solve utilization problems. Although it is fashionable to use the vocabulary of engineers and refer to service models produced by research and development as "products," these products are usually not apparatuses that can be put to work with proper instructions. They consist rather of complicated, often incomplete and overly general guidelines for practitioners. Proper use may require substantial training and changes in work habits and practice beliefs, all of which may encounter agency and staff resistance. Unlike a physical apparatus, practice models can readily be picked apart by users who may incorporate some elements into their own practice, usually after refashioning them somewhat, and junk the rest.

As a result of these and other obstacles, the dissemination of service models of proved effectiveness into an ongoing program provides no assurance whatsoever that the model or the parts of it that come to be used in the program will be effective. It does not even provide assurance that the methods will be used at all. For example, following a nine-month effort to train the staff of a state department of public welfare in the use of task-centered methods, the author and his colleagues assessed the impact of the training through comparing samples of staff case recording before and after the program. Despite an implementation effort of more than usual intensity—one that included several workshops and staff applications of the model—the evidence suggested that the training had a limited effect on the staff's performance.

Such disquieting experiences are likely to be repeated until more effective methods of dissemination are devised. The challenge is particularly great when the attempt is made to transplant practice models cultivated under the protected conditions of special projects into the turbulent climates of ongoing agency programs.

Correlational Studies of Practice

So far this article has limited its focus to various forms of experimentation, whether carried out in single projects or within the framework of research and development programs. In correlational strategies, the researcher does not manipulate practice, but rather studies it through determining patterns of association among its different elements: among types of clients, practitioners, problems, processes, outcomes, and so on. In studies most directly relevant to improving practice, independent variables are drawn from the characteristics of clients, practitioners, and treatments; the dependent variables are usually measures of outcome. In other words, the usual purpose is to identify factors that might help explain variations in outcome.

Thousands of such studies have been carried out in social work, psychology, and psychiatry. Almost every variable known to clinician and researcher has served time in a correlation matrix. Although a good deal has been learned, the yield of consistent findings that have proved useful for the improvement of clinical practice has been distressingly small, and there is little evidence that this body of research has had a significant impact on practice.

Why is this so? In the first place, it has proved difficult in correlational designs to

provide adequate evidence of causal relations because of (1) the sizable number of variables that need to be controlled to provide explanations of outcome, (2) the use of samples of insufficient size to permit simultaneous control of more than a few of these variables, (3) problems in determining time sequences between events, and (4) the pervasive shortcomings of measurement. In addition, variables of great potency that prove to be strongly and consistently correlated with outcome across varied conditions have yet to be discovered, even though, as Parloff, Waskow, and Wolfe observe, "researchers continue to persist in the belief that such variables exist."[12] As a result, predictor variables in such studies tend to correlate weakly, if at all, with outcome variables. What is more, the correlations can often be explained by other factors and are likely to come and go from study to study.

The weaknesses of correlational approaches become especially striking when attempts are made to examine the relation between particular treatment methods and outcome, a relation of fundamental importance in research to improve practice. A correlation between the use of a method and an outcome measure is always open to interpretation in either direction. For example, the use of verbal encouragement by the practitioner may be positively correlated with increases in a measure of the client's self-concept, but one does not know whether the use of the method brought about change in the client's self-concept or if changes occurring for other reasons elicited the encouragement from the practitioners. One would need repeated measures on change in the client's self-concept to tell if the change in the client preceded or followed variations in the use of encouragement.

It may be argued that this is another example of the researcher's obsessive search for certainty, but one observation needs to be made in rebuttal: when correlations between the use of an intervention and an outcome are positive, there seems to be a tendency to interpret them in the obvious direction. Isn't it logical that use of encouragement would enhance the client's self-concept? But when the correlations are negative, interpretations in the opposite direction are favored. It may be logical to interpret a positive correlation between number of interviews and outcome as suggesting that the more service provided, the more the client is helped, and Beck and Jones, for instance, made such an interpretation.[13] But when confronted with a negative correlation between the number of contacts and outcome, Wallace favored an interpretation in the opposite direction: families that received more contacts did less well because they required more service.[14]

The same shortcomings are found, of course, when correlational methods are used within the context of experimental designs in attempts to isolate the specific ingredients of treatment that might have accounted for the observed effects. Although such analyses of treatment components may be worth conducting, one should not expect the findings to be particularly revealing.

Apparent exceptions to the rule that correlational studies have yielded little that would contribute to the improvement of practice often turn out to be more appearance than exception. A first wave of studies may produce some consistent and interesting correlations, but these findings often fail to withstand subsequent critiques or to reappear in subsequent and possibly more refined research. For example, the largely correlational evidence that the presence of the so-called core therapeutic conditions (warmth, empathy, and congruence) contributed to successful outcomes once appeared

strong.[15] It became increasingly less convincing as old studies were more closely examined and as new studies accumulated.[16]

Although correlational methods have a role in research to improve practice—for example, in the study of nonmanipulable factors and in generating hypotheses for experimental testing—they have been overused as means of investigating the effects of treatment variables that can be manipulated and hence tested more definitively through experimental designs. Moreover, in the process of creating experimental interventions, one can make use of previous studies to design forms of treatment that may be better than those existing. In correlational research, one is limited to searching for clues about what might be better from whatever forms of treatment are available for study.

Computerized Information Systems

Agency information systems that can store, retrieve, and manipulate routinely collected and computerized data on clients, staff, services, and outcomes are potentially a major resource for improving practice.[17] With their capacity for generating huge data sets—thousands of cases in one recent study—information systems can provide researchers with the large numbers desirable for correlational analyses of practice variables.[18] Field experiments can be run with minimal effort by using existing machinery of data collection. Since the data flow is endless, studies can be repeated over time. Studies that would normally take years can be completed in weeks and the results make readily available to program decision-makers. More important, practice can be studied and influenced as it actually occurs across entire programs.

Questions about how well a given form of service is actually being implemented in agency programs become open to empirical inquiry.

The development of information systems with these capacities can in itself be thought of as a research strategy, one that would lead to the creation of "perpetual research machines."[19] Conducting studies or monitoring practice with data provided by information systems would be a continuation of the strategy.

At their present state of development, however, information systems rarely collect the kind of data on service processes and outcomes that would be needed to modify agency practice. Service and outcome data tend to be extremely crude and supplied largely by practitioners themselves without provision for assessment of reliability. For example, a counseling service may be described with no greater precision than a recording of the number and type of interviews held. Since large numbers of cases are involved, the costs of collecting precise and reliable data are considerable; moreover, it is difficult to devise a single set of measures that would satisfy a variety of information and research purposes.

But solutions for some of these problems are being developed. Measurement approaches that delineate both service focuses and outcomes, such as Goal Attainment Scaling and measures based on direct observation of changes in clients' behavior, are being incorporated into information systems.[20] As a study by Fanshel illustrates, it is also possible to develop modules calling for particular measures that can be inserted into routine data collection procedures for limited periods of time.[21] As such progress continues, information systems should become an increasingly important means for research to influence services where it matters most—within the context of agency programs.

Improving the Researchability of Practice Approaches

Some forms of practice are more suitable than others to testing and development through research. Approaches amenable to research are those consisting of clearly stated, reproducible procedures that are addressed to targets capable of being measured with a reasonable degree of precision, that can produce results quickly, and that can predict specific effects from the application of particular methods. This final criterion is of central importance. It means that the sequence of events intended to produce desired effects—for example, the chain of practitioner and client actions likely to alleviate a problem—needs to be explicated in clear and measurable terms. With such mapping, research can be used to determine how particular modifications in the sequence affect outcomes. Such specific relations are hard to ascertain if the processes of change are defined in terms of abstractions, such as "developing emotional insight" or "strengthening ego boundaries," that are difficult to define clearly and that are not broken down into sequences of discrete events. From the researcher's perspective, treatment then becomes a "black box," an amalgamation of processes that cannot be satisfactorily sorted out or studied.

One can investigate what happens when such black boxes are used, and there is evidence that some of them, such as psychodynamic practice, may presently be as effective for most purposes as more researchable modalities, such as behavioral intervention.[22] But as long as treatment remains a black box, it may be impossible to secure evidence on what leads to what and hence difficult to bring about improvements based on scientific knowledge. Practice that lends itself to modification through research has a long-term advantage.

It should be clear from the above discussion that research has its limitations as a tool for improving practice. With some forms of practice, these limitations may be so handicapping that more progress can be made through means other than empirical inquiry. Luborsky and Spence drew a similar conclusion following their review of research on psychoanalytic approaches:

> *Quantitative research on psychoanalytic therapy presents itself, so far, as an unreliable support to clinical practice. Far more is known now through clinical wisdom than is known through quantitative objective, studies.* Much of what is contributed by the quantitative literature represents a cumbersome, roundabout way of showing the clinician what he or she already "knows." [Emphasis in original.][23]

Although research on such forms of practice, particularly thoughtful qualitative studies of single cases, may yield benefits, it should not be regarded as a major means of improving service. By the same token, research cannot be relied on to provide firm evidence about what is really known or what really represents progress.

Any practice model, or at least parts of it, can be made more amenable to scientific scrutiny, however, through relating concepts and methods to measurable events and through ordering these events in the form of specific, testable hypotheses. For example, if it is posited that educative methods will enhance the client's reality testing, the treatment theorist would need to explicate what practitioner behaviors constitute educative methods, what specific client responses denote reality testing, and the steps by which the former affect the latter.

If such terms and relations are spelled out with rigorous testing in mind, then the stage is set for truly informative research. What is being suggested is a proto-research strategy that would help provide the kind of raw material needed for the best applications of the scientific method.

Conclusions

If it is correct to assume that the improvement of its individualized services is a central objective of social work and that research should provide a major means of pursuing that objective, then the conclusions to follow might be taken as suggestions for priorities in social work research. These conclusions are an attempt to synthesize and highlight certain themes that have already emerged in consideration of the separate strategies.

First, emphasis on experimental research seems to be of essential importance. Although other forms of study have their place in building practice methods, ultimately the methods must be tested to determine how they operate and with what results under varying conditions. But older experimental paradigms—in particular, the large-scale once-and-for-all evaluations of previously untested programs—need to be replaced by forms of experimentation, such as single-subject designs and micro and exploratory experiments, that are better suited to the progressive modification of practice methods. Regardless of the form it takes, experimentation can be used to best advantage if it is organized in research and development undertakings aimed at producing better practice models. Such undertakings, and practice experiments generally, need to be carried out by personnel with technical competence in both service and research methods. This is not to suggest that researchers should take over the job of developing service models, but rather that there is a need for a new breed of model developer, one who knows what is to be tested and how to test it.

Second, if improvement of practice is the goal, research strategies must be directed toward the eventual utilization of whatever they produce. That is, ways must be found to insure that service improvements arising from research efforts work in agency programs. One approach would be for agencies to place greater emphasis on research and development rather than to leave the initiative in academic or research centers. Another would be to utilize information systems as means of monitoring the introduction of modifications in service. Data on the use of a modification could be routinely collected to determine how well it was being implemented in a program or in an agency. These approaches, which could of course be used in sequence, would need to be combined with far more effective means of in-service training than are customarily used. Moreover, utilization itself should become the focus of research and development.

Finally, if research is to be used to improve practice as a whole, then all brands of practice need to be cast in forms more amenable to research. This direction would require the translation of abstract practice theories, concepts, and processes into operational terms and would encourage the abandonment of those that cannot be. With an increasing objectification of practice, more powerful and promising research strategies—such as newer forms of experimentation, research and development approaches, and information systems—can be used to better advantage. This movement should lead to and be furthered by single-subject and other forms of experimental testing of widely used methods that until now have been studied only through correlational research if at all; interpretation, paradoxical injunction, and accurate empathy are examples. Putting service into researchable forms and using a predominantly experimental methodology to improve it may ultimately be the only way that social work can make significant progress toward achieving its long-standing goal of a scientific base for its individualized services.

NOTES AND REFERENCES

1. Joel Fischer, *Effective Casework Practice: An Eclectic Approach* (New York: McGraw-Hill Book Co., 1978), p. 52.

2. See, for example, Joel Fischer, ed., *The Effectiveness of Social Casework* (Springfield, Ill.: Charles C Thomas, 1976); and Edward J. Mullen and James R. Dumpson, eds., *Evaluation of Social Intervention* (San Francisco: Jossey-Bass, 1972).

3. Mullen and Dumpson, eds., op. cit.

4. Andrew Weissman, "Industrial Social Services: Linkage Technology," *Social Casework*, 57 (January 1976), pp. 50–54.

5. For a more extended sample, *see* William J. Reid, "A Test of a Task-Centered Approach," *Social Work*, 20 (January 1975), pp. 3–9.

6. *See*, for example, Michel Hersen and David H. Barlow, *Single-Case Experimental Designs: Strategies for Studying Behavior Change* (New York: Pergamon Press, 1976); Harold Leitenberg, "The Use of Single-Case Methodology in Psychotherapy Research," *Journal of Abnormal Psychology*, 82 (August 1973), pp. 87–101; and Michael W. Howe, "Casework Self-Evaluation: A Single-Subject Approach," *Social Service Review*, 48 (March 1974), pp. 10–15.

7. R. Vance Hall, *Applications in School and Home*, "Behavior Management Series," Part 3 (Lawrence, Kans.: H. and H. Enterprises, 1971), p. 55.

8. *See*, for example, Edwin J. Thomas "Mousetraps, Developmental Research, and Social Work Education," *Social Service Review*, 52 (September 1978), pp. 468–483; and Jack Rothman, *Research and Development in the Human Services: Toward a Systematic Methodology of Applied Social Science*. To be published by Prentice-Hall.

9. *See*, for example, Robert M. McFall and Diane Bridges Lillesand, "Behavior Rehearsal with Modeling and Coaching in Assertion Training," *Journal of Abnormal Psychology*, 77 (1971), pp. 313–323; and Robert McFall and Craig Twentyman, "Four Experiments in the Relative Contribution of Rehearsal, Modeling and Coaching to Assertion Training," *Journal of Abnormal Psychology*, 81 (1973), pp. 199–218.

10. Ronald H. Rooney, "Prolonged Foster Care: Toward a Problem-Oriented Task-Centered Model." Unpublished doctoral dissertation, School of Social Service Administration, University of Chicago, 1978.

11. Thomas, op. cit., p. 47.

12. Morris B. Parloff, Irene Elkin Waskow, and Barry H. Wolfe, "Research on Therapist Variables in Relation to Process and Outcome," in Sol L. Garfield and Allen E. Bergin, eds., *Handbook of Psychotherapy and Behavior Change: An Empirical Analysis* (2d ed.; New York: John Wiley & Sons, 1978), pp. 233–282.

13. Dorothy Fahs Beck and Mary Ann Jones, *Progress on Family Problems: A Nationwide Study of Clients' and Counselors' Views on Family Agency Systems* (New York: Family Service Agency of America, 1973), p. 123.

14. David Wallace, "The Chemung County Evaluation of Casework Services to Dependent Multiproblem Families," *Social Service Review*, 41 (December 1967), p. 386.

15. Charles B. Truax and Kevin M. Mitchell, "Research on Certain Therapist Interpersonal Skills in Relation to Process and Outcome," in Allen E. Bergin and Sol L. Garfield, eds., *Handbook of Psychotherapy and Behavior Change: An Empirical Analysis* (New York: John Wiley & Sons, 1971), pp. 299–344.

16. *See*, for example, Kevin M. Mitchell, John K. Bozarth, and Charles C. Krauft, "A Reappraisal of the Therapeutic Effectiveness of Accurate Empathy, Nonpossessive Warmth, and Genuineness," in Alan S. Gurman and Andrew M. Razin, eds., *Effective Psychotherapy: A Handbook of Research* (New York: Pergamon Press, 1977), pp. 482–502; Parloff, Waskow, and Wolfe, op. cit.

17. William J. Reid, "Applications of Computer Technology," in Norman A. Polansky, ed., *Social Work Research: Methods for the Helping Professions* (Chicago: University of Chicago Press, 1975), pp. 229–253.

18. David Fanshel, "Parental Visiting of Foster Children: A Computerized Study," *Social Work Research and Abstracts*, 13 (Fall 1977), pp. 2–10.

19. William J. Reid, "The Social Agency as a Research Machine," *Journal of Social Service Research*, 2 (Fall 1978), pp. 11–24.

20. Thomas J. Kiresuk and Robert E. Sherman, "Goal Attainment Scaling: A General Method for Evaluating Comprehensive Mental Health Programs," *Community Mental Health Journal*, 4 (December 1968), pp. 443–453; and Howard L. Millman and Charles E. Schaefer, "Behavioral Change: Program Evaluation and Staff Feedback," *Child Welfare*, 54 (December 1975), pp. 692–702.

21. Fanshel, op. cit.

22. *See*, for example, Lester Luborsky, Barton Singer, and Lise Luborsky, "Comparative Studies of Psychotherapies," *Archives of General Psychiatry*, 32 (August 1975), pp. 995–1008; Mary Lee Smith and Gene V. Glass, "Meta-Analysis of Psychotherapy Outcome Studies," *American Psychologist*, 32 (September 1977), pp. 752–760; and R. Bruce Sloane et al., *Psychotherapy versus Behavior Therapy* (Cambridge, Mass.: Harvard University Press, 1975).

23. Lester Luborsky and Donald P. Spence, "Quantitative Research on Psychoanalytic Therapy," in Garfield and Bergin, eds., op. cit., pp. 331–368.

Making Research Relevant for Practitioners

FREDRICK W. SEIDL

AT THIS POINT in the history of the social work profession, it is clear that social work practitioners neither read, write, nor utilize research. Rosenblatt and Kirk, Osmalov, and Fischer have documented this problem.[1] Since 1903 schools of social work have taught courses in the methods and content of research, but the impact of such efforts on practitioners' utilization of research is negligible now.[2] Researchers have attempted to come to grips with the problems. Bloom has writ-

ten about how research from various disciplines might be utilized and how practice problems can be used to teach the concepts of research.[3] Briar has discussed using the concept of the clinical scientist to integrate research and practice.[4]

This article looks at the "front end" of the research process, that is, at how research problems can be formulated to maximize their relevance and utility for the direct service pratitioner, the social worker at the interface of the client and the service system. It (1) outlines criteria for determining which research problems are relevant, (2) suggests ways to develop such questions, and (3) discusses who might do such research and where it might be done. The article concludes with an argument for an increase in agency-based research within the context of several research roles available to social workers.

The author wishes to thank Robert Applebaum for his help in gathering information and constructing the argument; the staffs of the Dodge County Department of Social Service, the Dane County Department of Social Service, and the Dane County Mental Health Center for help in generating ideas and identifying problems; and the faculty of the School of Social Work at the University of Wisconsin–Madison for giving generously of their time and interest.

Characteristics of a
Relevant Research Problem

For a research problem to be relevant for
practice and for the results it generates to
be of use to practitioners, the problem
needs to have several characteristics: it
must involve variables that can be influenced by practitioners, it must be both
researchable and understandable, and it
must exhibit the qualities of both timeliness and space specificity. In the logical
positivistic view of science, propositions
of high relevance tend to meet the requirements for theory because they are
usually localized in space and time.[5] In
contrast, highly relevant research, although it too is bounded in space and
time, may not be theoretical at all. It may
focus instead on the particulars of the
situation and give little attention to the
general statements that can be abstracted
from those particulars. Propositions can
meet the requirements of relevance and
skirt those of theory and still be framed
as *if-then* conditional statements of
nonequivalence between an antecedent
and a consequent condition—between
independent and dependent variables.

Manipulable Variables. Social work
practitioners are constrained in what
they can do by their job descriptions, organizations, skills, and power.
They cannot have an impact on all things.
Much of the research carried out in the
hope of helping the direct service practitioner become more effective focuses on
variables over which practitioners have
no control. Nonmanipulable variables
such as personality, age, and sex are
favorites for researchers, and although
such research may be useful in triage or
case-management models and in program
planning and administration, such
studies are of little use to the direct service practitioner. At best, the focus on
variables that workers cannot influence

gives them perspectives about their own
limitations; at worst, it gives them a sense
of helplessness since it emphasizes that
the things which make a difference are
out of their hands. There are things the
practitioner can control, change, or manipulate, however, and the statement of a
research problem that is relevant to
practitioners should focus on these.

This injunction to focus on manipulable
variables places a special burden on the
outside researcher. To know which variables are subject to planned change, one
needs to know the specific job contingencies of the person who is to implement the
findings. Different workers have different
bases of power and influence. Hence, the
frequently heard response from workers is
that no matter how well intentioned the
researchers, if they are not intimately
familiar with the issues important to the
social workers in a particular situation,
the research will not be of much use.

Researchability. Relevance for practice is just one side of the equation;
the other side also requires explication.
Much of what direct service practitioners
need to know is not directly translatable
into research problems. For example, the
author and his colleagues asked a group
of participants in a continuing education
program questions about tasks required
by their jobs and about the knowledge
they needed both for these tasks and in
general. The knowledge they needed can
be distinguished as belonging to three
broad categories: skills to do things; information regarding systems, laws, and
procedures; and scientific means to
validate service techniques and to assess
clients' needs.

The most frequently cited needs were
for skills—counseling and leadership
skills, the skills needed to staff a committee, skills in treatment techniques and
communication, and skills associated
with linking people to resources. Al-

though learning a skill does not involve any scientific activity, the empirical validity of an activity that requires skill is a scientific problem. As Reid put it, "It took a lot of skill to bleed a patient."[6]

The second most frequently cited need for knowledge concerned information about systems, laws, procedures, and policies. How one executes a task through a system is determined by both formal and informal policies and procedures and is important in practice. Although researchers might inquire into the effects of various policies and procedures on workers, clients, and client systems, understanding the procedure is not a research problem since it is a product of management and legislation. Researchers may aim to increase the proportion of procedures that is scientifically based, but social work practice remains in large measure the learning and execution of skills and procedures regardless of their scientific merit.

The informal survey also pointed up a need for knowledge that clearly fell within the realm of scientific inquiry. The type of scientific knowledge workers most frequently said they needed were means of validly differentiating clients' needs so as to provide the most effective service. Questions about the effectiveness of various counseling techniques and other sets of skills were also cited. All these needs of direct service practitioners are for knowledge that can be discovered through research.

Problem Intelligibility. It is most difficult to implement what one does not understand. The researcher and practitioner may not understand one another, although this is like the British and Americans being divided by the same language. Although problems of intelligibility are not confined to differences of language, examples abound in language. One lies in the varying definitions of

"burnout." Practitioners have tended to define "burnout" as job turnover, and scholars have seen it in psychological terms relating to stress, exhaustion, and excessive demand. Social control is seen by researchers as the opposite of coercive control or as the actualization of some core value; practitioners tend to view social control as synonymous with oppression.

For maximum utility, a research problem needs to be cast in the language of the utilizer, the practitioner. This is difficult for two reasons. First, researchers are trained in translating everyday phenomena into the framework of the prevailing scientific paradigms. This makes the research relevant to the paradigm and not necessarily to practice. Second, the history of the researcher-practitioner relationship has made the practitioner wary of the researcher's language. Some practitioners in the author's field have come to call regression equations "aggression equations." Although the focus of social work educators has been to prepare students as consumers of research, little has been done to prepare researchers to write understandable research reports or to communicate effectively in some other way with those who might use the findings in practice. If researchers are to formulate problems intelligible to practitioners, they need to be trained to recognize what practitioners mean by their expressions, how they define a situation, and what they see as the problems that confront them.

Timeliness. Social work practice is dynamic, perhaps more dynamic than any other of the recognized professions. This dynamism results in part from the sanction for practice lying largely in public social policy. Such policy changes daily. Social service workers have become accustomed to rapid job shifts, changing target populations, and new technologies. To deal with this, research projects need to be completed within a short period of time. The four or five years associated with the large-budget research effort so valued by university-based researchers means that the findings will become available too late to make a difference in the day-to-day practice of social work. By then the program will have changed, and the social workers in the program will be doing something else. The payoff of such research is not in expanding the knowledge base of direct service practitioners, but in organizing and funding social services in the future. If the research problem is to be relevant to practitioners, however, it must address the problems they are encountering this year or this month. The premium, therefore, is on quickly executed research. Scholars often call it "quick and dirty," but there are many situations in which quick and dirty is better than long and clean. The hard-nosed requirements of truth tend to conflict with the immediate requirements of utility, so research that is timely is often hard to publish.

Space Specificity. From the point of view of direct service practitioners, the most relevant research is that done in their agency with that agency's clients and with consideration given to the unique configurations of the immediate practice situation. Although evaluation studies, for example, have eschewed direct and deliberate appraisal of administrative performance because such findings are not easily generalizable, an appraisal of administrative performance may be just what direct service practitioners need to understand what is happening to their caseloads. If it is to be useful, research cannot ignore local variability because it has little theoretical relevance. This has been among the problems of several pieces of behavioral research—space-specific variables were

potentially instrumental in whether the manipulation had effects, but these variables were ignored.

Generating Relevant Problems

There are quite a number of ways to formulate research problems that exhibit the five characteristics of relevancy—manipulability of the variables, researchability, problem intelligibility, timeliness, and space specificity. Consideration here will be given to three modal types: making deductions from paradigms of social work or social science, carrying out job analyses and defining needed bits of information, and involving practitioners in formulating definitions of problems. The first two of these need only brief attention here; involving practitioners in the process of formulating research problems, which is the approach most likely to produce practice-relevant research problems, requires closer examination.

Problems from Paradigms. Problems for research are most frequently drawn from paradigms of practice or models of problems borrowed from related social science disciplines. This is a legitimate scientific activity. Deriving a research problem from existing paradigms guides research so that its findings are useful in further articulation of the parent model. In social work, conceptual models have been built, but there is little consensus about which is most effective. The issue of *Social Work* devoted to this necessary and important task of the construction of satisfactory conceptual models indicated how divergent the views of the field and its mission are.[7] All such models, whether practice models or parent models drawn from other disciplines, are necessarily quite abstract, and as became clear in the earlier discussion of how research problems depend for relevance on particularities of time and space, such abstraction seriously compromises the relevance of the problem.

These problems are magnified by importing models from social science. Research that results in either the rejection or the further articulation of social work and social science models has considerable long-term impact on the activities of the direct service practitioner, but it is difficult to see the short-run benefits to day-to-day practice.

Job Analysis. An approach that has not been widely used but that appears to have potential is the empirically oriented job analysis. The basic idea is that if the job is known, it is possible to determine what knowledge is useful for its execution. The incentive to carry out meaningful job analysis has increased with the introduction of the reporting requirements of Title XX. One example is Teare's analysis of practice in Florida Public Welfare.[8] This study used factor analysis to isolate seven service tasks: personnel management, physical-personal care, direct services casework, community-program interface activities, case management, supply management, and skill training and mediation within groups. Early findings such as these have indicated that social work research efforts have placed disproportionate emphasis on psychotherapeutic research; the activities of social workers are much more highly concentrated in interorganizational linkages, coordination, and case management than in counseling. The data suggest that social workers are more accurately characterized as facilitators and determiners of resources than as changers of people. If this is true, research into the effectiveness of various services, assessment technologies, and

service outcomes is in order. Among Title XX agencies at least, models of case management need to be explored.

Practitioner Involvement in Formulating Research Problems

Although there is merit in formulating research problems either deductively by drawing them from models or inductively through empirical analyses of jobs, the involvement of practitioners in problem formulation has both pragmatic and political advantages. Since practitioners are expected to utilize the fruits of research, it is reasonable that they be consulted about the problems that research needs to address. Theoretically, if direct service practitioners have a major and perhaps a determining role in the formulation of research problems, the widespread and well-documented perception of research as being irrelevant to everyday practice might be changed.

This is not a revolutionary idea. Researchers in the past have attempted to involve practitioners in the formulation of problems. Lindeman carried out a Delphi survey of research priorities in clinical nursing and was successful in securing and pooling expert judgment as to future directions for nursing research.[9] Social work researchers have frequently been frustrated in similar attempts, and the frustration has been felt on both sides. Since the problem stems largely from the researcher's inability to tap the practice wisdom of professionals for important research topics, it is appropriate to suggest ways to solicit research problems from practitioners by using interviews, participant observation, and intrusive group approaches.

Interviewing. The most obvious approach is the most direct one, but as any social worker knows, interviewing is a skill that takes practice and wisdom. In one study, carried out in a system of correctional camps, administrators were concerned about the level of morale in some of the camps and about how the morale might be improved. They identified this concern and communicated it to a researcher who was known to be sympathetic to the concerns of the staff in the system. The researcher and colleagues then determined, through interviews and subsequently through a modified q-sort technique, what the administrators understood by the meaning of the term "morale." They also interviewed the administrators to discover what they thought affected morale. The definitions of "morale" that were finally operationalized were not those found in the criminological literature, but those that reflected what the term meant to the participants in the situation. Similarly, potential independent variables were operationalized using practitioner definitions.[10]

The researcher's task is twofold. It is essential, first, to exercise sufficient interviewing skills to understand the phenomenology of the practice situation, that is, to understand the meaning of the words participants use to describe their tasks and their environments, and, second, to be able to operationalize these meanings into reliable and valid measurements. The important point here is that the validity of the measurement lies in the definition of the concepts held by the practitioners. If each concept overlaps with a theoretical notion, all the better, but for research to be relevant to practice, the preferred option is to define things in the practitioners' terms.

Participant Observation. The most likely approach for the agency-based researcher is that of one who is both a participant and an observer or researcher. According to this model, the researchers gain familiarity with practice problems by directly observing them in their own practice and in the practice of their colleagues. Briar's clinical-scientist is one example of the use of the participant-observation approach to formulating research problems. Relevant research problems often stem from disagreements among staff as to the proper course of action in a certain situation. This may place the researcher in a difficult position, but it has promise as a way to generate problems of practice significance. The author carried out a study of the results of varying hours of field placement for social work students following a debate in the curriculum committee of his school of social work. The results, which took two months to collect, were fed back into the decision-making process of the committee and were used in the committee's deliberations.

Intrusive Group Approaches. Intrusive group approaches have been used to determine research priorities for the delivery of social services. The Social Services Research Workshop held in Washington, D.C., attempted to pool professional judgment concerning significant gaps in knowledge and to gather "recommendations for research needed to assist in reaching future decisions regarding social service programs and social policy."[11] Few, if any, of the participants were front-line social work practitioners; they were, instead, an elite of bureaucrats and scholars interested in service delivery problems. The author has used intrusive group approaches, most frequently the nominal group technique, with practitioners to define problems for research, particularly in the evaluation of the Wisconsin Community Care Organization, a large-scale demonstration project.[12]

The nominal group technique is a seven-step group process through which

Table 1. Research Priorities Identified in Nominal Group Process by Social Workers in a Rural County in Wisconsin

Item	Rank
What are the effects of federal legislation on programs, and practical impact on workers in the field?	1.0
How do you keep well-intentioned programs from being corrupted by the local power structure?	2.5
The burnout problem: effect on workers, reduction of worker effectiveness and contribution to high turnover.	2.5
Understanding the rules and regulations of paperwork.	4.0
How to develop credibility with the community, clients; the influence of community on program development.	4.0

professional judgment may be pooled. The approach was used as part of the proceedings of the Social Services Research Workshop. The heart of the process is a silent period during which participants generate ideas; this is followed by serial presentation of the ideas with opportunities for "piggybacking" new ideas. Although the validity and reliability of the nominal group technique has not been established, the author and his colleagues found the technique useful in three group sessions, two in departments of social service and one in a community mental health center. All three groups were asked to respond to the same question: "What are the most pressing needs of direct service practitioners that should have the attention of social work researchers?" Tables 1, 2, and 3 show the top five items from each of the groups. The first was a group of social workers in

a rural county's department of social services (Table 1). All were BA graduates who had trained as social workers; none were members of the National Association of Social Workers. Two were involved in adult services, and the remaining seven were involved in some aspect of child welfare. Ranks were established through a weighted voting procedure in which each worker rated his or her top five choices.

The second group was composed of workers from an urban department of social services. Almost all held MSW degrees; ten were direct service workers; one was a supervisor. The five top priorities of this group are represented in Table 2. In total, twenty ideas were generated by the rural group and fifty-two by the urban group.

The third group to generate potential research ideas consisted of the direct

Table 2. Research Priorities Identified in Nominal Group Process by Social Workers in an Urban County in Wisconsin

Item	Rank
Effect of worker time off on burnout; things that could be done to reduce burnout.	1.0
Effectiveness of substitute care, effects on children, placement.	2.5
How to get research to practitioners to keep them informed.	2.5
Develop a case-management system to coordinate services with clients and eliminate duplication of services.	4.5
Paperwork problems: how can workers do quality work with heavy paperwork load?	4.5

Table 3. Research Priorities Identified in Nominal Group Process by Social Workers in a County Mental Health Center in Wisconsin

Item	Rank
Effectiveness of treatment modalities in relationship to population being served and the characteristics of therapists.	1.5
Are mental health centers worth the money? Is the community mental health concept worth it?	1.5
Clearer guidelines to crisis situations—when they will occur (for example, suicide or murder).	4.0
Effect of goal setting (accountability) on treatment.	4.0
How to reach minority and low-income groups in need of mental health services.	4.0

service staff of a county mental health center. This group was far better trained than either of the other two groups and included two Ph.D.s. It was a productive group and slightly resistant to the nominal group format because the format imposed constraints on free-floating discussion. Table 3 shows the top five items generated by this group.

The lists of priorities drawn up by the practitioners in the three Wisconsin agencies require further clarification through follow-up with the participants in the group processes, perhaps using the Delphi technique, if any of the ideas are to become useful as research questions. Clearly, some of the problems do not meet all the criteria specified at the beginning of this article, and it would be difficult to satisfy the criterion of researchability with several of them. Nevertheless, the group process approach gives some assurance that the other criteria are met—that the problems involve manipulable variables, that they are intelligible to practitioners, and that they are pertinent to a particular time and place.

Who Should Do Relevant Research?

In 1929, the Milford Conference reported its conclusion that

there is no greater responsibility facing social case work at the present time than the responsibility of organizing continuous research into the concepts, problems and methods of its field. . . . Social case workers cannot leave the responsibility for research to foundations and universities. They must do it themselves and participation by social case workers in such research must be widespread.[13]

Much of what has been said in this article might have been written as a follow-up to Milford. If research is to be timely and space specific and to deal, in practitioner's language, with relevant and researchable variables, it can best be conducted where direct practice is carried out. In recent years, however, the trend has been strong toward university-based research and away from agency-based research and researchers. It is likely that social work research will continue to have difficulties of relevancy until this imbalance is corrected.

One of the major difficulties between 1929 and 1979 that makes the reconsideration of the Milford finding practical is the development of new research technologies. Developments in both single-subject and small-n research technology, as well as the advances in techniques for formulating research questions suggested here, make it possible to carry out research that is highly relevant to the needs to direct service practitioners.

Who should do the research? Obviously, it should be a person with a good deal of methodological skill, particularly in measurement. Since the technology of the direct service worker is complex, the researcher should have an intimate familiarity with agency technology.[14] Elaborate training in the theoretical paradigms of social science is probably not necessary; it may even interfere in understanding the unique idioms and concepts that develop among groups of practitioners at particular times. To borrow from Veblin, extensive training in social science paradigms may produce a "trained incapacity." It is best if researchers are direct service practitioners, as in Briar's notion, or in-house researchers who daily rub elbows with the practitioners whose work they study.[15] The researcher's significant reference group should consist primarily of practitioners who are concerned about the utility of the work, not the university committees who decide salaries and promotions. It is important, therefore, that such researchers not be required to publish.

There are ethical, political, and scientific problems in this type of research. What are the ethics involved in evaluating the work of a colleague? What special pressures will the practitioner-researcher face? What political problems will an agency-based researcher encounter, particularly in evaluation? Does an agency-based researcher have the same kind of publication rights as a university-based researcher? Will objectivity be compromised by being an agency employee? Will the work of such researchers degenerate into apologies for agency operations? This laundry list of questions could be much longer. Since many doctoral programs in social work are already training students to work as practitioner-researchers, it is important that such questions be addressed.

Another question raised by the practitioner-researcher model is who, then, will carry out the important role of the researcher-scholar? Many of the scientific discoveries that have become the foundation of the modern health care system were not made by practicing physicians. Neither Sir Alexander Fleming nor Jonas Salk practiced medicine. Practitioner-researchers or agency-based researchers who believe in the prevailing technology are not likely to ask hard, evaluative questions about it. Among the special requirements for the scholar-researcher whose work may have little immediate application to practice is considerable familiarity with the models and theories of social science. The introduction of behavioral approaches came from psychology, not social work, and important breakthroughs in the technology of practice will probably not come from research into the immediately pragmatic and relevant, but from fresh insights into old problems.[16] There is a need for scholars who know both social work and social science and who have training in the paradigms of both disciplines. There are important roles for both big thinkers and technocrats, and a series of roles in between.

Research is not one task, but many tasks. On a continuum of immediate relevance to practice, research done by Briar's practitioner-researcher is at one end and that of the social scientist–researcher at the other. Between these poles lie the agency-based researcher described here, the service system researcher typically employed by planning agencies, and the university-based researcher of generalized interventive strategies and social work practice models. The profession needs to examine the costs and benefits of all these roles for researchers and to determine the particular problems each might best deal with, the particular constraints under which each operates, and the short-run and long-run utility of each. The argument here has been for a renewal of interest in the agency-based researcher, who, when armed with new technologies of problem formulation, research design, and measurement, can contribute substantially to social work practice.

NOTES AND REFERENCES

1. Aaron Rosenblatt, "The Practitioner's Use and Evaluation of Research," *Social Work*, 13 (January 1968), pp. 53–59; and Stuart A. Kirk, Michael J. Osmalov, and Joel Fischer, "Social Workers Involvement in Research," *Social Work*, 21 (March 1976), pp. 121–124.

2. Betsy-lea Casselman, "On the Practitioners' Orientation toward Research," *Smith College Studies in Social Work*, 42 (June 1972), p. 211. For a glimpse into a period when research was not as alienated from practice as it is now, *see* the writings of Dorothea Dix, Charles Brace, Jane Addams, William Booth, and Mary Richmond.

3. Martin Bloom, "The Selection of Knowledge from Other Disciplines and Its Integration into Social Work Curricula," paper presented at the Annual Program Meeting of the Council on Social Work Education, Minneapolis, Minn., January 1968; and Bloom and William E. Gordon, "Measurement through Practice," *Journal of Education for Social Work*, 14 (Winter 1978), pp. 10–15.

4. Scott Briar, " Incorporating Research into Education for Clinical Practice in Social Work: Toward a Clinical Service in Social Work." Paper presented at the Conference on Research Utilization in Social Work Education, New Orleans, La., October 1977.

5. Ernest Nagel, *The Structure of Science* (New York: Harcourt, Brace & World, 1961), pp. 47–48.

6. William Reid, "Some Reflections on the Practice Doctorate." Paper presented at the Conference on Issues in Social Work Doctoral Education, Ann Arbor, Mich., November 1976.

7. "Special Issue on Conceptual Frameworks," *Social Work*, 22 (September 1977), entire issue.

8. Robert Teare, "An Empirical Analysis of Social Work Practice in a Public Welfare Setting." Paper presented at the Big Sky Summer Symposium on Competence in Social Work, Big Sky, Mont., August 1977.

9. Carol A. Lindeman, *Delphi Survey of Clinical Nursing Research Priorities* (Boulder, Colo.: Western Interstate Commission for Higher Education, 1974).

10. Mary Wirtz Macht, Frederick W. Seidl, and D. Richard Green, "Measuring Inmate Morale," *Social Work*, 22 (July 1977), pp. 284–289.

11. *Proceedings of Social Service Research Workshop* (Washington, D.C.: Public Technology, 1976), p. 1.

12. For a description of the nominal-group technique, *see* Andre Delbecq, Andrew Van de Ven, and David Gustafson, *Group Techniques for Program Planning* (Glenville, Ill.: Scott, Forseman & Co., 1975), pp. 7–13.

13. *Social Case Work: Generic and Specific*, a report of the Milford Conference (Washington, D.C.: National Association of Social Workers, 1974, reprint of 1929 ed.).

14. Mary Wirtz Macht and Fredrick W. Seidl, "A Contingency Approach to Evaluation: Manager's Guidelines." Paper presented at the Institute for Human Service Management Conference, Sacramento, Calif., June 1978.

15. Briar, op. cit.

16. For a discussion of this process, *see* Thomas Kuhn, *The Structure of Scientific Revolutions* (Chicago: University of Chicago Press, 1962).

PART 3

Improving Delivery of Services

Evaluation Research and Program Evaluation: A Difference without a Distinction

WYATT C. JONES

THE DEBATE BETWEEN social work practitioners and social scientists over the efficacy of social work research did not begin with the publication, in 1965, of *Girls at Vocational High*.[1] However, that study touched off a new round in the discussions, and the reverberations of that controversy are still felt in social work agencies and professional schools. It would be pleasant to say that this is a dead issue, but the best prognosis is that it is a dying issue. The advances in social work research during the ensuing years have helped to redefine the issues and to delimit the arguments. Recent theoretical and methodological developments allow a reassessment of these arguments.

As is the case with many intellectual arguments, the real controversy arises from some ambiguity, either in the concepts used or in the findings reported. A review of the extent and nature of these ambiguities may be instructive in the attempt to assess the future of social work research. For this purpose there is no need to limit the critique to social work examples, although they may be most relevant. In fact, social work research shares the ambiguities associated with all social science research and with scentific research in general.

Science, in one sense, is a search for order, for systematic variation on the basis of which predictions may be made that ultimately permit control of the phenomena under scrutiny. Covariation, however, does not involve a cause-effect relationship; the difference between correlation and causation is widely recognized. Correlational or associative studies are by no means useless. Astronomy and meteorology are respectable sciences that rely heavily on correlational analysis. However, causal relationships usually require experimental research for their demonstration. The classical model for experiments, of course, has been the laboratory. But field trials have been successfully used by demographers and, in a less controlled setting, by anthropologists. Social work researchers have sought to adapt the model of the experimental control group to their needs, with varying degrees of success.

Much social work research has been patterned after the work of sociologists and, to a lesser extent, social psychologists. It is my impression that instructors in research courses in schools of social work are predominantly from these disciplines. The emphasis on survey methodologies and small group research is one result of this affinity. However, certain research procedures have been adopted from economics, notably the recent emphasis on cost-benefit analysis. The social sciences, on which so much social work research has been modeled, have been less influenced than the natural sciences by the critical reexamination of the scientific method, particularly experimentation, that has followed recent developments in the history and philosophy of science, operations research, and statistical inference.[2] Another professional group, educational researchers, have been more sensitive to these problems and have wrestled with their implications.[3]

The systematic attempts to evaluate evaluations, to conduct what Cook has called secondary evaluation and Scriven metaevaluation, are now coming into prominence.[4] Social workers came early to this task with the Fordham Symposium of 1971, which reviewed in detail thirteen evaluations of professional social work interventions.[5] This was followed by Fischer's review in 1973 of casework studies.[6] In a later article with the provocative title "Does Anything Work?" Fischer extended this critique to fields other than social work.[7] The Fordham Symposium and Fischer restricted their reviews to experimental studies with control groups. Their findings were largely negative, but they have been overinterpreted by extending their criticism to all social work research and their negative findings to all social work interventions. Although such multievaluations are superior to any single study in assessing the validity and credibility of the reported results, they are subject to some problems. The available studies may be a biased sample (only the so-called best ones get published); comparable data across studies may not be available (suggesting the need to archive unpublished reports); and the unique features of each project can render them unsuitable for such comparisons. In general, the reviewer may need to disaggregate the reported results by asking, What different kinds of effects do different kinds of programs have on different kinds of people?[8]

Conceptual Ambiguity

The first ambiguity confounding social work research is conceptual. A lack of clarity characterizes much social science research and is especially evident in applied social research.[9] Although the distinction between basic and applied social research is not clearly drawn, the principal difference is in the purpose for which the research is carried out. Basic research is conducted to discover new knowledge, and applied social research is directed to the solution of some real-world problem. Coleman characterized basic research as "discipline-oriented" and applied research as "decision-oriented."[10] In this context, social work research is distinctly applied. It usually addresses a real-world problem and is designed to facilitate decision making about policies or programs of social intervention.[11] This statement is not meant to denigrate the value of social theory or the importance of developing social work knowledge; it merely states a fact about the current state of the art.

The conceptual levels, or the level of abstraction, at which research is conducted were categorized by Hyman and Zetterberg as (1) theoretical or experimental, which seeks understanding and emphasizes verification studies that test hypotheses (this is basic, discipline-oriented research, in Coleman's terms), (2) evaluative or programmatic, which tests the practical value of a program and emphasizes demonstration studies that measure effectiveness, and (3) diagnostic, which explores a new or unknown problem and emphasizes descriptive studies that develop taxonomies.[12] These conceptual levels are listed in descending order of complexity and generality. In actually carrying out research, the order would normally be reversed: exploratory studies would lead to demonstration studies, which would generate hypothesis-testing experiments with theoretical relevance. Evaluation research would fall, then, in the middle level.[13]

In recent years, policymakers—from congressmen to consumers—have become increasingly skeptical about the effectiveness and cost-efficiency of many public policies. The relatively new field of evaluation research has grown up to help answer some of these pressing questions, or at least to silence some of the blatant criticisms. The ambiguities in the application and interpretation of evaluation research have arisen because its place in the hierarchy of research studies has not been clearly understood. To the frequently identified conceptual problems of unspecified targets, vague goals, and ambiguous purposes must be added the unstated assumptions that underlie most research efforts. The basic assumption that only an experiment can demonstrate cause-effect relationships has been widely questioned.[14] In addition to the usual attention to Type I and Type II errors—the probabilities of accepting a false hypothesis or rejecting a true one—this criticism points out a Type III error—the probability of solving the wrong problem.[15] Boulding has called this the fallacy of suboptimization—"the attempt to find better and better ways of doing things that probably should not be done at all."[16] In its laudable efforts to be scientific, social work research has been guilty of "naive empiricism"—the assumption that data are neutral and independent of theory and that data alone are sufficient to test a theory.[17] Working from this radical perspective on research, Mitroff and Bonama argue that

> the appropriate way to do science is consistently to look for 'critical experiments' that help to discriminate between competing sets of assumptions. . . . The testing of any theory . . . in science therefore requires the existence of *at least one other* strong rival theory.[18]

Mitroff and Bonoma propose a dialectical or adversary model of inquiry, which

> does not begin by assuming that one of them is 'true' or 'false,' 'right' or 'wrong,' but that each viewpoint may be picking up a part of a yet-to-be-determined 'correct' viewpoint.[19]

Many social work researchers have been defensive of their particular theories and the assumptions they involve and have been unable to tolerate the ambiguity of competing positions and opposing ideologies. They have assumed that such disagreement represents a breakdown in the normal process of scientific inquiry. In other disciplines, this competition of ideas is viewed as the sine qua non of science, and anything else is judged to be unacceptable. Instead of avoiding theoretical and methodological disagreement, social workers might be advised to embrace it and build it into their research designs.

Methodological Ambiguity

This article has already hinted at the unrealistic standards of methodological purity that social workers have imposed on other people's research. Now that the impossibility of a pure experiment is recognized for the myth it is and that all contemporary inferential statistics have been demonstrated to be illogically founded,[20] social work researchers may be released to expand their methodologies and rethink some of their research priorities. Social workers and their critics have frequently denigrated social work research. They have criticized the research designs, the methodological acumen, the statistical sophistication, and the interpretation of findings. These are easy shots and cannot be generalized to all research done by social workers. Social work's designs, methodologies, statistics, and interpretations are not appreciably different from those used in other social science disciplines or other helping professions. To the extent that social workers may deal with more important, more public, and more expensive issues, their research may attract more attention. *Girls at Vocational High* was reported on the front page of the *New York Times*. Much of the flak, however, comes from those within the profession. In this respect, we social workers may have become our own worst enemies.

Before attempting to explicate some of the problems and possibilities of evaluation, which may be identified as the middle range of research, it will be useful to look briefly at the upper and lower levels, that is, at theoretical hypothesis-testing studies and descriptive taxonomic studies. At the lower level, need assessment, incidence and prevalence estimation, participation studies, and descriptions of caseloads, populations at risk, and the like are important and undervalued types of research. These are the bread and butter of agency research and are often overlooked in the rush to deliver service, any service to anybody, and

downgraded when compared with high-powered experimental research. At the other extreme, the fiscal and logistical limitations of experimental research are well known and the problems attendant upon such projects may put researchers off. However, the amount of solid theory to be tested and the number of situations in which randomly selected experimental and control groups can be negotiated are less than researchers might wish. In other words, we social work researchers do not do the kinds of research we might well do, and we cannot do the kinds we think we ought to be doing. It is possible that viewing the research enterprise as a continuum will increase and enhance social work research at all levels.

The diagnostic descriptive research at the first level is not evaluation. It is an important starting point, however. Efforts along these lines should be redoubled for these are the baseline data that must inform operations and management decisions. They are also the data base for higher order research that extends through evaluation to the development of new knowledge. The creation of management information systems (MIS), to which may be added some relevant outcome measures, including both worker and client reports, is an important step in this process. The imminent extension of the requirement for Professional Standards Review Organizations (PSROs) to social work will add a federal mandate for these data. Edwards and Guttentag propose a multiattribute utilities model and Bayesian statistical inference to meet the special requirements of evaluation research.[21] In this model, the values of different decision-making groups are made explicit and ordered in priority. Alternatives for action related to the decision are specified, and inferences about states of the real world are expressed:

> The insight and understanding gained from
> exploratory data analysis are at least as

important as confirmation of hypotheses and postulated effect obtained through designed experiments. The latter seek to confirm that we have the right answer, while the former help assure us that we have the right question.[22]

Evaluation Criteria

In developing a methodology for evaluation, it is important to state a set of criteria. First, of course, it must be good research. Campbell and Stanley agree that research must produce findings that are internally and externally valid—they must be true and they must be generalizable.[23] In addition, the results must be useful to some audience and must be worth more than they cost to produce. These three standards—technical adequacy, utility, and cost-effectiveness—have been spelled out by Stufflebeam in the form of eleven specific criteria. The four criteria of technical adequacy are (1) internal validity, (2) external validity, (3) reliability, and (4) objectivity. To meet standards of utility, evaluation research must be (5) relevant, (6) important, (7) adequate in scope, (8) credible, (9) timely, and (10) pervasively disseminated. Finally, research must meet the prudential criterion of (11) cost-effectiveness. Stufflebeam's administrative checklist for reviewing evaluation plans (see Fig. 1) is a useful tool.[24]

In general, evaluation may be said to serve two distinct purposes, which drastically affect what data are collected, how they are collected, how they are reported, and how others judge the results. If the purpose is to provide information for decision-making, researchers seek to maximize the utility of the data they collect and the findings they report. For policymakers to use evaluation results, the research must answer the questions decision-makers ask, not the academic hypotheses of the researchers. It must be

carried out within a reasonable time, feeding back results to enable project managers to revise their programs, retarget their interventions, add or retrench their services, increase or diminish their activities. A final report four years after the program has been abandoned is worse than useless.[25] Scriven has labeled evaluation for policy decisions as formative research; Rossi and Wright call it process evaluation.[26] I propose to call it program evaluation. Program evaluation begins by asking, Does this program, policy, or intervention work? This implies that policymakers must define what "working" means. A program can be evaluated on several levels, ranging from simply monitoring the clients served and accounting for the time and money spent, to a process analysis of the service delivery system and an assessment of the program's outcomes.[27]

The central issues for program evaluation have been enumerated by Rossi and Wright:

> (1) How can policy goals be defined for evaluation; (2) What are the most appropriate designs, measuring devices, and analyses to be employed, given the limitations imposed by sponsor and budget; (3) What are the appropriate audiences for findings of an evaluation research; and (4) how can evaluation research contribute maximally to the process of decision making in public policy?[28]

It has been argued that the major problems of program evaluation are vague goals, strong promises, and weak effects.[29] In the light of this criticism, whose goals or objectives are to be studied? Certainly the research design must be built into the implementation of the program, and the researcher must be in on the planning at the earliest possible moment. The objectives of all groups—sponsors, staff, clients, and community—should be anticipated in the planning and their questions should be answered by the research. Program

Fig. 1. An Administrative Checklist for Reviewing Evaluation Plans

Conceptualization of Evaluation
- ☐ *Definition* How is evaluation defined in this effort?
- ☐ *Purpose* What purpose(s) will it serve?
- ☐ *Questions* What questions will it address?
- ☐ *Information* What information is required?
- ☐ *Audiences* Who will be served?
- ☐ *Agents* Who will do it?
- ☐ *Process* How will they do it?
- ☐ *Standards* By what standards will their work be judged?

Sociopolitical Factors
- ☐ *Involvement* Whose sanction and support is required, and how will it be obtained?
- ☐ *Internal communication* How will communication be maintained among evaluators, sponsors, and system personnel?
- ☐ *Internal credibility* Will the evaluation be fair to persons inside the system?
- ☐ *External credibility* Will the evaluation be free of bias?
- ☐ *Security* What provisions will be made to maintain security of data?
- ☐ *Protocol* What communication channels will be used by the evaluators and the system personnel?
- ☐ *Public relations* How will the public be kept informed about the intentions and results of the evaluation?

Contractual/Legal Arrangements
- ☐ *Client/evaluator relationship* Who is the sponsor, who is the evaluator, and how are they related to the program?
- ☐ *Evaluation products* What evaluation outcomes are to be achieved?
- ☐ *Delivery schedule* What is the schedule of evaluation services and products?
- ☐ *Editing* Who has the authority for editing evaluation reports?
- ☐ *Access to data* What existing data may the evaluator use, and what new data may be obtained?
- ☐ *Release of reports* Who will release the reports and what audiences may receive them?
- ☐ *Responsibility and authority* Have the system personnel and evaluators agreed on who is to do what in the evaluation?
- ☐ *Finances* What is the schedule of payments for the evaluation, and who will provide the funds?

The Technical Design
- ☐ *Objectives and variables* What is the program designed to achieve? In what terms should it be evaluated?
- ☐ *Investigatory framework* Under what conditions will the data be gathered—for example, experimental design, case study, survey, or site review?
- ☐ *Instrumentation* What data-gathering instruments and techniques will be used?
- ☐ *Sampling* What samples will be drawn? How will they be drawn?

---

evaluation is a political process, and researchers must build support and acceptance by recognizing the priorities of all parties with a stake in the outcome. It is almost essential that formative evaluations be conducted by insiders who have direct access to the top management of the program. The methodologies to accomplish these design requirements are detailed in Tripodi, Fellin, and Epstein.[30]

If the purpose of the evaluation is to determine accountability, then objectivity and credibility require an outside researcher. Accountability requires a retro-spective approach that is similar to Scriven's concept of summative evaluation.[31] I would call it evaluative research. In contrast to program evaluation, which is conducted for the sake of determining policy, evaluative research addresses questions about outcome, assesses the merit of the goals, the adequacy of the research designs, and the efficiency of their implementation. Whereas formative research asks, What was done? summative research asks, Did it do any good? These broader questions involve considerations of morals, ethics, and utility, and

Fig. 1. (continued)

☐ *Data gathering* How will the data-gathering plan be implemented? Who will gather the data?
☐ *Data storage and retrieval* What format, procedures, and facilities will be used to store and retrieve the data?
☐ *Data analysis* How will the data be analyzed?
☐ *Reporting* What reports and techniques will be used to disseminate the evaluation findings?
☐ *Technical adequacy* Will the evaluative data be reliable, valid, and objective?

The Management Plan

☐ *Organizational mechanism* What organizational unit will be employed—for example, in-house, self-evaluation, or external agency?
☐ *Organizational location* Through what channels can the evaluation influence policy formulation and administrative decision-making?
☐ *Policies and procedures* What established and/or ad hoc policies and procedures will govern this evaluation?
☐ *Staff* How will the evaluation be staffed?
☐ *Facilities* What space, equipment, and materials will be available?
☐ *Data-gathering schedule* What instruments will be administered, to what groups, according to what schedule?
☐ *Reporting schedule* What reports will be provided, to what audiences, according to what schedule?
☐ *Training* What evaluation training will be provided, to what groups, and who will provide it?
☐ *Installation of evaluation* Will this evaluation be used to aid the system to improve and extend its internal evaluation capability?
☐ *Budget* What is the internal structure of the budget? How will it be monitored?

Questions of Morals, Ethics, and Utility

☐ *Philosophical stance* Will the evaluation be value free, value based, or value plural?
☐ *Service orientation* What social good, if any, will be served by this evaluation? Whose values will be served?
☐ *Evaluator's values* Will the evaluator's technical standards and values conflict with the client system's and/or sponsor's values? Will the evaluator face any conflict of interest and what will be done about it?
☐ *Judgments* Will the evaluator judge the program; leave that up to the client; or obtain, analyze, and report the judgments of various reference groups?
☐ *Objectivity* How will the evaluator avoid being co-opted and maintain objectivity?
☐ *Prospects for utility* Will the evaluation meet utility criteria of relevance, scope, importance, credibility, timeliness, and pervasiveness?
☐ *Cost-effectiveness* Compared to its potential payoff, will the evaluation be carried out at a reasonable cost?

SOURCE: Daniel L. Stufflebeam, "Meta-Evaluation," Occasional Paper No. 3, The Evaluation Center, College of Education (Kalamazoo: Western Michigan University, 1974). (Mimeographed.)

they consequently bring into play the philosophical stance of the evaluators. Will the researchers be value based, value free, or value plural? Whose values will dominate, those of the sponsor, the staff, the consumer, the researcher, or all of these?[32] In summative evaluation, the research report should present judgments, not merely descriptions. Stufflebeam has listed the questions to be asked about the results of a program:

What results were achieved? Were the stated objectives achieved? What were the positive and negative (unintended) side effects? What impact was made on the target audience? What long-term effects may be predicted? What is the relation of costs to benefits? Overall, how valuable were the results and impacts of this effort?[33]

To these could be added judgments supported by the demonstrated results: Should the program be continued, enlarged, replicated in other settings? How do its results compare with those achieved by other programs with similar objectives?

It is evident from this brief review that evaluative research is considerably more complex and demanding than program evaluation. However, it builds directly on the results of formative evaluation and asks equivalent questions in a larger context. Although summative evaluation can be conducted within a single program, evaluators frequently find it more productive to survey a number of related programs or a series of demonstration projects. This activity constitutes the field of metaevaluation.

Instructive reviews of multievaluations, that is, is evaluations of evaluations of evaluations, may be found in Cook and Gruder and in Rossi and Wright.[34] The programs involved in these reviews include the Head Start planned variation and follow through, the New Jersey–Pennsylvania Negative Income Tax experiments, a Performance Contracting experiment, "Sesame Street" evaluations, Manpower Training Programs, family planning, cost-benefit studies, and criminal justice and police experiments.[35] The reviewers also discuss the results of two independent assessments of evaluations undertaken by the Russell Sage Foundation and the Brookings Institution. Gilbert, Light, and Mosteller rated the effectiveness of thirty well-evaluated innovations of social, sociomedical, and medical experiments.[36] Bernstein and Freeman evaluated 236 ongoing federally financed programs.[37] Minnesota Systems Research studied 110 completed projects from seven agencies of the Department of Health, Education, and Welfare.[38] Bourque and Freeman assessed a group of federal programs for children.[39] Wholey et al. looked at federal evaluation policy in general.[40]

The conclusions about the general methodological adequacy of evaluations are uniformly pessimistic. Cook and Gruder believe

> that recent social experiments have not fulfilled the goal of providing valid, credible, and timely information that has helped in decision making. . . . These experi-

ments have "conveyed important messages to experimenters if not always to policymakers." However, this pessimism about current results is mitigated by optimism about potential, for the authors "find the long-term prospects for experimentation undimmed."[41]

I hope we social work researchers can be as optimistic about the future of our research. If we are to succeed, both schools and agencies must join in the struggle. Some beginnings have been made. Hudson suggests that schools might target their research courses to the interests and career goals of students.[42] Tripodi and Epstein opt for incorporating research methodology into social work practice.[43] Reid has visualized the experimenting social agency as an ongoing research machine.[44] The National Conference on the Future of Social Work Research should furnish some direction for schools of social work and some new fuel for that agency research machine.

NOTES AND REFERENCES

1. Henry J. Meyer, Edgar F. Borgatta, and Wyatt C. Jones, *Girls at Vocational High: An Experiment in Social Work Intervention* (New York: Russell Sage Foundation, 1965).

2. Imre Lakatos and Allen Musgrave, eds., *Criticism and the Growth of Knowledge* (Cambridge, England: Cambridge University Press, 1970); Ian Mitroff and Thomas V. Bonoma, "Psychological Assumptions, Experimentation, and Real World Problems," *Evaluation Quarterly*, 2 (May 1978), pp. 235–259; Michael J. Mahoney, "Experimental Methods and Outcome Evaluation," *Journal of Consulting and Clinical Psychology*, 46 (July 1978), pp. 660–672; and Walter B. Weimer, *Notes on Methodology* (Hillsdale, N.J.: Erlbaum, 1979).

3. *See* the series of papers from the evaluation centers at the colleges of education at Ohio State University and Western Michigan University.

4. Pedro Tamesis Orata, "Evaluating Evaluation," *Journal of Educational Research*, 33 (July 1940), pp. 641–651; Thomas

D. Cook, "The Potential and Limitations of Secondary Evaluations," in Michael J. Apple, Michael J. Subkoviak, and Henry S. Lufler, Jr., eds., *Educational Evaluation: Analysis and Responsibility* (Berkeley, Calif.: McCutchan, 1974), pp. 155–172; and Michael Scriven, "An Introduction to Meta-evaluation," *Educational Product Report*, 2 (February 1969), pp. 36–38.

5. Edward J. Mullen, James R. Dumpson, and Associates, *Evaluation of Social Intervention* (San Francisco: Jossey-Bass, 1972).

6. Joel Fischer, "Is Casework Effective? A Review," *Social Work*, 18 (January 1973), pp. 5–20.

7. Joel Fischer, "Does Anything Work?" *Journal of Social Service Research*, 1 (Spring 1978), pp. 215–243.

8. *See* Thomas D. Cook and Charles L. Gruder, "Metaevaluation Research," *Evaluation Quarterly*, 2 (February 1978), pp. 5–51.

9. Peter H. Rossi, James D. Wright, and Sonia R. Wright, "The Theory and Practice of Applied Social Research," *Evaluation Quarterly*, 2 (May 1978), pp. 171–192.

10. James C. Coleman, "Problems of Conceptualization and Measurement in Studying Policy Impacts," in Kenneth M. Dolbeare, ed., *Public Policy Evaluation* (Beverly Hills, Calif.: Sage Publications, 1973), pp. 19–40.

11. Darrell F. Hawkins, "Applied Research and Social Theory," *Evaluation Quarterly*, 2 (February 1978), pp. 141–152.

12. Herbert H. Hyman, *Survey Design and Analysis* (Glencoe, Ill.: Free Press, 1955); and Hans L. Zetterberg, *On Theory and Verification in Sociology* (Totowa, N.J.: Bedminister Press, 1963).

13. *See* Edward A. Suchman, *Evaluation Research* (New York: Russell Sage Foundation, 1967).

14. *See* Mitroff and Bonoma, op. cit.

15. Ian I. Mitroff and Tom R. Featheringham, "On Systematic Problem Solving and the Error of the Third Kind," *Behavioral Science*, 19 (November 1974), pp. 383–393.

16. Kenneth E. Boulding, "Reflection on Poverty," in *Social Welfare Forum, 1961* (New York: Columbia University Press, 1961), pp. 45–58.

17. Charles West Churchman, *The Design of Inquiring Systems: Basic Concepts of Systems and Organizations* (New York: Basic Books, 1971); and Paul Feyerabend, *Against Method: Outline of an Anarchistic Theory of Knowledge* (London, England: Humanities Press, 1975).

18. Mitroff and Bonoma, op. cit.

19. Ibid.

20. Ian I. Mitroff, "Systems, Inquiry, and the Making of Falsification," *Philosophy of Science*, 40 (June 1973), pp. 255–276; and Weimer, op. cit.

21. Ward Edwards and Marcia Guttentag, "Experiments and Evaluation: A Reexamination," in Carl A. Bennett and Arthur A. Lumsdaine, eds., *Evaluation and Experiment: Some Critical Issues in Assessing Social Programs* (New York: Academic Press, 1975), pp. 409–461.

22. Bennett and Lumsdaine, eds., op. cit., pp. 23–24.

23. Donald T. Campbell and Julian C. Stanley, *Experimental and Quasi-Experimental Designs for Research* (Chicago: Rand McNally & Co., 1966).

24. Daniel L. Stufflebeam, "Meta-Evaluation," Occasional Paper No. 3, The Evaluation Center, College of Education (Kalamazoo: Western Michigan University, 1974) (mimeographed), pp. 5–11. *See also* Stufflebeam, "Meta-evaluation: An Overview," *Evaluation and the Health Professions*, 1 (Spring 1978), pp. 17–43.

25. Carol H. Weiss, ed., *Evaluation Research* (Englewood Cliffs, N.J.: Prentice-Hall, 1972).

26. Michael Scriven, "The Methodology of Evaluation," in Ralph W. Tyler, Robert Gagné, and Scriven, eds., *Perspectives on Curriculum Evaluation*, "AERA Monograph Series," No. 1 (Chicago: Rand McNally & Co., 1967), pp. 39–83; and Peter H. Rossi and Sonia R. Wright, "Evaluation Research: An Assessment of Theory, Practice, and Politics," *Evaluation Quarterly*, 1 (February 1977), pp. 5–52.

27. Robert S. Weiss and Martin Rein, "The Evaluation of Broad-Aim Programs: Difficulties in Experimental Design and an Alternative," in Carol H. Weiss, ed., *Evaluating Ac-*

tion *Programs* (Boston, Mass.: Allyn & Bacon, 1972), pp. 236–249.

28. Rossi and Wright, op. cit., p. 11.

29. Peter H. Rossi, "Testing for Success and Failure in Social Programs," in Rossi and Walter Williams, eds., *Evaluating Social Programs* (New York: Seminar Press, 1972).

30. Tony Tripodi, Phillip Fellin, and Irwin Epstein, *Differential Social Program Evaluation* (Itasca, Ill.: F. E. Peacock Publishers, 1978).

31. Scriven, "The Methodology of Evaluation."

32. *See* Edwards and Guttentag, op. cit.

33. Stufflebeam, "Meta-evaluation: An Overview," p. 18.

34. Cook and Gruder, op. cit.; and Rossi and Wright, op. cit.

35. For a review of family planning evaluations, *see* Elizabeth T. Hilton and Arthur A. Lumsdaine, "Field Trial Designs in Gauging the Impact of Fertility Planning Program," in Bennett and Lumsdaine, eds., op. cit., pp. 319–408. For reviews of cost-benefit studies, *see*, John H. Noble, Jr., "The Limits of Cost-Benefit Analysis as a Guide to Priority-Setting in Rehabilitation," *Evaluation Quarterly*, 1 (August 1977), pp. 347–380; and Stanley Masters, Irwin Garfinkel, and John Bishop, "Benefit-Cost Analysis in Program Evaluation," *Journal of Social Service Research*, 2 (Fall 1978), pp. 53–62. For reviews of criminal justice and police experiments, *see* Joseph H. Lewis, "Evaluation of Experiments in Policing," *Evaluation Quarterly*, 2 (May 1978), pp. 315–330; and Leslie T. Wilkins, *Evaluation of Penal Measures* (New York: Random House, 1969).

36. John P. Gilbert, Richard J. Light, and Frederick Mosteller, "Assessing Social Innovations: An Empirical Base for Policy," in Bennett and Lumsdaine, eds., op. cit., pp. 39–193.

37. Ilene N. Bernstein and Howard E. Freeman, *Academic and Entrepreneurial Research* (New York: Russell Sage Foundation, 1975).

38. *Final Report: Evaluation and Prediction of Methodological Adequacy of Research and Evaluation Studies* (Minneapolis: Minnesota Systems Research, 1976).

39. Linda A. Bourque and Howard E. Freeman, "Evaluating Evaluation Studies: A Review and Appraisal of Current Research on the Impact of Federal Programs for Children" (Los Angeles: Institute for Social Science Research, University of California at Los Angeles, 1977). (Mimeographed.)

40. James S. Wholey et al., *Federal Evaluation Policy* (Washington, D.C.: The Urban Institute, 1970).

41. Cook and Gruder, op. cit., p. 41.

42. Walter W. Hudson, "Research Training in Professional Social Work Education," *Social Service Review*, 52 (March 1978), pp. 116–121.

43. Tony Tripodi and Irwin Epstein, "Incorporating Knowledge of Research Methodology into Social Work Practice," *Journal of Social Science Research*, 2 (Fall 1978), pp. 43–52.

44. William J. Reid, "The Social Agency as a Research Machine," *Journal of Social Service Research*, 2 (Fall 1978), pp. 19–31.

Harnessing Research to Enhance Practice: A Research and Development Model

JACK ROTHMAN

IN THE HISTORIC GULF between research and practice in social work, researchers have pursued one set of interests and practitioners another. At least this is how each of the parties has perceived the other. The author recently interviewed research and operational people in British social service departments and found counterpoised attitudes. Researchers were described as aloof and divorced from practice. They were said to stand

This article is adapted from publications of the Community Intervention Project of the University of Michigan, Ann Arbor, supported by the National Institute of Mental Health, in particular, the author's book, *Social R&D: Research and Development in the Human Services*, published in 1979 by Prentice-Hall, and *Developing Effective Strategies of Social Intervention: A Research and Development Methodology*, by Rothman, Joseph G. Teresa, and John L. Erlich, available from the National Technical Information Service, Springfield, Va. (PB-272454 TR-1-RD, 1977). The author also expresses his appreciation to his associates for their contributions to the ideas presented in this article.

apart from the goals of the agency and from its operational problems and processes; they were accused of not taking sufficient interest in the basic tasks of practice or in the pressures faced by operational people. Informants observed that researchers do not extend themselves to form personal associations with operational people. Researchers' stance of objectivity, it was reported, had led not to an informed understanding of practice, but rather to a disdainful detachment— they stood not only apart from agency practice, but also above it.

Practitioners did not escape from their share of blame for the existence of a research-practice chasm. Respondents in the study spoke of practitioners as irrationally attached to particular techniques and ways of work, intensely sensitive to criticism, and highly protective of their autonomy, all of which tends to close out new knowledge. They were said to prefer an intuitive style of performance that relies on a "feel for the situation" rather than on data from outside "experts." This was further complicated by an alleged lack of adequate knowledge about research and by ingrained hostility by some toward it.

To a considerable degree, researchers have been deficient in responding to research needs as defined by practitioners. Practice research is a turbulent and messy arena. Methodologies for studying practice have been inadequate. Certain types of applied research, including program evaluation, were frowned on by the social science mainstream as tainted and inferior. Suchman struggled in virtual isolation for years in his efforts to perfect and legitimate a methodology for evaluative research. Social work research has never been well established or widely supported, and the researchers were already in a fragile enough position without venturing into areas that were suspect in the eyes of their research peer group in other disciplines. It was safer and more reliable to follow standard canons of research, even though these were often aimed away from concerns central to practice. The questions posed were those that could be answered by standard methodology, and not enough effort was made to bend the methodology to respond to the questions that needed to be asked. An engineering orientation to practice research was largely absent.

Social work practitioners were, of course, no help in this. Their appreciation and encouragement of researchers in the field has always left much to be desired. The attitudes of many practitioners provided an inhospitable environment for social work researchers to work in.

There are some indications that the separation between research and practice has begun to narrow. Methodologies have begun to emerge that permit a reconciliation and blending of research and application. The model of the pure researcher

using classic study designs has begun to lose its monopolistic hold. Social researchers now have methodologies and models that permit them to thrust themselves into practice situations and concerns without a sense of downgrading their professional standards. The time has arrived when research can be harnessed to enhance social practice; research technology can be shaped to advance practice technology.

The potential for harnessing research to serve practice stems from two contemporary developments: improved methods of retrieving and storing social science research, and new methods of conducting research related to practice. A much larger and richer body of research is available to inform practice than has existed before. Since World War II there has been a burgeoning of research knowledge in every field of social science inquiry. Improved methods of retrieving, synthesizing, and storing this information are being perfected. Computerized data banks are one of the major advances along these lines. Some of these data systems are broad in scope, such as the Smithsonian Scientific Information Exchange, and some are specialized, such as MEDLARS for medical information and ERIC for educational data. There are also more and improved indexes to literature, services which provide reviews on various subjects, such as Project Share of the Department of Health, Education and Welfare, and synthesized works, such as the *Annual Review of Sociology* and the *Annual Review of Psychology*. In addition, a profession of specialists in information science has made its appearance, so that technicians and consultants are available to assist in inventorying and extracting information. Some schools of social work and their affiliated research centers have employed such specialists. The author's experience in working with existing social science research sources has convinced him that this is an avenue of tremendous potential for enhancing practice.

Among the new methodologies for conducting research, advances in program evaluation and other forms of evaluative research have been striking, and the implications for testing and assessing practice are immediate and significant. It is becoming possible to know with some assurance what works in intervention and under what conditions, as well as what does not work and should be discarded. Single-case designs and other quasi-experimental approaches lend themselves to conducting research that is enmeshed in the realities and complexities of practice.[1] These approaches permit the assessment of patterns and techniques of intervention and the construction of operational guides and procedures to channel effective practice. These new designs constitute an interlocking of practice and research in a way that is highly compatible and interdependent. In reviewing his work with these approaches, Briar made this observation:

> We could no longer maintain a distinct and clear separation between research and practice. As students began to apply what they were learning in the field, they not only incorporated the research-practice model into their practice, but research and practice became fused and we found that when we addressed research we also were talking about practice and vice versa.[2]

Social work researchers have begun to apply these contemporary research perspectives and tools to practice. Among these steps are Briar's efforts to define and operationalize a clinical scientist, Thomas's thrust in the direction of development research, Reid and Epstein's sustained activity in refining task-centered casework, and the author and his associates' work in formulating a research and development (R&D) methodology for social intervention.[3] There are

some different themes and emphases among these approaches, which is a useful diversity at this early stage in the emergence of this new approach, but there is also a common thread marking a new and promising research direction.

The remainder of this article presents the R&D formulation in succinct form, indicating some of its characteristics and discussing some of its methological aspects. The R&D approach has particular advantages in that it requires the incorporation of both important advances identified earlier—the retrieval of existing research knowledge and the employment of new tools for conducting research. It also allows those in the social sciences and social work to build on the substantial experience and knowledge of the physical sciences and industry in applying research to the creation of products and procedures having practical utility. From the standpoint of the practitioner, R&D's essential output is practice technology that can be put to immediate and easeful use.

R&D Model

Since the R&D research utilization model has been elaborated in detail elsewhere, it is necessary here to convey only its basic features and dynamic flow.[4] References to the Community Intervention Project (CIP), a long-term action-research study that both applied and helped refine the social R&D model, will help clarify how the model works and provide a platform for discussing a number of conceptual issues concerning the use of the R&D approach.

The model is composed of six material stages linked by five operational steps. An updated version is diagrammed in Figure 1. To indicate how the model interfaces with the various concepts of research and development found in the lit-

Fig. 1. Schematic Representation of the Research and Development (R&D) Model of Research Utilization

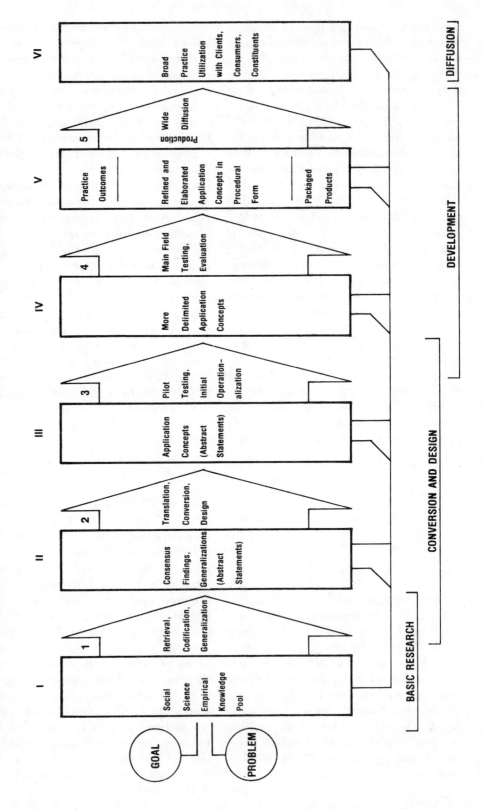

erature, the four basic phases of R&D are indicated at the bottom of the figure. In CIP, the research team started with the problem of low levels of participation in agency programs. Problems and goals are opposite sides of the same coin, and problems can often be restated as goals. In CIP, the goal was to develop a means of increasing participation rates in agency programs. The first step in the application of the R&D model is to identify sources of research literature that bear on the subject. In the CIP experience, the R&D team went to selected journals in the disciplines of sociology, psychology, political science, and applied anthropology, as well as to periodicals in applied professions such as social work, public health, and adult education. A carefully structured retrieval program was used to survey and assess the designated pool of research material in a systematic way. The team codified studies dealing with participation and looked for consensus findings. A consensus finding emerges when numerous investigators working under varying conditions converge on similar conclusions. The R&D team then expresses the consensus finding as a generalization concerning the subject under inquiry. In the CIP example, a consensus finding permitted the formulation of a generalization on participation, which was stated roughly as follows: The amount of voluntary participation in an organization depends on the benefits gained from the participation.

A generalization is usually passive in form; it describes relationships among social phenomena. For R&D purposes it must be converted into an active form that prescribes a means of modifying some social phenomenon or state of affairs. This conversion results in an application concept, which is an intervention inferred directly from the generalization. The process of conversion entails technical, synthetic, and artistic components

that have been analyzed in another publication.[5] In the CIP situation, the application concept extrapolated from the generalization read as follows: To foster participation in organizations, programs, and task groups, practitioners should provide or increase relevant benefits.

An application concept is generally considered by its framer to have high potential as an intervention strategy because it is founded on research evidence and, ideally, is further supported by personal experience and practice literature. Nevertheless, devising the concept involves the use of inference and conjecture to reshape a generalization. Thus the application concept represents an informed supposition about the effects of a given type of intervention. This supposition requires empirical testing.

Exposing the application concept to real-world scrutiny is the development phase of R&D. Development begins with a pilot test to determine whether the application concept can be made to work in action and to experiment with various means of devising a working model or demonstration. In CIP, eight practitioners carried out the application concept in their usual agency settings and carefully recorded their activities and the results. This pilot phase explored whether practitioners can acquire and manipulate relevant benefits and whether these have some discernible effect on rates of participation.

If the pilot test yields a positive assessment, the next step is main field testing. In this phase, a larger number of field staff and implementation sites carry out the application concept, but with tighter and more refined procedures. In the CIP case, the field staff included twenty-one agency-based practitioners with a part-time commitment to the project. Standardized recording forms were used, and a rigorous evaluation plan was put into effect that used a carefully selected panel of judges to rate the outcome of each intervention. The main field test permits the application concept to be specified in a firmer and more detailed way. For example, the CIP field test delineated the variety of benefits practitioners were providing to clients. The instrumental benefits included such material benefits as obtaining a loan or grant or securing needed information or authorization, and such anticipatory benefits as obtaining a verbal commitment as a step toward the material gain. Expressive benefits included the interpersonal rewards of making new friends and having an enjoyable social experience, and the symbolic satisfactions of receiving an award or mention in a newspaper article that represented public recognition of an individual's participatory activities. The field test also determined that the practitioners typically offered multiple benefits involving combinations of these different types of benefits.

The product of these development efforts for CIP was a practitioners' handbook, which brought the R&D team into the last step of development—operational field testing. In this case, the handbook was tested in an informal way. Potential users—practitioners, students in graduate training, and faculty—were asked to review or use the handbook as a planning or training instrument. The field sample at this stage closely approximates the ultimate target population of users, and it reveals user reactions, bugs, useful improvements, and the like, permitting corrections and modifications to be made in the final version. The basically cyclical character of development is evident in the repeated testing and refining.

The development phase culminates in a product that has concrete utility. In CIP this was the final version of the practitioners' handbook, which encapsulated successful implementations of the application concept and offered practitioners specific directions for increasing participation. Such an operational or procedural guidebook outlines techniques that describe effective practice behaviors and increases the likelihood that others will be able to use the application concept effectively. The CIP handbook indicated the steps for implementing the application concept, obstacles that might be encountered, circumstances that might either facilitate or limit implementation, and recommendations for dealing with these circumstances—all derived from successful implementation cases. The booklet was packaged in an attractive, highly readable format, was relatively brief, and was written in practice-relevant language.[6]

The last step in R&D is the active diffusion of the R&D product so that it becomes available to potential users who are experiencing a similar problem. An important part of R&D is a vigorous and responsible attitude toward getting practice products into use, a form of "social marketing" which is unabashedly aggressive.[7] In the CIP program, a two-pronged national diffusion campaign was carried out using high-intensity workshops and low-intensity mass communication techniques. The intention was to make the handbook known and to stimulate its utilization by professionals in community mental health and family service agencies, two types of agencies that CIP participants believed lacked skills in maintaining community or organizational participation. The CIP team tried and evaluated different types of diffusion approaches to inform further diffusion efforts.

Although some filling in of details follows in the remainder of this discussion, this bare-bones overview of R&D leaves a great deal unsaid. The basic concept of R&D probably appears both logical and obvious to the reader. Nevertheless, the method is rarely used in the human service fields and in the social sciences. An apt description of the R&D approach and support for it as a way of improving social intervention has been expressed by Etzioni:

> It is fairly standard practice in the engineering of new spacecraft, weapons, airplanes, even toys, to move systematically from a theoretical concept to a pencil-and-paper design, to a small scale model that is subject to various tests, leading to the production of one or a few full-scale prototypes—all before mass production is authorized. Normally, at each stage modifications are made on the basis of experience gained. . . . New government [social] programs need to go through as full and as careful a process of research and development as new technologies.[8]

Conceptualizing Development

In earlier writings, the author has discussed retrieval and conversion designs.[9] This discussion focuses on development as an aspect of social R&D. Further details are available in a technical report of the CIP project, which the CIP R&D team prepared.[10]

Development requires that an application concept derived from the research literature be fully tested, evaluated, and detailed so that it can be used with facility and dependability. This is what makes development so difficult and demanding. Radnor et al. of the Center for the Interdisciplinary Study of Science and Technology point out that readiness for use is the distinguishing characteristic of development:

> Development involves a process of converting knowledge into *User-ready* products. [Emphasis in original.] The emphasis or focus of development is on the User. The end-product must be something the User can use (with at most some minimal fitting or tailoring).[11]

The concept of user-ready materials, techniques, and program is elementary and important, yet it is absent from the social sciences and human services. In these disciplines, a new policy or program is usually conceived and promulgated by a policy group or administrative staff. It is then widely disseminated without a formal evaluation of its performance criteria or effectiveness. Occasionally, some preliminary pilot application is conducted, but this usually involves no more than questions of feasibility. Hundreds of programs sponsored by the departments of Housing and Urban Development, Labor, and Health, Education and Welfare in such areas as housing, job placement, and rehabilitation are carried out in this way. Occasionally, evaluation is encouraged or mandated, as with Office of Economic Opportunity Community Action Programs or, more recently, in Community Mental Health. Evaluation typically occurs only after the programs have been described and are in widespread—often national—operation. These programs often involve millions of clients, but they have no clear-cut, systematic procedures for evaluation findings to redirect the design of the program. Compared to industrial R&D, these approaches appear primitive, inept, and wasteful.

Why development has been overlooked in the social field is an enigma. There has been some retrieval and synthesis in what has been referred to as propositional inventories at the retrieval end of R&D. There has also been a considerable amount of research and theory building on the diffusion end. Program evaluation has also been receiving increasing attention. But use of the techniques and insights of development in a coherent manner has been rare. This constitutes a huge intellectual and technical void in the social sciences and allied professions.

A sad, but unfortunately typical example of what occurs when development is neglected was reported by Gross, Giaquinta, and Bernstein, who attempted to implement a new instructional approach called the catalytic role model in a public school system. The authors described the innovation as follows:

> This role is to maximize the potential talents and interests of each child, to help children to develop their interests and capacities, to help them learn how to learn, and not to teach them a set of standard concepts or facts. Children are seen as different types of candles to be lit; the task of the teacher is to light each candle.[12]

After eight months the attempted innovation ended in failure, leaving staff disillusioned and cynical:

> Our findings showed that the failure to implement the innovation was attributable essentially to a number of obstacles that the teachers encountered when they attempted to carry it out [including] . . . lack of clarity about the new role model, . . . lack of skills and knowledge required to carry it out, . . . unavailability of required materials and equipment, . . . a set of organizational arrangements that were incompatible with the innovation.[13]

This is a case of an intervention that was imprecisely conceived and described. The requirements of role performance were only generally stated, the expected outcomes of implementing the innovation were not clearly formulated, and there was no training to provide the new skills that the teachers needed to implement the intervention. All these limitations would be immediately discernible with an R&D approach.

The research task of development can be usefully posed in terms of the relationship between an intervention, X, and an outcome, Y. Here are some examples of this relationship that were drawn from CIP studies.

● Increasing participation in community organizations (Y) through providing appropriate benefits (X).

● Promoting acceptance of an innovation (Y) through initially using a limited portion of target system (X).

● Changing organizational goals (Y) through shifting the structure of influence within an organization (X).

● Increasing effectiveness in practitioner role performance (Y) through achieving role clarity and consensus among appropriate superordinates (X).

A key intent of development is to determine those factors involved in treatment X that are associated with its optimal implementation, that is, with the successful attainment of outcome goals. This is inherent in the logic of the research and development process. In this formulation, outcome Y is the independent variable; intervention X is the dependent variable. The Xs may also be referred to as process variables—a constellation of operative variables associated with the intervention. There are also antecedent variables. These may be viewed as constituting a predisposing, initiating set, which defines the baseline situation and influences the process of implementation.

Conceptually, four social-psychological factors fall within the category of antecedent variables and are hypothetically of relevance to the effectiveness of intervention X: (1) personal factors, such as the personal attributes and attitudes of the practitioner, (2) organizational factors, principally the structure of the organization or agency employing the practitioner and in which the intervention is carried out, (3) client factors, specifically the nature of the client system or target group with which the practitioner is engaged, and (4) community factors, including the structure of the community in which the intervention takes place.

The variables may be conceptualized in

terms of what Rosenberg has referred to as the conjoint or concomitant variables in a given theoretical relationship.[14] Further, these process variables may have a facilitating or limiting effect on outcome. The purpose of R&D is to determine which process variables that come up in the implementation of intervention X are associated with favorable outcomes.

Another way of saying this is to define the research task as one of engineering rather than traditional knowledge building. The objective is not primarily to determine whether something is true (X is related to Y, or X causes Y), but how something works (by what means does X bring about Y). By assessing carefully what happens in different kinds of conditions when the application concepts are implemented, the R&D team determines how these concepts can be operationalized as process variables. The natural settings of practice are the field sites for the study. Evaluation, or performance testing, is conducted to determine whether outcome goals are adequately achieved. The aim is to demonstrate the feasibility and workability of an application concept, but not usually in comparison with an alternative theoretical or conceptual approach. Effectiveness in attaining an objective at a given outcome rate or level typically suffices for development purposes. A practical end is sought, and pragmatic methods are used. Thus, control groups and the customary accoutrements of experimental design are often unnecessary. However, the newer methods of single-subject study and quasi-experimental designs are pertinent.

Every development undertaking includes the production of useful tools and procedures. Research and practical ends are intertwined. The development of a new practice technique through R&D methods necessitates the accumulation of systematic data about how practice is carried out and about the context in which practice occurs. The weight given to immediate and practical as opposed to long-term and generalizable considerations varies from one development project to another. A pressing decision in every development program, therefore, concerns striking a balance between these two orientations. Development carried out at a university is likely to arrive at a balance point that is on the side of knowledge generation—with concomitant implications for its methodology—than is a project sponsored by a national service agency.

The overall tasks of development may be set forth as follows:

1. Development determines if an application concept devised during design and conversion will work in action. Can users make it work in real-world conditions?

2. Development determines how an application concept works in action, that is, what it takes in human and material terms to operationalize the principle in field conditions. This involves specifying the detailed procedures of implementation.

3. Development evaluates whether the application concept works effectively and efficiently in action. Can the concept attain the intended objectives with a reasonable degree of success and reliability, and at an acceptable cost?

4. Development devises means to capture and package the specifications of operationalization in a form that permits easy communication and replication. In industry this may mean mass production; in the human services it means widespread practice adoption.

A fairly complex set of factors go into establishing a development program. The CIP experience suggests that a framework for development planning include a range of considerations:

The general plan or design of the field test

Administrative responsibilities, arrangements, and lines of authority

Staff composition, functions, and size; auxiliary staff

Staff supervision, training, support, relationships

Field settings (agencies, implementation sites)

Instruments for measuring process, outcomes, antecedent variables, participant characteristics, social structural variables, and so on

Sampling requirements and methods

Data analysis procedures

Data processing methods and costs

Materials handling

Space requirements

Finances, including salaries, equipment, and operating expenses

Timing and duration of development

Communications

Relationships to the funding or sponsoring body

Procedural problems and design flaws

Other considerations could be added to this list, but these suffice to indicate the scope of technical, human, and organizational concerns that must be encompassed. Fairweather carried out the principle of development in his work, terming his approach experimental social innovation.[15] He evolved his application concepts not from previous research, but from observation of natural behavior. His writings provide valuable direction for working with the framework of development.

The framework of development involves close articulation between pilot and main field testing. Pilot testing is the first step in substantiating an application concept in the real world. As such, it is an extremely important step in moving from theory to practice. Pilot work explores on a small scale whether the R&D objectives are likely to be achieved in a main field test. It provides direction for constructing and testing the development framework. In this sense, it assents to or vetoes a large-scale implementation of the project. It also provides the tools and procedures through which the large-scale undertaking with a fully articulated framework can take place.

Main field testing in development involves a number of interrelated purposes and methods. The main field test requires a larger number of users and user settings than did the pilot study. This is necessary to determine whether the application concept will work in a broader range of typical user circumstances than prevailed in the pilot situation.

Some illustrations from the CIP experience may clarify aspects of development work. CIP pilot staff worked only with the general statement of the application concept. They had no manual or handbook available to them, and they used open-ended log recording forms to report their experiences. These participating practitioners may be termed front-end social engineers or development engineers, because it was necessary for them to work at the edge of theory. Their tasks consisted of converting aspects of theory into real-world processes.

The core of the development work was done with an expanded field staff. This group had not only the application concept to work with, but also a preliminary version of the handbook, which had been composed from the experience of the pilot staff. The field staff used more structured, checklist-type recording instruments with categories derived from the pilot study's logs. The field staff also had a well-defined methodological procedure to guide their efforts.

Although participants in the main field study were still performing the social engineering functions of converting and operationalizing theoretical formulations, they had materials to work with that had already begun to take formative, operational shape. Consequently, they needed less theoretical competency and required less supervisory support than did the pilot group. The result of all this performance testing is the determination of specifications for implementation.

Performance-Testing and Specifications

The need for attention to performance is evident when viewed in the light of R&D objectives: it is essential to find out if the application concept works. Industrial R&D carries this analysis a step further. It holds that evaluation indicates not only whether the solution works, but also its reliability and the conditions under which it works. This has given rise to the field of reliability engineering, which tries to establish tests for measuring and assessing parameters of reliability. Since it assesses the consistency of a certain performance within a given set of operating conditions, reliability engineering is potentially as useful a notion in social R&D as it is in industrial R&D.

Five important factors need to be examined in connection with performance-testing. These are outcome evaluation, process evaluation, instruments for recording interventions, quantitative analysis, and the formulation of specifications.

Outcome Evaluation. The literature on the theory of program evaluation is the main source of information on the methods of outcome assessment in the social sciences. The last decade has seen an outpouring of theoretical and methodological literature on evaluation by such scholars as Caro, Guttentag, Weiss, Rossi, Williams, Suchman, Epstein,

Tripodi, and Fellin.[16] These authors generally agree on the definition and purpose of evaluation research, differing only slightly in emphasis. Weiss, for example, sees such research as a way of measuring the effects of a program against the goals it set out to accomplish.[17] This provides useful input for decision-making about the program and for improving future programming. Caro agrees, stating that evaluation research "attempts to provide a program administrator with correct information on the consequences of his actions."[18] Tripodi, Fellin, and Epstein define evaluation as a management technique for the systematic feedback of information to be used to improve social programs.[19] Others, such as Suchman, emphasize the scientific function of enabling inferences to be made about the effects of given intervention.[20] All these expressions highlight a particular feature of evaluation research—the use and adaptation of scientific methods to further practical social goals. This is the same blend described here as characteristic of R&D. Workable forms of evaluation should evolve from the pilot phase of an R&D project.

Ample technical information is available about evaluation methods and will not be repeated here. It is enough to locate evaluation as a function within the R&D model.

Process Evaluation. Whereas outcome evaluation concerns itself with the results of an intervention, process evaluation concerns itself with the means. Outcome evaluation asks the question, To what degree are application concepts successful when applied in the field? Process evaluation asks, Does the implementation of the application concept embody the fundamental form of the concept? This examines whether the concept materializes, that is, whether X is actualized. The concreteness and coherence of processes are less tangible in social than in physical applications; it is more difficult to be clear about the operational reality of a social process than of a machine.

Process evaluation has not received the same degree of attention in the literature as outcome evaluation, but this has been changing. The literature deals with the treatments, programs, and interventions used to bring about given outcomes. As Chommie and Hudson state,

> An alternative and complementary strategy of evaluation aims to conduct research that facilitates program changes and enhances understanding of it. This strategy looks at program processes to explain outcomes and in general to learn more about intervention.[21]

Hesseling sees process evaluation as taking place during the progress of a program. In his view, it involves a "systematic observation and recording of the activities of a program."[22] Specific methodological details can be found in the evaluation literature and in the CIP technical report.[23]

Instruments for Recording Interventions. The R&D approach makes practice its main point of focus and consequently requires sophisticated and powerful measuring tools to track and record the process of implementing an application concept. There are three important ways of gathering the data the social scientist seeks: direct observation; interviewing, directly or through questionnaires, those participating in the experience; and self-reporting by those participating in the experience. Straight observation requires the observer to be on hand in the immediate environment. This sometimes introduces an unnatural element and risks distorting the social process; the observer may be an intrusive, causative element in that process. Interviewing lessens this risk, for the in-

terviewer intrudes only periodically, and this can be done outside the interventive situation. Interviews, however, are less likely to capture subtle changes in direction, thought, or process that are readily apparent in ongoing observation. Self-reporting offers a natural way of gathering data on complex, internal thought processes, but is susceptible to distortion, since participants may not perform their reporting tasks with the expected diligence, may view their experiences with various distortions of ego or stress, or may even report what they believe the experimenter wants to hear without regard to the true facts of the situation. As Trow observed,

> Different kinds of information about man and society are gathered most fully and economically in different ways, and . . . the problem under investigation properly dictates the methods of investigation. . . . The inferences we make from data, and the theory from which they derive and to which they contribute, may, indeed, be nothing more than "educated guesses"—but that is the nature of scientific theory. Our aim is to make them increasingly highly educated guesses.[24]

The full range of measuring instruments available to the social sciences for knowledge-building purposes can also serve social R&D. A period of careful experimentation and creative guesswork lies ahead in matching such instruments to the special requirements of R&D. The discussion by Fairweather previously referred to is useful in guiding the selection of instrumentation for measuring intervention.[25]

Quantitative Analysis. The objective of development is to observe intervention in a natural setting and thus to facilitate the success of future interventions by others in the same types of settings. The rationale for this was provided in part by Mackie and Christensen:

To the extent that stimulus conditions differ in research and real-life contexts, the need for translation and confirmatory research increases. When stimulus conditions are highly abstract, or nonsensical, the findings of a study can do little more than generate hypotheses for validation studies, i.e., translation is not possible.

In general, studies will be more translatable and have a higher likelihood of application if the investigator employs "natural" stimuli (stimuli as they exist in some operational environment). The use of "natural" stimuli, or carefully constructed facsimiles, should be encouraged; the temptation to invent stimulus (task) conditions to suit one's convenience, experimental apparatus, or theoretical viewpoint should be resisted.[26]

One consequence of studying natural phenomena is the creation of multivariable, "messy" research situations. This circumstance, and its particular virtues, was analyzed by Stagner in connection with the use of research on learning to improve classroom teaching:

The research strategy of the "pure" experimentalist is typically designed around the single criterion; and, indeed, if the environment so constrains the organism that only one dimension of behavior variability is permitted (e.g., speed of running down an alley), not much more can be gotten. But anyone who has done learning research knows that different criteria of learning often give different outcomes. The experimenter cuts this Gordian knot by arbitrarily choosing one and discarding data relevant to the others. But he, too, might achieve more penetrating insights into the consequences of his independent variables if he adopted a multiple-criterion approach to his dependent measures.[27]

Data analysis in these circumstances is complex and sometimes perplexing. Some of the difficulties and requirements of this approach are spelled out by Guetzkow:

Many social situations have large numbers of highly interrelated variables with feedbacks. Instead of being able to work with quasi-isolated miniature models—as the natural scientist does—the user of social

science must immediately work with an interrelated system. Even though scientist and applier try to simplify, both are forced to reckon with the interplay among their variables, because variables often cannot be held constant without disrupting the social process itself.[28]

Tukey, an expert in multivariate analysis, has suggested that analysis techniques should seek "scope and usefulness" rather than the security of established and neat procedures.[29] He speaks of multivariate heuristics involving a kind of venturesome detective work. Such analysis is concerned with the dynamic interrelatedness of measures of given subjects or phenomena. Another specialist, Kendall, defines the task of technical analysis in this way:

The variates are dependent among themselves so we cannot split one or more off from the others and consider it by itself. The variates must be considered together. Procedures for combining the variables in an optimal way need to be formulated.[30]

There is no question but that this places a strain on statistical technology.

Multivariate analysis involves such complex and interrelated procedures as factor analysis; canonical, multiple, and partial correlation; multivariate analysis of variance; and discriminant and classification functions. Matrix algebra is an indispensable tool for carrying out these analytical procedures, as is the use of appropriate computer programs. Fortunately, methodological guides are available, as can be seen in works by such authors as Tukey, Horst, DuBois, and Harris.[31]

It is evident that the staffs of R&D programs need not only able program evaluation specialists, but also research analysts with specialized competency in multivariate techniques. The alternative is for the R&D program to make provision for ample consultation by such experts. Expansion of social R&D will stimulate the improvement of multivariate statistical techniques. At the same time, social R&D depends on such advances for its own development.

Formulation of Specifications. The ultimate result of performance testing is the specification, in quantitative terms, of how various procedures of implementation affected the success of different interventions—the parameters and central tendencies determining the conditions of adequate or successful intervention. Such standards are common in the physical sciences and industry—in performance requirements for an automobile using a newly designed engine, for example. Repeated tests with the engine under varying road conditions indicate a normal speed and maximum limits of speed within which safety can be assured. Similar tests might specify a range of driving speeds for maximal gas economy.

Analogues in the social field are rare. The CIP team experimented with devising specifications, and it was able to state, for example, the largest, smallest, and modal number of community groups contacted by practitioners who attained their intended goals with different interventions. The team further designated the maximum and minimum number of individuals of various types who were contacted in different types of practice implementations. Similarly, the types of individuals and groups who most significantly affected outcomes were indicated—for example, board members versus agency staff, or voluntary associations versus public agencies. The team also quantified the different strengths of various facilitating and limiting factors impinging on different interventions, among them supervisor support and client disinterest. Examples of how to present such quantitative specifications to guide practice can be found in a plan-

ning manual developed by the CIP program for training graduate students.[32]

Specifications can be developed for areas of social work practice. For example, the optimal range for the number of sessions a week for group therapy could be designated, as could the optimal number for an entire course of therapy. It is also possible to establish similar specifications for home visits, for supportive comments during a session, or for instances of denying privileges in different types of treatment.

Although quantitative constructs such as these are valuable, the approach also can be overdone. The CIP team's experiences and the reported results of others indicate that qualitative materials and presentations are especially appreciated by operational people and that utilization is favorably affected by such presentations.[33] The quantitative aspect has been highlighted in this discussion, but an enlightened R&D program will be evenhanded in employing a variety of quantitative and qualitative methods.

Conclusion

This overview of R&D has been presented with the recognition that it is one of several variations of a new pattern of research that is heavily intertwined with practice, that promises to be of high utility to practice, and that provides a way of closing the gap that has separated research and practice over the years. The new orientation makes use of an engineering perspective and offers an alternative and additional methodological style for social work researchers. Ben-David, a respected student of the sociology of science, advocates that social scientists discard the classic form and turn instead to the engineering and other alternatives:

Social scientists have done a disservice to their own work by trying to mold it according to the model of basic natural science. . . . My main recommendations have been that social scientists should organize their work according to models which suit their own purposes, rather than distort their work to fit the requirements of some ideal (or idealized) models. I have shown that the models which suit social science are those of clinical medicine, engineering, geology and genetics, rather than those of physics. . . . The implication for the social scientist in the definition of his role is that in those cases where he is actually a social clinician or engineer, he will have to face this fact much more consciously than he has done before. The growth in professional employment (on a permanent or contractural basis) of social scientists has made it difficult to maintain the attitude that the social scientist be concerned only with the conception of ideas, and not with the problem of putting them into practice.[34]

This author's position of advocacy is less pronounced. It is appropriate and propitious that multiple styles of inquiry exist in the social sciences and human services to address different problems and types of situations. Until now, R&D and similar engineering approaches have been underrepresented and underdeveloped. It will serve the profession well to give these approaches a sustained push in the period ahead to arrive at a balanced array of research technologies. It is fortuitous that this move toward breadth and balance also moves toward reconciliation with practice.

NOTES AND REFERENCES

1. Michel Hersen and David H. Barlow, *Single-Case Experimental Designs: Strategies for Studying Behavior Change* (New York: Pergamon Press, 1976); Donald T. Campbell, "Reforms as Experiments," *The American Psychologist*, 24 (April 1969), pp. 409–429; and James A. Caporaso and Leslie L. Roos, Jr., *Quasi-Experimental Approaches: Testing Theory and Evaluating Policy* (Evanston, Ill.: Northwestern University Press, 1973).

2. Scott Briar, "Incorporating Research into Education for Clinical Practice in Social Work: Toward a Clinical Service in Social Work." Paper presented to the Council on Social Work Education Conference on Research Utilization in Social Work Education, New Orleans, La., October 1977, pp. 10–11.

3. Ibid.; Edwin J. Thomas, "Mousetraps, Developmental Research and Social Work Education," *Social Service Review*, 52 (September 1978), pp. 468–483; William J. Reid and Laura Epstein, *Task-Centered Casework and Task-Centered Practice* (New York: Columbia University Press, 1972 and 1977, respectively); and Jack Rothman, *Research and Development in the Human Services* (Englewood Cliffs, N.J.: Prentice-Hall, 1979).

4. Jack Rothman, *Planning and Organizing for Social Change: Action Principles from Social Science Research* (New York: Columbia University Press, 1974).

5. Jack Rothman, "Conversion and Design in the Research Utilization Process," *Journal of Social Service Research*, 2 (Winter 1979), pp. 117–131.

6. Jack Rothman, Joseph G. Teresa, and John L. Erlich, *Fostering Participation and Innovation* (Itasca, Ill.: F. E. Peacock Publishers, 1978).

7. Philip Kotler, *Marketing for Nonprofit Organizations* (Englewood Cliffs, N.J.: Prentice-Hall, 1975).

8. Amitai Etzioni, "An Earth-NASA: The Agency for Domestic Policy Development," *Human Behavior*, 5 (December 1976), p. 11.

9. Rothman, *Planning and Organizing for Social Change*; and Rothman, "Conversion and Design in the Research Utilization Process."

10. Jack Rothman, Joseph G. Teresa, and John L. Erlich, *Developing Effective Strategies for Social Intervention: A Research and Development Methodology*, (Springfield, Va.: National Technical Information Service, PB–272454 TR–1–RD 1977).

11. Michael Radnor et al., *Agency/Field Relationships in the Educational R/D & I System*, "A Policy Analysis for the National Institute of Education" (Evanston, Ill.: Center

for the Interdisciplinary Study of Science and Technology, Northwestern University, October 1976), p. 72.

12. Neal Gross, Joseph B. Giaequinta, and Marilyn Bernstein, *Implementing Organizational Innovations: A Sociological Analysis of Planned Educational Change* (New York: Basic Books, 1971), pp. 12–13.

13. Ibid., pp. 196–198.

14. Morris Rosenberg, *The Logic of Survey Analysis* (New York: Basic Books, 1968), pp. 159–196.

15. George W. Fairweather, *Methods for Experimental Social Innovation* (New York: John Wiley & Sons, 1967).

16. Francis G. Caro, ed., *Readings in Evaluation Research* (2d ed.; New York: Russell Sage Foundation, 1977); Marcia Guttentag and Elmer L. Struening, eds., *Handbook of Evaluation Research*, Vols. 1 and 2 (Beverly Hills, Calif.: Sage Publications, 1975); Carol H. Weiss, *Evaluation Research: Methods of Assessing Program Effectiveness* (Englewood Cliffs, N.J.: Prentice-Hall, 1972); Peter H. Rossi and Walter Williams, eds., *Evaluating Social Programs* (New York: Seminar Press, 1972); Edward Suchman, *Evaluative Research: Principles and Practice in Public Service and Social Action Programs* (New York: Russell Sage Foundation, 1967); Irwin Epstein and Tony Tripodi, *Research Techniques for Program Planning, Monitoring and Evaluation* (New York: Columbia University Press, 1977); and Tripodi, Phillip Fellin, and Epstein, *Social Program Evaluation: Guidelines for Health, Education and Welfare Administrators* (Itasca, Ill.: F.E. Peacock Publishers, 1971).

17. Weiss, op. cit.

18. Caro, op. cit., p. 88.

19. Tripodi, Fellin, and Epstein, op. cit.

20. Suchman, *Evaluative Research*, p. 38.

21. Peter W. Chommie and Joe Hudson, "Evaluation of Outcome and Process," *Social Work*, 19 (November 1974), p. 682.

22. P. Hesseling, "Principles of Evaluation," *Social Compass*, 11 (1964), p. 19.

23. Rothman, Teresa, and Erlich, *Devel-oping Effective Strategies for Social Intervention.*

24. Martin Trow, "Comment on Participant Observation and Interviewing: A Comparison," *Human Organization*, 16 (Fall 1957), pp. 33–35.

25. Fairweather, op. cit., pp. 122–144.

26. Robert R. Mackie and Paul R. Christensen, *Translation and Application of Psychological Research*, Technical Report 716–1 (Goleta, Calif.: Human Factors Research, 1967), pp. 39–40.

27. Ross Stagner, "Presidential Address to Division 14 [Industrial Psychology] of the American Psychological Association," *Newsletter of the Division of Industrial Psychology*, 3 (1966), p. 2.

28. Harold Guetzkow, "Conversion Barriers in Using the Social Sciences," *Administrative Science Quarterly*, 4 (June 1959), p. 70.

29. John W. Tukey, "The Future of Data Analysis," *Annals of Mathematical Statistics*, 33 (March 1962), pp. 1–67.

30. Maurice G. Kendall, *A Course in Multivariate Analysis* (London, England: Charles Griffin & Company, 1957), p. 5.

31. John W. Tukey, *Exploratory Data Analysis* (Reading, Mass.: Addison-Wesley Publishing Co., 1977); Paul Horst, *Factor Analysis of Data Matrices* (New York: Holt, Rinehart & Winston, 1965); Philip H. DuBois, *Multivariate Correlational Analysis* (New York: Harper & Row, 1957); and Richard J. Harris, *A Primer of Multivariate Statistics* (New York: Academic Press, 1975).

32. Jack Rothman, John L. Erlich, and Joseph G. Teresa, *Promoting Innovation and Change in Organizations and Communities* (New York: John Wiley & Sons, 1976).

33. Mark Van de Vall, Cheryl Bolas Mark, and Tai S. Kang, "Applied Social Research in Industrial Organizations: An Evaluation of Functions, Theory and Method," *The Journal of Applied Behavioral Science*, 12 (April, May, June 1976), pp. 158–177.

34. Joseph Ben-David, "The Search for Knowledge," *Daedalus*, 102 (Spring 1973), pp. 39–51.

Beyond Knowledge Utilization in Generating Human Service Technology

EDWIN J. THOMAS

THE THESIS OF THIS ARTICLE is that more than knowledge utilization is required in the generation of human service technology. This thesis derives from a conception of research that emphasizes the methodology of technological innovation for human service rather than the more familiar behavioral science research methodology oriented toward knowledge building. The thrust toward knowledge utilization so common in contemporary writing on research in recent years derives largely from the behavioral science model of research, whereas the present emphasis on additional processes needed to generate social technology derives from a conception of developmental research. Because of the importance of developmental research for the generation of social technology and the understanding of the processes to be highlighted here, this model of research is described briefly at the outset.

Overview of Developmental Research

Developmental research is a new and different paradigm of inquiry, inasmuch as it places primary emphasis on those methods by which interventional innovations and other aspects of social technology are analyzed, designed, created, and evaluated. Social technology is what developmental research yields, not knowledge about human behavior. It is thus that this emerging model of research is to be contrasted with the more familiar behavioral science model oriented toward building knowledge about human behavior. The introduction of developmental research into the fields of human service increases the number of available research methods and promises to enhance the capability of social work and related fields of human service to accomplish their objectives.

A brief overview of the conception of and rationale for developmental research is presented here for the benefit of readers not familiar with earlier statements.[1] Selected theses taken from earlier, more detailed explications, are summarized below.

1. Social technology is the primary means by which social work accomplishes its objectives. There are at least nine genera of social technology: physical frameworks (for example, the architecture and grounds of a residential facility for the aged); electromechanical devices (such as tape recorders, television, and computers); information systems (for example, computer-assisted record keeping); assessment methods (for example, interviewing guidelines for gathering client data in assessment); intervention methods (such as insight treatment and contingency contracting); service programs (such as adoption and day care); organizational structures (bureaucratic, decentralized, or equalitarian); service systems (such as community mental health agencies and state welfare departments); and social and welfare policy (for example, welfare policy of a given presidential administration).

2. There is continuing need to generate new social technology in human service fields such as social work.

3. The research methodologies of behavioral science and social work generally subserve the objective of building knowledge of human behavior, whereas those of developmental research are oriented especially toward the generation of social technology.

4. It is now possible to begin to formulate the main activities of developmental research. The phases of developmental research proper are analysis, development, and evaluation. Two additional phases—diffusion and adoption—are mainly concerned with utilization of the social technology. The full sequence of phases with their constituent steps and conditions is called developmental research and utilization. Each of these phases has its distinctive operational steps and material conditions.

5. There are at least eight sources of basic information that may be drawn on in the process of generating social technology. These sources are basic research, applied research, scientific technology, allied technology, legal policy, social innovation, indigenous research, and practice.

6. There is a generation process that must be undertaken by the developmental researcher in order to make use of basic information in the creation of a new technological product. The generation process involves procedures by which information from a basic source is converted, extended, adapted, and otherwise transformed in behalf of achieving interventional and other social technological innovation.

7. Among the distinctive research methods of developmental research are those that are involved critically in the generation process by which information from a source is transformed into innovative social technology.

8. Because developmental research consists of methods directed specifically toward the analysis, development, and evaluation of the very technical means by which social work objectives are achieved, developmental research may be the single most appropriate model of research for social work.

Although new, developmental research has been done and can be done. However, it involves a new concept that requires explication and a methodology that is not yet recognized or mature. In an effort to explicate and extend the emerging methodology of developmental research, this article specifies and illustrates five processes involved in the generation of social technology for human service fields such as social work. These processes are critical to the generation of social technology because they intervene between the basic, raw information out of which social technology may be composed or assembled and the operational realization of a social technological product. The purpose here will be to present, illustrate, and contrast these generation processes and to highlight directions for subsequent methodological development in this area.

Generation Processes

Developmental research ordinarily begins with some aspect of a problematic human condition, such as child abuse, poverty, disordered family relationships, that is judged to merit human service attention. The task of developmental research, in a word, is to generate suitable social technology to address this problematic condition. By what process or processes does the innovational generation come about? Posed in this way, the question is indeed challenging, for it appears that one is asking no more or no less than what it is that makes it possible for one to invent social technology. It is clearly not enough to indicate that creativity, insightfulness, and ingenuity are required. And there is more to generation than a grand creative leap. More particularly, certain behavior is engaged in under given conditions with specific sources of information in behalf of particular objectives in order to evolve a given type of human service technology. With attention to particulars such as these, the purpose here will be to try to identify some of the critical elements and distinctive processes that enter into the innovation of social technology so that eventually, with further analysis and inquiry, a stronger methodology of interventional generation

will become available to the human service fields.

To begin with, the developmental researcher starts with identifiable sources of information and, at some later point and following several intervening steps, ends up—if everything goes well—with a design for one of a number of identifiable genera of social technology. The sources of basic information available for the generation of social technology are important to identify and keep in mind because they provide significant leads to the particular inventive transition required to make use of the information for purposes of interventional generation. These sources of basic information, as indicated in Figure 1, consist of the contributions from basic, applied, and indigenous research; technology from science, allied technologies, social innovation, and practice; values and ideology; legal policy; and practice experience. There are at least five generation processes: knowledge utilization, technological transfer, value realization, legal interpretation, and experiential synthesis. As may be seen in Figure 1, each basic source of information relates to one of these five generation processes. Each of these processes, in turn, must be carried out before achieving technological accomplishment indicative of one of the nine genera of social technology.

It should be immediately evident to the reader familiar with social research and development and related models of research utilization that innovational generation in developmental research relies on more than the utilization of knowledge from one or another area of research. In the present view, knowledge utilization is but one generation process along with four others; it is important but not the only, the best, or even the essential activity involved in interventional generation. Indeed, it is the author's impression that more social work technology derives

Fig. 1. Sources of Basic Information, Their Particular Generation Process and Types of Social Technology

SOURCES OF BASIC INFORMATION	GENERATION PROCESSES	TYPES OF SOCIAL TECHNOLOGY
1. SCIENTIFIC TECHNOLOGY 2. ALLIED TECHNOLOGY 3. SOCIAL INNOVATION 4. PRACTICE	TECHNOLOGICAL TRANSFER	PHYSICAL FRAMEWORKS ELECTROMECHANICAL DEVICES INFORMATION SYSTEMS
5. BASIC RESEARCH 6. APPLIED RESEARCH 7. INDIGENOUS RESEARCH	KNOWLEDGE UTILIZATION	ASSESSMENT METHODS INTERVENTION METHODS
8. VALUES AND IDEOLOGY	VALUE REALIZATION	SERVICE PROGRAMS
9. LEGAL POLICY	LEGAL INTERPRETATION	ORGANIZATIONAL STRUCTURES SERVICE SYSTEMS
10. PRACTICE EXPERIENCE	EXPERIENTIAL SYNTHESIS	SOCIAL AND WELFARE POLICY

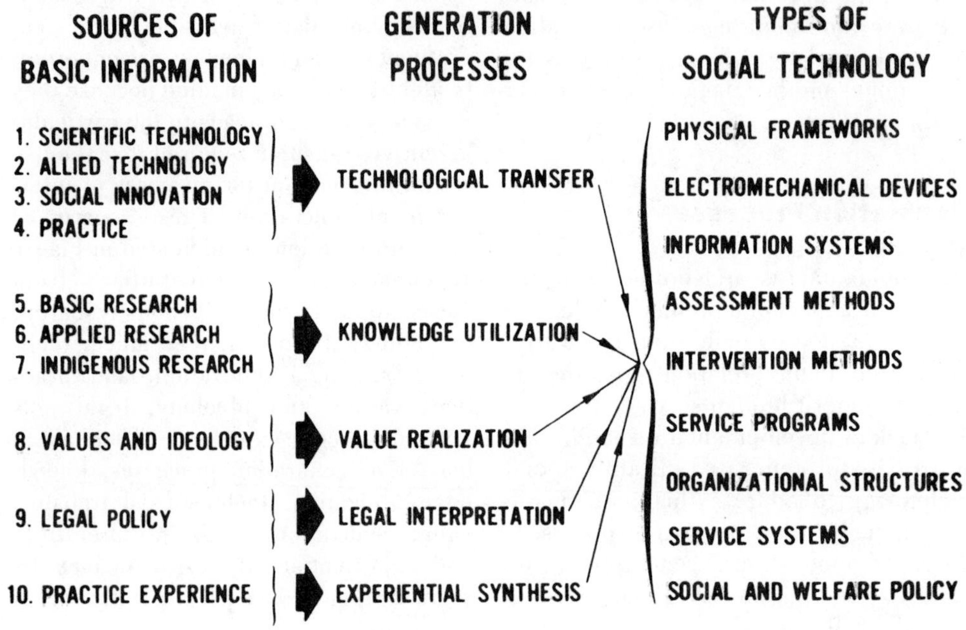

from the transfer of other technologies than from the utilization of knowledge from research. Although less well understood than knowledge utilization, the other generation processes of technological transfer, value realization, legal interpretation, and experiential synthesis are distinctive processes that have a place in the larger picture of technological innovation that cannot be matched or replaced by the methodology of knowledge utilization. With this as overview, attention will now be turned to discussion of each of the five generation processes.

Knowledge Utilization

Knowledge utilization is that process by which knowledge from research is transformed into social technology. The knowledge may be in the form of facts, concepts, hypotheses, empirical generalizations, or theories. Among the important sources of such knowledge are basic research (which embraces the contributions from such fields as psychology, sociology, anthropology, political science, and economics), applied research (for example, the research findings in psychotherapy or applied behavior analysis), and indigenous research (such as social work research). Illustrative of social technological products based in important measure on knowledge utilization are the action principles for community organization formulated by Rothman and his colleagues, practice principles to enhance client compliance with practitioner instigations proposed by Levy and Carter, and the eclectic approach to casework proposed by Fischer.[2]

Beginning largely in the 1960s, research was directed toward the utilization process itself. Havelock described this emerging discipline as "the science of knowledge utilization."[3] Research centers for study of the utilization of scientific knowledge were established, and there was a great deal written in the 1960s and 1970s on the process of utilization. Models of research utilization have been proposed, the phases of the utilization process have been distinguished, selection criteria for the utilization of knowledge have been identified, and sophisticated literature retrieval models to generate intervention guidelines have been developed.[4] Work along all these lines continues. Knowledge utilization is the best understood and most thoroughly explicated generation process of those considered here, and, therefore, will not be described further. There is a rich and informative literature to which the reader may turn for details.[5]

When scholars and researchers first became seriously interested in problems of knowledge utilization some twenty years ago, the process was not well understood, codified, and explicated, and, indeed, it seemed to many to be a mysterious and inscrutable enterprise. Through the careful identification and specification of component activities that comprise the process of knowledge utilization, what approximates a methodology of utilization is now available that enables practitioners, scholars, researchers, and students to utilize knowledge systematically to generate useful contributions to human service technology. The other generation processes deserve the same careful attention that knowledge utilization has received so that they too can be rendered more explicit and carried out systematically in behalf of the generation of interventional innovation.

Technological Transfer

Technological transfer involves the process by which technology is transferred from one area of technology to another. In the case of social work, the transfer entails transmission from technological areas outside the field as well as from some areas within the field to other areas in which that technology has not yet been employed. Clearly, the availability of a sufficiently well developed and potentially applicable technology in another area is essential to technological transfer. Technological transfer is perhaps the major means by which social work technology is expanded. If it is correct, as the slogan has it, that technology begets technology, the growth of technology through its spread from one area to another is made possible by the process of technological transfer.

There are at least four major sources of technology from which social technology may be transferred. The first of these is scientific technology, which embraces technological information from such fields as engineering, electronics, and telecommunications. Examples of scientific technology that have been applied to social technology in the human services are computer applications to assessment and change, automated intake, information systems and data management, and the use of videotaping in practice training.[6]

A major source of technological information bearing on social technology derives from allied technologies. Such fields as hospital administration, public administration, business administration, public health, behavior therapy, architecture, clinical psychology, nursing, and medicine are among the main fields that have allied technologies potentially relevant to human service technology in social work. Examples of technological contributions from these fields include such applications as break-even analysis in budget planning, use of the Problem-Oriented Medical Record, behavioral assessment and modification methods, environmental design, psychoanalysis, and epidemiological research methods.[7]

A third source of technology derives from social innovation. Self-help groups, such as Alcoholics Anonymous, Synanon, Al-Anon, Parents Anonymous, Neurotics Anonymous, and Overeaters Anonymous, are illustrative. Another type of social innovation is the curious one that might be called popular psychology, as is illustrated by est and such self-help books as *Your Erroneous Zones*.[8] Also illustrative are Transcendental Meditation, Yoga, and Zen Buddhism, aspects of oriental religions that have taken root in this country.

A fourth source of social technology derives from social work practice itself. Current social work practice in interpersonal helping and administration and in carrying out programs and policy may be rich sources of technology for potential use in areas of social work practice in which they have not yet been applied. The spread of group methods, developed initially in recreation and group work settings, to settings in which direct service to individuals and families is provided would be illustrative. So would the adoption of skills of community action and planning by caseworkers in settings providing direct services. Because of differences in clientele, setting, and objectives, the transfer of technology from one domain of social work to another may entail as large a transition as borrowing technology from outside fields.

The transfer of technology can be thought of as implicating at least five stages: (1) selection of technological information (or the technology itself) from among relevant sources, (2) retrieval of the relevant information (or technology), (3) collation and assembly of such information (or technology), (4) evaluation of the other technology in terms of such criteria as its relevance to human service technology, its potential efficacy, and its transferability, and (5) design of a "product" suitable for use in the social technology of human service.

The stages can be moved through quickly and easily when a technological innovation is borrowed directly from another field and is used essentially without modification. This *direct importation* of technology from an allied field is illustrated by the use of behavior modification procedures in social work practice. Most behavioral methods of intervention, such as contingency contracting and point and token systems, have been taken over essentially without modification to be employed, generally with other helping methods, in endeavoring to achieve social work objectives. Although direct importation merits careful selection and evaluation of suitability for human service in social work, it does not necessitate redesign in order for it to be capable of being used. In contrast, transfer by *selective alteration* involves at least some redesign of the technology to make it suitable for use in its new domain. For example, rather than being taken over directly in exactly the form it was used for medical recording, Problem-Oriented Medical Recording has been modified somewhat in its applications in social work.[9]

Still another mode is *transfer by extension*. For example, it would appear that indigenous innovation tends to be used to augment social work technology rather than to be taken over and included as an integral part of it. Thus, the social worker endeavoring to assist an individual with a problem of alcohol abuse might readily refer the client to Alcoholics Anonymous with the idea that the client would attend Alcoholics Anonymous while also continuing in treatment with the worker. Most self-help groups, as Killilea has observed, are lay, inspirational movements that stress anonymity and that have arisen in part to fill gaps in the service system.[10] Thus, they represent a type of helping method that cannot readily be taken directly into the helping methods that social workers could provide directly themselves. Popular psychology, if it is used at all by the professional helper, is likewise likely to be adjunctive. For example, at an appropriate point the social worker might assign a self-help aid such as *Your Erroneous Zones* as one component of therapy. Likewise, Transcendental Meditation could be employed adjunctively, if it served treatment objectives. It is too early to say whether indigenous social innovation is mainly adjunctive. There may be constituent features of social innovations that can be taken over and incorporated directly into social work helping methods. Careful analysis of the processes involved in social innovations may facilitate the shaping of helping methods along similar lines.[11]

Central to the process of technological transfer is determination of the fit and applicability of the new technology. Whether it is outright adoption or more hard-wrought adaptation depends on the applicability and fit of the proposed technology. All this is in contrast to the methodologies of making and assembling new technology, which are the principal considerations involved with the other generation processes.

Value Realization

Value realization involves the materialization of social technology, which is directed toward attaining the objectives of values and ideology. As a basis of social technology, values and ideology derive largely from social, political, and religious movements. Illustrative values are belief in sexual and racial equality, the humane treatment of human service clientele, and civil rights. Political ideology is illustrated by the creeds of communism, socialism, and capitalism, and religious ideology by the belief systems of Christianity and Judaism. Examples of social technology based on values and ideology are pastoral counseling, feminist therapy, consciousness-raising groups, radical therapy, client advocacy, and gay counseling.[12] All social technology, of course, has some basis in values and ideology, so it is appropriate to inquire concerning what it is that marks value realization as worthy of being designated as a distinctive generation process. With value realization, in the pure case, there are strong values and ideology crying for realization for which there is no fully suitable social technology to serve as an instrument to achieve the objectives of the values and ideology, and these values and ideology serve as the main impetus and guide in shaping the new technology.

Some of the elements of value realization are illustrated by the emerging technology of advocacy, as portrayed in the analysis by Panitch.[13] The analysis in question began with exposition of the value and ideological basis for advocacy. It was noted that the Ad Hoc Committee on Advocacy of the National Association of Social Workers had indicated that the social worker has a moral obligation under the Code of Ethics of the association to be an advocate and that this obligation requires more than merely urging certain actions by adversaries. Further, drawing on different sources, there was detailed specification of the dehumanizing conditions and abusive treatment that can be afflicted upon clients which would justify practitioner advocacy. With the above as a basis in values and ideology, the author then endeavored to extend the technology of advocacy through presenting fourteen "techniques of intervention." Among these were expert testimony, position-taking, administrative redress, petitions, persistent demands, and demonstrations and protests. Other more familiar techniques also described were intra-agency committees, education, demonstration projects, direct con-

tact with officials and legislators, and the use of coalition groups and of client groups.

Some of these techniques are better developed and established than others. When applied to advocacy, established techniques may require adaptation, and these as well as the less well-developed techniques may necessitate considerably more explication. It would appear, then, that the main tasks of value realization are to assemble appropriate social technology for attainment of value-based objectives when such technology exists or, when it does not, to evolve new technology.

Legal Interpretation

Legal interpretation, as the term is used here for a particular generation process, involves the transition by which legal policy in the form of litigation or legislation is transformed into guidelines for the provision and conduct of human service. Through such activities as interpretation and stipulation, this process converts legal regulation to human service technology consistent with the prescriptions of the regulation. For example, consider the court decision of *Wyatt* v. *Stickney*.[14] The reader will recall that in this decision the court focused on the fundamental conditions for effective and adequate treatment. The court enumerated many rights that must be met, among them a right to the least restrictive conditions necessary for treatment, the right to be free from isolation, a right not to be subjected to unusual or hazardous treatment procedures without expressed and informed consent after consultation with counsel, and the right to keep and use personal possessions. In response to this court decision, articles then appeared dealing with some of the specific implications of this decision for the rights of the committed—thus setting the stage for altered intervention technology.[15] Although the process of legal interpretation may affect any aspect of human service technology, it generally entails at least the specification of guidelines involving client rights or practitioner, agency, program, or institutional responsibilities.

Resulting social technology may take the form of administrative regulations. For example, the Department of Public Welfare of the State of Minnesota has adopted a set of guidelines for aversive and deprivation procedures, partly in response to *Price* v. *Sheppard*.[16] This state plan requires external review of all suggested aversive procedures before implementation, continuing review of their affects, supervision of implementation by persons "knowledgeable and experienced in the theory, ethical considerations and application of behavior modification techniques," and assurance that aversive procedures are a component of an overall plan based on positive reinforcement principles. Many specific guidelines are proposed. Thus, in regard to goods or services to which the client is ordinarily entitled, it is specified that the client has the right to possession of, control over, and access to legitimate earnings and allowances. The resulting social technology may also take the form of guidelines of a professional organization. In response to recent litigation and legislation, national organizations such as the Research Advisory Committee of the National Association for Retarded Citizens and the Association for the Advancement of Behavior Therapy have proposed guidelines regarding the ethical treatment of clientele. As a consequence of extending due process hearings to many social welfare clients, new administrative and organizational strategies have been proposed in the professional literature.[17] As a result of his review of recent legal

developments dealing with the conduct of human services in schools, corrections, and mental health, Martin has prepared over one hundred questions, in the form of a review checklist, that human service professionals should be able to answer satisfactorily in connection with protecting particular rights of clients.[18]

Experiential Synthesis

The practice experience of practitioners can serve as an important basis for genuine innovation. A significant portion of human service technology was probably introduced in this way originally. The process by which practice experience of the practitioner is transformed into innovative human service technology is called experiential synthesis, for want of more apt identification. Practice is broadly conceived here to embrace direct experience in practice and what one has learned about practice through consultation, supervision, training, reading, and personal experience. These experiences come together and are thus synthesized in behalf of achieving interventional innovation. Examples might be the first time a psychotherapist saw a family together instead of a designated client alone to address a problem of family dysfunction; the first time a psychodynamic therapist, such as Freud, interpreted the meaning of an unconscious wish as part of therapy; the first time a token economy was used to accelerate desirable responding of clients in an institution; and the first time systematic desensitization was used as a method to reduce phobic anxiety.

The innovations may range from specific, isolated techniques to comprehensive approaches. They may be groundbreaking, as in some of the above examples, or they may be ordinary. In any event, a key feature of the outcome is that it is an initial application of social technology rather than a novel application. With an initial application, one is speaking essentially of the first or very early application of innovation (such as the first time a token economy was used) whereas a novel application is an unusual application of social technology already developed elsewhere for other purposes (such as application of a token economy in the classroom following its initial development and use in a mental hospital). Novel applications, involving transfer as they do, implicate the process of technological transfer, whereas initial applications derive from what is here called experiential synthesis.

It is useful to distinguish two ways in which experiential synthesis may result in innovation. One is through the initial introduction of an actual innovation, as in the above examples. The other is through innovation design wherein the technological innovation is laid out in "blueprint," as in writing in a book, article, or manual, but the innovation thus designed has not yet been fully carried out. Ideally, of course, the design of innovation as expressed in writing or other form of codification should be based on the innovation as actually carried out by the writer or others. In either case, however, there is a synthesis and creative blending of practice experience that can result in important advances not attainable by other means.

It is interesting to speculate concerning where the contributions of such writers as Sigmund Freud, Carl Jung, and Alfred Adler fit into this. They were indeed creative, described their new methods in writing, and were to varying degrees truly innovative in their practice. How about the seminal writings of such authors as Mary Richmond, Gordon Hamilton, Florence Hollis, Bertha Reynolds, Grace Coyle, Charlotte Towle, and Helen Perlman? These practitioner-theorists probably combined both types of experiential synthesis inasmuch as the innovations they described and recommended also derived at least in part from their own experience with these innovations. The same might be said for such present-day practitioner-theorists as Eric Berne, Fritz Perls, Salvador Minuchin, Murray Bowen, Virginia Satir, Albert Ellis, and Joseph Wolpe, except that the procedures are happily becoming more specific and replicable.

One approach to understanding experiential synthesis more thoroughly is to place emphasis on conditions that may increase the likelihood of the researcher-practitioner being genuinely innovative. At least four of these facilitative conditions come to mind. The first entails a problem-solving approach to assessment, intervention, and evaluation in which the unique difficulties and challenges presented in each practice situation are addressed. In the author's experience, practice situations are highly diverse and frequently present problems for which existing helping methods are not fully adequate. Endeavoring to evolve suitable procedures allows for innovation. Second, the practitioner can adopt a judicious experimental approach to intervention in which selective innovations can be tried on a provisional basis. It is important, of course, that such experimentation be carried out ethically and with sound rationale and be directed toward a solution of the practice problems under conditions for which other, better established procedures would not be adequate. A third condition would be to carry out systematic, empirically based practice as a means to strengthen the adequacy of the data that serve as the experiential basis for possible innovation.[19] Such practice would involve operational specification of the target behaviors and their measurement and monitoring during the different phases of intervention combined with the use of an evaluation design. Empirically based practice also calls for careful recording of the intervention procedures used so that they are subject to scrutiny, duplication, and appraisal by the practitioner and others. Finally, intimate familiarity with the literature and with current methods applicable in the area of intervention provides an excellent basis for recognizing limitations of methods and gaps in technology for which innovation would be appropriate.

Mixed Sources and Combined Processes

Although each generation process may be understood and applied as a distinctive process, the actual generation of social technological innovation most typically implicates more than one generation process. The generation processes are applied in particular combinations depending on the mix of sources of basic information. The generation of any aspect of social technology implicates values relating to human service, and, in this sense, involves value realization; and it is difficult to imagine the construction of any human service technology without utilizing relevant knowledge of human behavior and transferring applicable technology from other areas.

Although any given social technology need not be directly related to and based upon legal policy and the generation process of legal interpretation, all social technology is shaped by legal policy or is otherwise consistent with it. Further, the process of converting legal policy into relevant social technology is very likely to entail other generation processes such as technological transfer and knowledge utilization. Experiential synthesis is likewise a process that is unlikely to be carried out without concurrent technological transfer and knowledge utilization. And further, the practice experience that is the source of information for experiential synthesis is generally critical in guiding and shaping the construction of interventional innovation.

Conclusion

In support of the thesis that more than knowledge utilization is required in the generation of human service technology, four other processes involved in innovational generation have been presented and described. These additional processes are technological transfer, value realization, legal interpretation, and experiential synthesis. Each has its distinctive contribution to make to the task of generating human service technology. Each generation process needs to be analyzed and explicated more thoroughly in order to strengthen and extend the emerging methodology of research oriented toward the development of human service technology in social work.

NOTES AND REFERENCES

1. *See* Edwin J. Thomas, "Generating Innovation in Social Work: The Paradigm of Developmental Research," *Journal of Social Service Research*, 2 (Fall 1978), pp. 95–116; and "Mousetraps, Developmental Research, and Social Work Education," *Social Service Review*, 52 (September 1978), pp. 468–484.

2. Jack Rothman, *Planning and Organizing for a Social Change: Action Principles from Social Science Research* (New York: Columbia University Press, 1974); Rona L. Levy and Robert D. Carter, "Compliance with Practitioner Instigations," *Social Work*, 21 (May 1976), pp. 188–193; and Joel Fischer, *Effective Casework Practice: An Eclectic Approach* (New York: McGraw-Hill Book Co., 1978).

3. Ronald G. Havelock, *Planning for Innovation through Dissemination and Utilization of Knowledge* (Ann Arbor: Institute for Research, University of Michigan, 1973), p. 3.

4. *See,* for example, ibid.; Edward M. Glaser, *Putting Knowledge to Use: A Distillation of the Literature Regarding Knowledge Transfer and Change* (Los Angeles: National Institute of Mental Health, Mental Health Services Development Branch, 1976); Edwin J. Thomas, "Selecting Knowledge from Behavioral Science," in *Building Social Work Knowledge: Report of a Conference* (New York: National Association of Social Workers, 1964), pp. 38–47; Thomas, "Types of Contributions Behavioral Science Makes to Social Work," in Thomas, ed., *Behavioral Science for Social Workers* (New York: Free Press, 1967), pp. 1–3; Martin Bloom, *The Paradox of Helping: Introduction to the Philosophy of Scientific Practice* (New York: John Wiley & Sons, 1975); Tony Tripodi, Phillip Fellin, and Henry J. Meyer, *The Assessment of Social Research: Guidelines for the Use of Research in Social Work and Social Science* (Itasca, Ill.; Peacock Publishers, 1969); Tripodi, *Uses and Abuses of Social Research in Social Work* (New York: Columbia University Press, 1974); Rothman, op. cit.; and Edward J. Mullen, "The Construction of Personal Model for Effective Practice: A Method for Utilizing Research Findings to Guide Social Interventions," *Journal of Social Service Research*, 2 (Fall 1978), pp. 45–65.

5. In addition to sources such as those cited above, *see* Jack Rothman, "Conversion and Design in the Research Utilization Process," *Journal of Social Service Research*, 2 (Fall 1978), pp. 117–133.

6. *See,* for example, Thomas A. Williams, James H. Johnson, and E. L. Bliss, "A Computer Assisted Psychiatric Assessment Unit," *American Journal of Psychiatry*, 132 (175), pp. 1074–1076; Kenneth E. Hansen, Johnson, and Williams, "Development of an On-Line Management Information System for Community Mental Health Centers," *Behavior Research Methods and Instrumentation*, 9 (1977), pp. 139–143; Johnson and Williams, "The Use of On-Line Computer Technology in a Mental Health Admitting System," *American Psychologist*, 30 (March 1975), pp. 388–391; Fred W. Vondracek, Hugh B. Urban, and William H. Parsonage, "Feasibility of an Automated Intake Procedure for Human Services," *Social Service Review*, 48 (June 1974), pp. 271–278; David W. Young, "Management Information Systems in Child Care: An Agency Experience," *Child Welfare*, 53 (February 1974), pp. 102–111; and David Katz, "Videotape Programming for Social Agencies," *Social Casework*, 56 (January 1975), pp. 44–51.

7. *See,* for example, Roger A. Lohmann, "Break-Even Analysis: Tool for Budget Planning," *Social Work*, 21 (July 1976), pp. 300–307; Rosalie A. Kane, "Look to the Record," *Social Work*, 19 (July 1974), pp. 412–419; Harold Leitenberg, ed., *Handbook of Behavior Modification and Behavior Therapy* (Englewood Cliffs, N.J.: Prentice-Hall, 1976); Edwin J. Thomas, ed., *Behavior Modification Procedure: A Sourcebook* (Chicago: Aldine Publishing Co., 1974); and Thomas Walz, Georgiana Willenbring, and Lane De Moll, "Environmental Design," *Social Work*, 19 (January 1974), pp. 38–47.

8. Wayne W. Dyer, *Your Erroneous Zones* (New York: Avon Books, 1977).

9. *See* Kane, op. cit.; Wilma M. Martins and Elizabeth Holmstrup, "Problem-Oriented Recording," *Social Casework*, 55 (November 1974), pp. 554–561.

10. Marie Killilea, "Mutual Help Organizations: Interpretations from the Literature," in Gerald Caplan and Killilea, eds., *Support Systems and Mutual Help: Multi-Disciplinary Explorations* (New York: Grune & Stratton, 1976), pp. 37–93.

11. *See,* for example, the empirical and conceptual analysis of Leon H. Levy, "Self-Help Groups: Types and Psychological Processes," *Journal of Applied Behavioral Science*, 12 (July-August-September 1976), pp. 310–323.

12. *See,* for example, Carol Wesley, "The Women's Movement and Psychotherapy," *Social Work*, 20 (March 1975), pp. 120–125; Carol G. Radov, Barbara R. Masnick, and Barbara B. Hauser, "Issues in Feminist Therapy: The Work of a Women's Study Group," *Social Work*, 22 (November 1977), pp. 507–509; Susan Amelia Thomas, "Theory and Practice in Feminist Therapy," *Social Work*, 22 (November 1977), pp. 447–454; Sharon B. Berlin, "Better Work with Women Clients," *Social Work*, 21 (November 1976), pp. 492–497; and Arnold Panitch, "Advocacy in Practice," *Social Work*, 19 (May 1974), pp. 326–332.

13. Panitch, op. cit.

14. For more details, *see* Reed Martin, *Legal Challenges to Behavior Modification: Trends in Schools, Corrections and Mental Health* (Champaign, Ill.: Research Press, 1975), pp. 178–179.

15. *See*, for example, Charles S. Prigmore and Paul R. Davis, "*Wyatt* v. *Stickney*: Rights of the Committed," *Social Work*, 18 (July 1973), pp. 10–19; Frank M. Johnson, Jr. "Court Decisions and the Social Services," *Social Work*, 20 (September 1975), pp. 343–347.

16. "*Price* v. *Sheppard*," *Law and Behavior*, 2 (Winter 1977), pp. 3–4.

17. Donald T. Dickson, "Law in Social Work: Impact of Due Process," *Social Work*, 21 (July 1976), pp. 274–278; and Joseph J. Senna, "Changes in Due Process of Law," *Social Work*, 19 (May 1974), pp. 319–325.

18. Martin, op. cit.

19. For approaches to this kind of practice, see Fischer, op. cit.; Bloom, op. cit.; Edwin J. Thomas, "Uses of Research Methods in Interpersonal Practice," in Norman A. Polansky, ed., *Social Work Research: Methods for the Helping Professions* (Chicago: University of Chicago Press, 1975), pp. 254–284; and Edwin J. Thomas, "The BESDAS Model for Effective Practice," *Social Work Research and Abstracts*, 13 (Summer 1977), pp. 12–16.

Evaluation, Policymaking, and Budgeting: Starting from Scratch in Wisconsin

PETER J. TROPMAN

THE EFFECTIVE APPLICATION of social research to the process of policymaking has long been a goal; it has not, to any significant degree, been a practical reality. Principally, this results from the failure to integrate research into the processes of policymaking at the conceptual, organizational, and staff levels. If policymaking is to be informed by social research, it is necessary to develop a conceptual role for research in the policy development process, to design organizational strategies that formally integrate evaluation into the organizational structure, and to develop technologies for research and staff roles for researchers that are suited to an organization whose primary responsibility is the delivery of human services. Of equal importance is the need to correct the long-standing failure to apply research to program management.

Program evaluation is a type of applied social research that is easily conducted within human services organizations. It has been developed in response to the need to apply research to policymaking and program management—to help organizations develop rational policies and implement stated policy objectives effectively and efficiently. In Wisconsin, initial steps have been taken to make program evaluation an integral part of both the policymaking process and the program management function of the Department of Health and Social Services, the state's umbrella human services agency.

To the department as an organization and to program evaluation as a field, this represents both an opportunity and a challenge. For the department, it presents the opportunity to base policy and program management decisions on a clearer understanding of programs' outcomes and impacts, their efficiency and utilization patterns, their cost benefits, and the adequacy of the services they

104

provide. The introduction of program evaluation challenges the department to develop a capacity for critical self-evaluation and then to use it. For the field of social research and program evaluation, this Wisconsin innovation not only represents an opportunity to put words and theory into action in a statewide comprehensive human services organization; it also presents a tremendous challenge to deliver evaluation products that are useful to policymakers and program managers.

This article discusses the role of program evaluation in the policy development and program management processes of the Wisconsin Department of Health and Human Services. It focuses on the background and rationale for the development of a program evaluation capacity, on the conceptual design of the policymaking process and program evaluation's role in it, and on organizational and operational strategies for implementing the program evaluation.

Program Evaluation and Human Services

In the human services, the integration of evaluation into the processes of policy development and program management is the result of demand, not choice. The need to coordinate service delivery and to integrate policies; the need to improve the management of human services programs; the increasing demands for internal and external accountability; the organizational desire to maximize effectiveness; the present size, complexity, and stratification of the human services system; and the decreasing availability of new program dollars for human services—all these forces have sharply changed the focus in the human services from external questions of program development to internal questions of organization, management, and effectiveness,

from issues of growth to issues of quality. The central questions facing the field today, and for the foreseeable future, are not what new services or programs will be needed, but how can existing programs do what they are doing better? This reality is aptly and accurately described by Attkisson et al. in the introductory paragraph of *Evaluation of Human Service Programs*. In outlining the critical challenges facing human services programs, the authors state,

> The effectiveness of human services systems during the next decade will depend upon the skillful completion of several difficult organizational tasks—these include:
> • Reorganization of the human services network to achieve coordination, efficiency, and integration among specialized services.
> • Preservation and further enhancement of the unique contribution and expertise of specialized programs that currently function with relative autonomy in a categorical approach to service delivery.
> • Increasing the administrative skills of program leaders and fostering the application of more effective organizational designs.
> • Linkage of professional, paraprofessional, and generalist training to the goals, objectives, and realities of restructured human services network.
> • Use of program evaluation capacity as an internal management tool within every level of program organization and especially at the local community level where services are delivered.[1]

In this view, the critical demands are internal to the human services field, and program evaluation is a critical means of addressing these demands. By its very nature, program evaluation is the analytical tool most suited to the task of providing the critical information and analysis needed to make reorganizational decisions, improve the effectiveness and coordination of services, and improve administrative performance. It is thus an analytical discipline that is central to the development of the kinds of policy responses present conditions demand. It gives insight into what is working, what is not working, and why. To be effective, program evaluation must be internalized into the structure of the human services it is to serve. If the human services field fails to meet this challenge, there is a clear danger that an agenda of human services reform will be set by individuals and circumstances that are hostile to the goals of the field.

Definitions

Several critical questions need to be addressed: What is program evaluation? What is policy? What is program management? Where and how does program evaluation fit into the process of policy development and program management? What useful role does program evaluation play?

Program evaluation is a form of social research that is at the extreme of the applied end of the research continuum. In an excellent operative definition, Attkisson and Broskowski describe it as follows:

> 1. A process of making reasonable judgments about program effort, effectiveness, efficiency, and adequacy
> 2. Based on systematic data collection and analysis
> 3. Designed for use in program management, external accountability, and future planning
> 4. Focuses especially on accessibility, acceptability, awareness, availability, comprehensiveness, continuity, integration, and cost of services.[2]

Planning and budgeting are the tangible means of developing, describing, and quantifying both policies and programs. Although planning may be defined superficially as rational forethought—or humorously, as a process in which there is no last word, only the latest word—it is actually the process of defining goals, objectives, and expected outcomes and

then of designing and implementing the programs to accomplish them.

Budgeting is a planning process that addresses the critical question of procuring and allocating resources. The glib but useful distinction often made between plans and budgets is that all budgets are plans, but not all plans are budgets. For an agency delivering services, the budget is the most important plan and the most definitive and quantifiable policy statement. It is the acid test of an organization's commitment to the implementation of any policy. This would be true even if the budget were merely a fiscal document, but most human services budgets are also policy development documents in which policy definitions and redefinitions are integrated with the allocation, procurement, and reallocation process. The biennial budget for Wisconsin's Department of Health and Social Services, for example, combines in a single piece of legislation both the appropriations and the program policy decisions. A reorganization of the Wisconsin Department of Health and Social Services; the establishment of statewide, community-based, combined mental health and developmental disabilities programs; major initiatives for integrating human services; and the enactment of certificate of need legislation for hospitals and nursing homes are just a few of the substantive policy decisions contained in the department's budget request.

Program management is the process of implementing plans and budgets in compliance with policy decisions and directives. "Policy" is a difficult term to define in a comprehensive way. An understanding of what policy is, however, is central to defining program evaluation's role in relationship to it. A traditional definition of policy is contained in the *Dictionary of the Social Sciences:* a policy is "a course of action or intended action conceived as deliberately adopted, after a review of possible alternatives, and pursued or intended to be pursued."[3] In elaboration of this definition, the term might be said to refer to a series or set of programs aimed at achieving some set of objectives or goals.

A limitation of this definition is that it identifies policy too narrowly as an isolated phenomenon of front-end decision-making. In an organization, policy is more correctly viewed as the product of the interface between planning, budgeting, evaluation, and program management. Put in its simplest terms, policy is not just what we say we are going to do; it is what we are actually doing. A failure to view policy in this comprehensive, dynamic way represents a serious conceptual deficiency in defining the process of policymaking in any human services agency. The narrow definition also precludes a contributing role for program evaluation in policy development. Program evaluation's most critical role in the policy process is that of a tool which elaborates and refines definitions and descriptions of policy, and, through clearly defined feedback loops, provides a set of evaluation products, reports, studies, and analyses which meet the needs of planners, budgeters, and program managers to define, implement, and improve policy.

The Policy Process

The critical problem is not that human services organizations have failed to de-

vote resources to evaluation efforts, because they have. Rather, they have not conceptualized or implemented a role for program evaluation that integrates it comprehensively into every part of the policy process. The diagrams represent these points graphically. Figure 1 displays the model that is, regrettably, most descriptive of the policy process as it operates in most agencies. Planning, budgeting, and program management operate as progressive, cyclical steps in the process, with evaluation playing a nebulous and clearly external role. In this model, evaluation has no clear lines of access to any of the critical components in the policy cycle. Evaluation efforts are confined to isolated studies of individual programs and are initiated only as they are needed or as mandated components of special grant or pilot programs. More often than not, evaluation reports are written for external rather than internal consumption. It is this model that produces the cliché about the evaluation reports that gather dust on some shelf.

Figure 2 depicts the traditional textbook model of the policy cycle. In this model, evaluation is integrated into the process, but offers feedback only to the plan development or redevelopment phase. Policy is made at the planning and budgeting stage and implemented at the program management level. Evaluation then makes some judgment, after the fact, about how well the program worked. Presumably this is done to influence future planning. Conceptually, it is a neat model, but to the extent that evaluation enters the process at a late stage, it can easily fail to address the key questions of

Fig. 1. Policy without a Clear Role for Evaluation

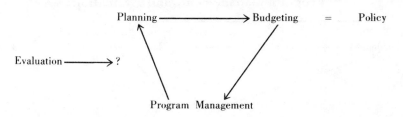

Fig. 2. Evaluation Limited to One Stage in Shaping Policy

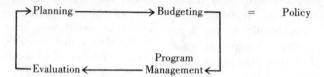

policymakers and program managers or fail to measure the key goals and objectives identified by the policymakers. Conducted in accord with this model, evaluation is often feared and misunderstood by program managers and ignored by policymakers; its isolated role causes its products to be ignored.

Figure 3 depicts policy as the result of the interface of planning, budgeting, program management, and program evaluation. In this model, evaluation is an integral component of the policy process. Although not viewed as a primary policymaker, evaluation plays two critically important roles: it is a definer and describer of what policy has been implemented, and it is a tool that provides critical feedback to all participants in the policy process.

Why are these roles so important? If a clear, rational policy is to be developed, it must be done with an understanding of what present policy is, how well it is working, and why or where it is not working. Evaluation reports are essential tools that enable policymakers and program managers to monitor and maximize the effectiveness of programs as they develop, to allocate and reallocate resources to appropriate and highly effective programs, and to develop and implement program management and program delivery schemes that are consistent with policy. Program evaluation thus provides timely and useful information to all actors simultaneously. This insures that its products are too useful to gather dust on the shelf. As Attkisson and Broskowski point out, program evaluation is

> a practical matter, of use to others primarily to the extent that it informs their current decision making, fulfills environmental demands for accountability, and points to future program improvement and efficiency. Program evaluation, therefore, is a part of the essential but basic process of internal planning and controlling of human services operation; in brief, it is an integral part of the managerial process and must be linked to long- and short-range planning efforts, as well as to varying control systems that seek adherence to, and signal deviations from, plans.[4]

Case Study

The development and implementation of a juvenile deinstitutionalization policy in Wisconsin illustrates how policy direc-

Fig. 3. Policy Resulting from the Interface of Planning, Budgeting, Program Management, and Evaluation

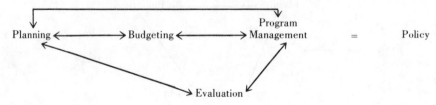

tion and policy implementation often differ and what role program evaluation can play in the policy process. At the planning-budgeting phase of the process, a policy decision was made to deinstitutionalize juveniles who were inappropriately placed in state institutions. The removal of status offenders—runaways, truants, and uncontrollable youths—from juvenile corrections institutions became a top priority. The objective was to place these youths in families or in community-based treatment centers. The expected outcome was a program that would be more effective because it addressed the juveniles' problems where the problems originated—in the communities. It was further expected that the community approach would be more humane and less costly than institutional programs. Operational and budgetary plans were developed, two of four juvenile institutions were closed, and the populations of state correctional institutions were cut in half.

With all this, it would seem clear that the policy of the state of Wisconsin was one of deinstitutionalization. But was it? And are its anticipated outcomes being achieved? It appears now that the actual policy of the state may not be deinstitutionalization, but reinstitutionalization. To be sure, children are out of state-operated institutions, but the numbers of children in private child care institutions are increasing significantly, and the children are remaining in these new institutions for longer periods at higher per month costs than was the case in the state institutions. Pretrial incarceration of status offenders is increasing at alarming rates; many new high-cost group homes have been established; and few new in-home services have been initiated.

What went wrong? Was the plan ill conceived? Did the planners lack adequate understanding of the population in need? Did the plan neglect to provide the appropriate complement of community-based services? Did the policy collapse occur because the budget failed to provide adequate resources to meet the needs of a community-based program? Or did it come about because the budget created financial incentives for placements in private institutions? Did the program's managers fail to implement the policy adequately or seek to redefine the policy to suit their needs and biases? Did management fail to understand the plan or to recognize what was happening when implementation became inconsistent with the policy? It also needs to be asked whether the program achieved its expected treatment outcomes and whether the community approach worked any better than the institutional approach.

These are questions that must be answered if future plans, budgets, and management decisions are to be made and adjusted in a way that insures that policies are implemented as intended, improved if this is appropriate, or abandoned if they are ineffective, unmanageable, or not cost beneficial. These are questions that can be most effectively answered by a program evaluation capacity that is fully integrated into the policy process.

Integrating Evaluation into Organizations

The development and integration of evaluation as a new partner in policymaking confront an organization with significant challenges. These challenges become tremendously complicated in a large, complex, and structurally stratified organization like a state department or a large county agency, but they are surmountable. In Wisconsin, several strategies have been developed to address these challenges and are now being implemented in the form of organizational components. Three major components will be discussed in detail:

• The establishment of a central policy unit that contains planning, budgeting, and evaluation capabilities and that is responsible for managing the process of policy development throughout the organization.

• The integration of the planning, budgeting, and evaluation functions horizontally within the central policy unit and vertically with the organization as a whole.

• The development of integrated management systems to provide the information needed for both the policy development and program management functions.

Each of these components is central to the policy process as a whole, and each needs an individualized strategy for its implementation. The remainder of this article describes the general design requirements of each component and explains how this design relates to the program evaluation function.

The Central Policy Unit

Coordinated and integrated policies designed to direct, improve, and coordinate service delivery do not just happen. In the highly complex organizations that are responsible for the delivery of human services, the development of policy must be viewed as a distinct organizational task. Ideally, this takes the form of a central staff unit whose members report directly to the chief administrative and policymaking officer of the organization. It is essential that this unit include the individuals with primary responsibility in planning, budgeting, and evaluation to insure a balanced impact of these policymaking disciplines and perspectives on critical policy decisions.

This is necessary for two reasons. Program managers who are primarily responsible for the administration of specific programs on a day-to-day basis often do not have the time or the perspective to conceptualize or develop broad, coordinated policy initiatives. Second, the categorical organization of human services programs inhibits the ability of the organization to comprehensively review and develop policies that are consistent and coordinated across program lines. A policy unit that is functionally divorced from program management and organizationally responsible for providing a comprehensive review of policy and program development is the only effective way to achieve the desired policies.

In Wisconsin, a central policy unit was created and called the Division of Policy and Budget. The following statement of purpose indicates its policy and functional responsibilities:

> The purpose of the Division of Policy and Budget is to develop and assist in the establishment of major policy directions for the Department of Health and Social Services. In this role the Division serves as the primary planning, budgeting and evaluation staff to the Department Secretary. The Division is responsible for identifying, analyzing and planning new policy initiatives and is responsible for securing and allocating resources necessary for all Departmental programs. The Division is responsible for enhancing the effectiveness of the Department's programs by assuring that all policies are appropriate, coordinated and consistent and by assuring that programs are continually monitored and evaluated in light of intended objectives. These objectives are achieved through a variety of highly complex processes including policy analysis and development, legislative proposal development, budget analysis and allocation, organizational development services, program planning, statistical and data analysis services and program evaluation services.[5]

In the clear recognition that policy is not just a "top down" exercise, policy development procedures focus the staff's attention on the principal mechanisms through which policy is made and clearly identify the critical points for decision-making by central policy staff and program administrators. In Wisconsin's Department of Health and Social Services, the central policy unit manages twenty-six discrete policymaking processes, which fall into three general categories: (1) budget development and monitoring processes, (2) plan development and review processes, and (3) evaluation plan development and evaluation product delivery.

The role of central policy staff, therefore, is one of managing policy processes, and it incorporates responsibility for initiating and giving direction to the formation of policy, for providing technical assistance during policy development, for carrying out analyses of policy options, and for monitoring the implementation of policies.

Implications for Evaluation. The integration of program evaluation as a co-equal participant in the process management role of a central policy unit has important implications for the kind of work program evaluators perform. These implications are apparent in four specific tasks program evaluation must address if it is to have an impact on policy: plan development, technical assistance, the production of studies, and training.

The first and most important step for program evaluation is to define for the organization what the system of program evaluation is and why, how, and when it will contribute to policy development. This information must be explained in a carefully prepared statement or plan, and this plan for the evaluation program must be understood and accepted by all the participants in the policy process—the planners, the budget developers, and the program managers. After completing the

conceptual design and planning for the evaluation, the evaluators must then function as process managers. As the program evaluation is implemented, evaluation products are produced and the results are incorporated into the policy debate.

Assuming responsibilities as process managers means that the program evaluators have to spend considerable time doing things other than evaluation studies. This role is critical, however, if central evaluation staff is to maximize the use of evaluation resources at all levels of the department.

The program evaluators must also provide technical assistance to agency staff who are, or ought to be, developing evaluation components for plans and budgets. The assistance assures (1) that program evaluation is incorporated wherever necessary, and (2) that evaluations are done in the best and most professionally sound way. Program evaluation is a highly technical art, and most who have not been trained in it simply do not know how to do it. Building measurable objectives into plans, developing good program monitoring systems, writing good evaluation components to demonstration projects, developing good contracts for evaluation products that are produced by outside specialists, and doing evaluations in a cost beneficial way are all routine tasks for evaluation personnel. The evaluation team must produce evaluation products—outcome evaluations, goal attainment and quality assurance studies, cost-effective analyses, and so on—that meet the needs of the policymakers, policy analysts, and program managers. It must then (1) determine policy analysis and program management needs that these reports can service, (2) determine whether the reports can or should be done on a special project or ongoing basis, and (3) go into production.

Out of recognition that evaluation is at

best misunderstood and at worst feared, the evaluators must also devote time in training the key policymakers and program managers to understand what evaluation is, how it can be used, and why it is useful. If evaluation is to be used, it must be understood not just as a necessary evil, but as a tool that planners, budgeters, and program managers can seek out and use in their daily work. At the same time, evaluators, especially those who have technical "how-to-do-it" evaluation knowledge but who have not worked in a real-world bureaucracy, need to train themselves in planning, program management, and budget development, so that they can understand the requests of the nonevaluators.

Horizontal and Vertical Integration

Establishing a policy development unit with responsibility for planning, budgeting, and evaluation does not insure that service delivery will be coordinated and effective or that policy will be consistent, interrelated, implemented, evaluated, or even improved. Since policy results from the interface between budget, planning, evaluation, and program management, specific organizational strategies have to be developed to integrate these functions and thus insure that critical policy issues are identified and addressed, and that the various perspectives, skills, and needs of each part of the policy process are known and considered. If planning, budgeting, evaluation, and program management are allowed to operate independently, the agency may well make the same mistakes it always has. What is needed is a tightly integrated policy development and program management process: the knowledge and responsibility necessary for all planning, budgeting, and evaluation functions must be integrated horizontally within the central policy unit, and then

this integration must be maintained in a vertical form so these functions are taken up by the subunits of the department primarily responsible for program management. This vertical integration is critically important. It is the mechanism that incorporates the program management function and perspective into the thinking of the central policy unit, which is not responsible for the daily operation of service delivery.

Two management strategies have been developed in Wisconsin to insure horizontal and vertical integration:

1. Horizontal integration is achieved through a matrix approach to management. Budget, planning, and evaluation tasks and inputs are all viewed as essential to the comprehensive and effective management of each policy process. Consequently, in the central policy unit, the management of each major decision-making process is the joint responsibility of two or all three analytical units, that is, the budgeting, planning, and evaluation units. At the same time, primary responsibility for each decision-making process is assigned to one analytical unit with secondary responsibility to one or both of the other two units. To insure that each process receives adequate, appropriate, and timely input from all three units, the manager of the unit with primary responsibility must first meet and negotiate with the units having secondary responsibility and then prepare specific statements that describe the internal division of labor and responsibility. These statements must include, in addition to a statement of the role and responsibilities of the primary unit, first, a specification of when during the year the contributions of the secondary units will be needed, and second, a description of which points in the process provide an opportunity for the resolution of any disagreements that may develop between primary and secondary units.

2. Vertical integration is achieved through formalized role definitions. For a policy process to be managed effectively, it must progress in a clearly defined and orderly way. The department's administrative officer, the central policy unit, and the units operating the programs must understand the purpose of the policy process, the expected policy products, and the time schedule for development, implementation, and evaluation. They must also understand each policy process's relationship to other policy processes and the relative roles and responsibilities of all participants in the policy process. The assumption is that this is best accomplished in a formalized way through clearly written statements or guidelines that define the overall parameters of each policy process in the Department of Health and Social Services and the relative roles and responsibilities of all the participants at various levels of the department. The ultimate purpose of these statements is to make clear how the process will operate vertically for that particular policy, and each statement does the following:

• Opens by stating the purpose of departmental involvement in that policy process, that is, why it would not be good enough to give each program unit free rein in this policy area.

• Expresses any overall direction that is to be followed by all divisions participating in the process.

• Lays out the timetables that will govern the operation of the process within the department.

• Specifies the policy products that are to be generated during the developmental stages.

• Describes the relationship that should exist, or be developed, between each policy process and other major policy processes that bear, or should bear, on the one described.

This approach to vertical integration is not fancy. It is a nitty-gritty and mechanistic approach, but it is firmly grounded in the belief that unless this level of detailed and managed interface is achieved, policy will surely not be integrated or even fully analyzed.

Responsibility of Program Evaluation. Like the establishment of a central policy unit, this strategy of horizontal and vertical integration has major implications for the four principal tasks of program evaluation: evaluation plan development, technical assistance, the production of evaluation studies and training. In developing an evaluation plan to accomplish the horizontal and vertical integration of evaluation, the initial step for evaluation staff is to define the role of program evaluation in each major part of the policy development process. This must be done in cooperation with colleagues in the central policy unit and in the vertical organization. This definition must be based on an analysis of each policy process to determine whether an evaluation component is presently built into that process and how it should be included. This analysis should also determine where, when, and how evaluation should affect each process.

Second, each of the major nonevaluation participants in the policy process should determine which of their evaluation questions typically go unanswered. The plan for the evaluation program should incorporate means of answering those questions. Third, the plan should include a system for discriminating between ongoing, routine evaluation operations and special one-time evaluation studies and should project the capacity to address both needs. Evaluation procedures that use information systems and that routinely analyze the information the systems produce are the most effective way of addressing routine questions. The development of a special study capacity is the way to handle the more detailed or in-depth evaluations. Many special studies are the result of questions raised by the analysis of routine information. Fourth, the evaluation plan should be an action plan that balances evaluation needs with evaluation capacity, determines evaluation priorities, and develops products which address those priorities.

The plan should implement the evaluation agenda by managing the evaluation resources and projects of the department. It should identify the key evaluation staff and resources already available to the department and provide for the acquisition of any new resources that may be necessary. These procedures will involve the central policy staff in a formal review and approved role. These five steps describe the management plan for the evaluation program of the agency, and they assure that the evaluation products will be integrated throughout the organization both horizontally and vertically.

The plan for the evaluation program should incorporate an evaluation training plan. It should determine the need for training among evaluation users at the central policy and program management levels and design a mechanism for setting priorities for delivering evaluation training. Similarly, the evaluation program plan and the analysis of each discrete policy development process should identify the specific areas in which technical assistance is needed. For example, planners may need technical assistance in developing measurable objectives or needs assessment information at the front end of the planning process or in analyzing utilization or cost-effectiveness information at the monitoring end. In another case, program managers may need assistance in designing quality assurance or case-monitoring systems that will give them good management information. The plan should determine these needs, set priorities, and then implement the appropriate technical assistance services. This will maximize the useful application of evaluation.

Finally, the plan should set forth an agenda for the evaluation products that will be delivered during the upcoming period. It should spell out the special studies and the system development work that will be done, as well as the regular reports that will be generated. It is important that this agenda identify the appropriate and answerable evaluation questions and provide for the delivery of the necessary evaluation products to the right persons at the right time—before a policy decision is made, not after. It is the responsibility of the central evaluation staff to follow through during the implementation of the evaluation findings or, at a minimum, insure that those findings become an integral part of the policy debate.

Integrated Management Systems

Information is the raw material that policymakers and program managers need for making decisions, and the collection and use of this information is the central feature of an evaluation capability. A management information system must be developed and implemented to provide the policymakers and program managers the information they need to make critical and routine decisions. As Sorensen and Elpers pointed out, information systems should be designed to meet two broad organizational needs:

1. To make better *plans*—plans that relate to organizational goals and objectives based on the relative benefits and costs of alternate courses of action.
2. To have better *control*—control that assures efficient and effective action in pursuing the organization's objectives. [Emphasis in original.][6]

Just as the appropriate information is critical for the effective performance of the budgeting, planning, and program management components of the policy process, it is absolutely essential for a strong program evaluation function. Without it, programs are incapable of producing the comprehensive evaluation products that program managers and policy analysts need, and evaluators are forced to generate separately all the information needed for each study. That is time consuming, expensive, and, given present technology, unnecessary. Most important, an information system that provides uniform information to all participants in the policy process gives the evaluation function the necessary level of credibility. If all participants are using the same information, the charge that evaluation staff developed the data, information statistics, and so on to justify its conclusion becomes moot. The policy debate can then more appropriately focus on the meaning of the information. An integrated management information system, therefore, is a technology that every organization needs if it is to have a comprehensive and day-to-day evaluation capacity and if program managers, planners, and budgeters are to understand and evaluate their decisions.

The Department of Health and Social Services in Wisconsin has given priority to the development of an Agency Integrated Management System (AIMS), which accomplishes the information-gathering objectives just outlined. Because this system is of critical importance to the policymaking process of the department, the central policy unit has primary responsibility to conceptualize and develop this system. Obviously, this effort is not starting from nothing in that many information systems are already operational. The need is to develop a system that is comprehensive—one that serves both the policy development and

program management functions. Program evaluation must play a major role in planning, implementing, and operating this system to insure its usefulness to the functions of program evaluation.

Information Systems and Evaluation.

A management information component, like the central policy unit and the system of vertical and horizontal integration, has implications for each of the four major tasks of evaluation. The plan for the evaluation program must insure that any information system developed provides the information necessary for evaluation. This includes information that

- Assesses the pattern of service delivery (e.g., Who receives what types and amounts of services?)
- Defines how current resources are required and being consumed (e.g., How are professional staff deployed?)
- Provides monitoring aids for various human service providers and managers (e.g., Were particular admissions of client entries into the program inappropriate?)
- Develops data for multiple reporting requirements (e.g., Reporting to federal or state funding agencies or payment agents such as the Social Security Administration or PSRO review)
- Assesses outcomes of rendered services (e.g., Level of functioning of client, changes in symptoms).[7]

This information must then be delivered to the policy analysts and program managers through evaluation reports.

Both during the information system's development and once it is in use, evaluation staff must provide planners, budgeters, and program managers with the technical assistance and training they need if they are to use the system's products in accord with the principles of sound evaluation. This multiplies the impact of program evaluation by making it a part of all major policy processes. In providing technical assistance, the program evaluation staff needs to help develop the technical instruments that are of special importance to the other functions. The development of the systems to gather good needs assessment information and of a uniform set of service and program definitions are two technical efforts that program evaluation is working on in Wisconsin.

Information system reports are, in many ways, program evaluation products. Routine program management and policy decisions can be made most effectively and efficiently in the light of the reports routinely supplied by the information system. The evaluation plan must insure that these reports contain the information essential to evaluation. Planners, budgeters, and program managers need technical assistance and training if they are to use these reports effectively.

Final Thoughts

Wisconsin is attempting to incorporate a program evaluation function into the mainstream of both the policymaking and the program management functions of the Department of Health and Social Services. The horizontal interaction of program evaluation with short-term budget development and long-term plan development, coupled with evaluation's verti-

cal interaction with program management, are the key strategic underpinnings of this effort. Critical to the success of this effort, however, will be the ability of the program evaluators to provide useful and understandable answers to the practical questions asked by top departmental program managers and decision-makers.

NOTES AND REFERENCES

1. C. Clifford Attkisson et al., eds., *Evaluation of Human Service Programs* (New York: Academic Press, 1978), p. 1.

2. C. Clifford Attkisson and Anthony Broskowski, "Evaluation and the Emerging Human Service Concept," in Attkisson et al., eds., op. cit., p. 24.

3. William H. Harrison, *Dictionary of the Social Sciences* (New York: The Free Press, 1964), p. 509.

4. Attkisson and Broskowski, op. cit., p. 23.

5. "Organization and Responsibilities of the Division of Policy and Budget," (Madison, Wisc., Department of Health and Social Services, March 1, 1978), p. 1.

6. James E. Sorensen and J. Richard Elpers, "Developing Information Systems for Human Service Organizations," in Attkisson et al., eds., op. cit., p. 127.

7. Ibid., p. 128.

PART 4

Services to Client Groups

Research on Social Work in Health Care: Progress and Future Directions

CLAUDIA J. COULTON

RECENT TRENDS INDICATE that the field of health care is taking on increasing importance in the social work profession. Approximately 40,000 social workers are now employed in a variety of roles in health care.[1] More than 16 percent of the Title XX expenditures last year were for health-related social and home care services.[2] Sixty percent of the nation's hospitals now have social service departments.[3] Social workers, moreover, are the largest professional group in health planning.[4]

The expansion of the number and functions of social workers in health care has its origin in a variety of developments:

- Accreditation standards for hospitals require social work services.
- Technological advances have been increasingly successful in prolonging the lives of chronically ill and disabled people who require a variety of social supports.

- Pressures for shortening lengths of stay in hospitals require the facilitation of timely admissions and discharges.
- The concept of health care is expanding to include psychological and social treatment.
- Community health centers now focus on the health of the family and the environment.
- The promotion of prevention and self-care requires that the health care professional help the patient understand and change health habits and behaviors.
- Programs of community health planning have frequently been expanded to include roles for social workers.
- Competition to fill beds has inspired hospitals to take an interest in patient satisfaction with the interpersonal aspects of care.
- Long-term care is broadening its scope and bringing such traditional social services as foster care, day care, and homemaker services under the health system umbrella.

The author would like to thank David Vielhaber for his comments on an earlier draft of this article.

These and other developments make it likely that social work research in health care will continue to develop and expand. They also indicate the need for a review of the research in the health field, an emphasis that previous surveys of social work research have not adopted.[5] This discussion has two purposes. First, it describes the present state of research related to social work in health care, identifying the areas in which research can inform practice and reviewing recent research reports in each area. The second purpose here arises naturally out of the questions that remain unanswered following the review—to suggest directions for future social work research in health care. Questions regarding the resolution of methodological issues are also discussed.

Since health care, social work, and research are concepts that are variously defined, it is important to establish some definitions as guides for discussion. First, what is research? Here it refers to written reports of studies based on systematic, empirical observation to describe a phenomenon or test a hypothesis, and it includes only those studies that exert some control over observer bias or unwarranted inference.

Social work practice, for purposes of this review, includes more than those services delivered by professional social workers. Many of the social services needed by the physically ill or disabled are provided by other types of personnel, such as homemakers, companions, transportation workers, home health aides, and friendly visitors. Although a package of such services may at times be provided personally by the social worker, they are services that the professional social worker is now more likely to manage, arrange, or coordinate.

Health care, again for purposes of this review, includes both institutional and community-based medical and related services for physically ill and disabled persons and their families. Research on mental health care is not included here, but studies of long-term care for the physically impaired are discussed.

Given these definitions, what research topics should be included in a discussion of social work research in health care? Should it include only research done by social workers? Probably not, since much relevant research is multidisciplinary or conducted by other professions. Should it include only research on social work practice per se? Probably not, because many studies have implications for social work practice even though that is not their primary focus. Nevertheless, a review cannot focus on every topic of research that may, however remotely, be useful to social workers in health care.

Consequently, this analysis focuses on empirical research that has relatively direct applicability to social work practice in health care.[6] "Practice" here is broadly defined in terms of function, but is limited to that which is associated with the prevention or treatment of physical illness or disability.

Research questions relevant to social work in health care can be divided into several broad areas:

• What implications do the psychosocial causes and consequences of physical illness and disease have for effective practice? Specifically, in which of the causes and effects of illness can social workers intervene?

• What are the practice and policy implications of factors affecting patients' reactions to and utilization of health care? For example, what aspects of health care organizations should be targets for social work intervention?

• What affects the ways social services are delivered in health care organizations? Who uses services and how are they organized?

• What are the effects of social services on patients and their families? In other words, what kinds of services produce desired outcomes?

In each of these broad areas, a variety of questions can be identified, and the available research findings suggest some beginning answers. This review summarizes these questions and answers, emphasizing those studies in which social workers have participated or that were designed to have clear implications for social intervention.

Psychosocial Factors in Health and Illness

Knowledge about the psychosocial causes and consequences of health and illness has traditionally provided direction for social work intervention. For practice to be effective, it should be guided by answers to the following questions:

• What are the effects of illness and disability on patients and their families? What accounts for the differences in these psychosocial outcomes?

• What psychosocial conditions are associated with the occurrence of physiological symptoms?

• What psychosocial factors affect the way people form their health habits and use health services?

Social work research has tended to focus mainly on the psychosocial consequences of illness. However, if social workers are to contribute to primary and secondary prevention, they must also increase their understanding of the psychosocial factors affecting service utilization and the life circumstances that seem to lead to disease.

Psychosocial Consequences. Much of social work practice in health care is directed toward ameliorating the psychosocial consequences of illness and disability. Considering the importance of this area, it is surprising that only a small proportion of the research on these topics has been conducted by social workers or designed to yield implications for clinical practice.

Much of the research on the psychosocial reactions to illness has been conducted by sociologists primarily for the purpose of testing sociological propositions and concepts. There is now fairly strong evidence that people with acute conditions tend to adopt the sick role in predictable stages.[7] For some, illness seems to be an acceptable way to avoid responsibility for failing to meet certain role expectations.[8] Also, values and beliefs about health and illness have been found to be related to ethnicity and group membership.[9] Beliefs seem to influence whether a person lives in health or illness.[10] Since these sociologically oriented studies were not conducted for the purpose of informing social work practice or programs, their implications for practice can only be inferred.

More directly applicable to social work practice is a smaller group of studies that are clinical in nature and that focus on the personal, interpersonal, and family problems faced by people with a disease or disability. Some of these studies were done by social workers, but many were carried out by physicians with some assistance from social workers.

Supporting patient's efforts to cope has frequently been a function of social work. Weisman and Worden, examining the coping strategies of cancer patients, found that 40 percent of the patients experienced their point of maximum distress during the first eight to ten weeks of their illness.[11] Physical symptoms, work, and finances were the areas of greatest concern. The most effective coping strategies were confrontation of the problems, redefinition of the problems, and compliance with authority. The least successful strategies were suppression, acting out, withdrawal, blaming others, blaming self, and denial. The authors recommend that patients be given assistance in learning to use the effective strategies.

Other studies also found denial to be an ineffective coping strategy. Chaklin and Warfield found patients who denied the stigma associated with amputation made less rehabilitation progress.[12] Kaplan, Grobstein, and Smith found that families who openly communicated information about a leukemic child's condition and impending death experienced fewer postmortem problems.[13] Starr found that children who failed to acknowledge facial deformities had poorer self-esteem and more behavior problems when they reached adolescence.[14]

Unfortunately, few controls were possible in any of these studies of coping mechanisms. Therefore, it is not clear whether avoidance or denial actually results in better adjustment or whether some other characteristic affects both adjustment and the tendency to use denial. More controlled studies of coping are required to answer this question.

Many studies found that chronically ill people report facing multiple psychosocial problems.[15] Among the problems reported were decreased income and increased expenses, difficulty in filling leisure time, isolation, depressed mood, impaired sexual functioning, anxiety about pain, and change in family routines. Braham et al. found that multiple sclerosis patients rated 48 percent of their resources for social and personal care as inadequate.[16] Only 20 percent of the care they received came from community agencies with the rest delivered by family and friends. There was evidence that this burden had an adverse effect on family adjustment.

These studies, as well as some yet to be discussed, illustrate the difficulties of operationalizing for research purposes the concepts of need and problem. In some instances, the categories were defined by professionals; others used definitions supplied by patients. This lack of consistency hampers the drawing of valid generalizations from the findings.

The effect of caring for a chronically ill family member can be seen in a study by Stone and Shapiro.[17] They hypothesized that over time families would become more proficient in caring for the patient. After 1½ years, only 40 percent of the families had mastered these caring tasks, and others reported much stress. The successful families were quite autonomous in many areas, suggesting that careful assessment is required to determine whether a family can carry the burden of providing full-time care for a chronically ill member.

The presence of an extensive social network may also help to explain the successful adaptation of the chronically ill person and his family. Findlayson found that postmyocardial infarction patients of lower socioeconomic status tended to rely more on family and friends than did more affluent patients.[18] She found further that the more numerous their sources of lay assistance, the better their physical and psychosocial outcomes.

Psychosocial Preconditions. Psychosocial factors are also frequently considered to contribute to illness and disability and, hence, should be of interest to social workers in suggesting avenues for prevention. Socioepidemiological studies have found that people of lower socioeconomic status tend to experience more days of illness and more chronic and disabling illness.[19] The relative influence of such factors as stress, downward mobility, inaccessible medical care, poor nutrition, and inadequate housing in explaining these findings is not clear. However, these studies do support the notion that social and psychological factors contribute to illness and disease.

Although not conducted primarily by social workers, a growing body of research suggests that stressful life events can affect physical health. Hinkle and Wolf, who compared episodes of illness with stressful life events, concluded that about one-third of the episodes of illness were associated with the individual's attempt to adapt to situations he encountered.[20] Other studies linked changes in people's situations with social stress and episodes of disease.[21] Similar conclusions were reported by Bergin, a social worker who compared patients admitted to the hospital with congestive heart failure with patients admitted for other reasons.[22] She found that significantly more of the patients with congestive heart failure than with other ailments had experienced an acute emotional event within three days prior to admission.

Utilization. Social workers are frequently involved in facilitating the use of medical care services because psychosocial factors seem to affect utilization. Research in sociology and public health shows that persons with low incomes and members of certain ethnic groups tend to use emergency services and illness-related services to a greater extent than do individuals with higher incomes and of northern European descent. Conversely, persons with lower incomes and members of minority groups use fewer services for preventing illness and maintaining health than do those who have greater incomes and are members of majority groups.[23] These differences seem to be partly related to beliefs about the etiology of illness and the effectiveness of Western medical practices.[24] Reference group norms also seem to influence behavior in both health and illness, but there is evidence that these patterns can be changed

through modification of the ways services are delivered.[25] Health Maintenance Organizations (HMOs) seem to have been particularly successful in reducing barriers to utilization of primary and secondary preventive services.[26]

Social workers' studies in this area most often focused on patients using obstetrical and gynecological services. Watkins compared 120 mothers initiating prenatal care early with those initiating it late. Early initiators were younger, had fewer pregnancies, reported fewer social problems, had more positive feelings toward pregnancy, and had previous history of fetal loss.[27]

Two studies have focused on women seeking abortions. A comparison of women who actually obtained an abortion with those who dropped out after counseling revealed that those who dropped out had less education, were further along in pregnancy, and had partners who were negative towards abortion.[28] An examination of women seeking abortions showed that 45 percent of the patients did so for social reasons, 53 percent for psychological reasons, and 5 percent for medical reasons.[29]

Studies of compliance with medical care recommendations are also relevant to social work practice. Some of these have shown that reinforcement contingencies can have a marked influence on following medical advice, and others suggest that the quality of the communication between patient and provider may affect compliance.[30] Studies of the impact of the attitude and behavior of health care providers show that it is particularly important that practitioners and patients share common definitions of the problem and that patients feel accepted and valued by the provider.[31]

Summary and Future Directions. The literature contains a fairly clear picture of the kinds of psychosocial problems faced by the physically ill or disabled person. Although families are presently providing most of the personal care, they differ in their abilities to carry this burden. The presence of extensive social networks helps both patients and families cope with illness. In general, denial seems to be an ineffective strategy for coping with illness, and the confrontation and redefinition of problems seem most effective.

It is also known that patients from certain ethnic groups, of lower socioeconomic status, and with little education tend to use health services for episodic rather than primary care. They perceive symptoms later and take longer to get to the appropriate service. Their beliefs about health care are frequently inconsistent with the tenets of Western medicine. HMOs and neighborhood health centers have been somewhat successful in changing this behavior through reducing the barriers to utilization. Compliance with medical recommendations has been enhanced through improved communication and the manipulation of reinforcement contingencies.

Finally, there is beginning evidence that stress can result in physiological symptoms. Social networks seem to serve as a buffer against the impact of stressful events.

Comparing what is known about the psychosocial causes and consequences of illness and disability with what social workers need to know suggests several major directions for further research in this area. First, the concept of coping seems important to social work functions, but present research gives little idea of how to facilitate effective coping. Can certain strategies be learned? What social work techniques are most likely to result in this type of learning?

Second, since a large proportion of personal care is provided by the patients' families, it is important to learn more

about the impact of such activities on family functioning. Is it possible to identify those family characteristics associated with success or failure in providing this care? If professional care is substituted, what impact does this have on family stability and on the expressive aspects of care? What are the consequences for child development and marital satisfaction of caring for a chronically ill family member?

Third, since social networks seem to facilitate coping and serve as a buffer for stress, it is necessary to know more about how such networks occur. Which is more important, the quantity or the quality of the relationships? Is it possible to create social networks for people who have limited relationships? How can health professionals strengthen such networks when they do exist?

Fourth, there is a need to learn more about the role of stress in illness. Are economic and living conditions major contributors to stress? Why are some people in identical circumstances affected more than others? Can certain types of social services mitigate harmful effects?

Fifth, the ways in which psychosocial factors affect utilization and compliance in medical care need to be investigated. Can beliefs about health be changed? How can health professionals be influenced to change their own patterns of communicating with patients? How might reinforcement contingencies be incorporated into routine health care so as to facilitate compliance?

Health Care Organizations

The second area of research that was identified as important to social workers examines the effect of health care organizations on patients. The way health services are delivered influences patients in a variety of ways. The organizational climate of a hospital or nursing home can affect a patient's comfort, anxiety, self-esteem, identity, and so on. The accessibility of health services affects how patients use them. These aspects of health service organizations should be of concern to social workers because they have implications for social work intervention with the structure and personnel of health care facilities.

Organizational Climate. Although there is increasing interest in humanizing hospital care, there has been little systematic social work research on the psychosocial impact of the hospital environment. However, a few studies have focused on the climate of long-term care. Felton found that a person's fit with his or her environment in a nursing home affected morbidity and mortality.[32] Similarly, Kahana discovered that the nature of the nursing home environment had a profound impact on well-being.[33] These findings indicate that social workers can play a role in matching people to health care environments or modifying environments to be more congruent with patients' characteristics.

A number of studies have documented the impact of the relocation of patients on their health. Killian found that mortality rates were much higher for long-term care patients who were transferred than for a comparison group that remained in one facility.[34] These findings emphasize the importance of preparing patients for movement from one setting to another.

Access. Many studies have demonstrated the importance of the accessibility of care to a patient's understanding of how to use it. Berloff found that the availability of a comprehensive health care team changed the health care utilization patterns of thirty-one multiproblem families.[35] Their increased use of such services as nursing counseling, psycho-social guidance, and health education, together with a decreased use of physician services, suggested that these families had moved from an illness orientation toward a health orientation.

Health planning activities have the potential of making services more accessible, but the community health perspective does not always predominate. Murphy found that physicians in solo practice had the least favorable attitude toward community health compared to other health professionals. Other direct practitioners, including social workers, also had less interest in community health than did planners and administrators.[36]

Summary and Future Directions. Since the majority of social workers in health care have functioned as clinicians, it is not surprising that little social work research has focused on the climate of care or access to care. However, the few studies reviewed here show that these concepts are crucial to patient well-being.

We know that the climate of an institution influences its patients and that individuals respond differently to particular environments. To translate this knowledge into guidelines for social work practice, several other questions need to be answered. What aspects of institutional environments are most salient? What characteristics of people determine whether a particular climate will be suitable for them? What attributes of institutional environments maximize well-being for most patients? How can existing settings be modified to resemble these ideals? What procedures and arrangements can reduce the mortality associated with relocating patients?

Answering any of these questions requires the measurement of environments. Social science has devoted much attention to measuring the attributes of people, but has found fewer ways of measuring characteristics of environments. Scales are needed that are capable of assessing institutional environments on dimensions that are important to patient well-being. It will also be necessary to assess individuals along these same dimensions so that practitioners can determine whether they are suited for particular environments. This type of information could eventually influence placement decisions or plans for environmental modification.

Accessibility of care affects utilization, especially of primary and secondary preventive services. How can existing services be made more accessible? What supportive services can minimize the impact of geographical and logistical barriers? Since health centers obviously cannot be located on every street corner, social workers are bound to be involved in facilitating access to care. Answers to the above questions will help social workers plan programs to accomplish this goal.

Social Service Delivery

The third research area useful to social workers concerns the actual provision of social services. The ways in which social services are organized and delivered have frequently been emphasized by social work researchers, and the studies have had a variety of focuses:

• Consumers: Who uses services, what are their problems, and who needs services the most?

• Social workers: What role do they play, how do they function on a team, how do others see them, and what do they do?

• Other professionals: How do they perceive social workers, how do they work with social workers, and what is the nature of the team?

• Services: How are they organized? How are service functions influenced by the larger facility or community in which they are delivered?

Consumers. Who needs and uses health-related social services? This is a difficult question to answer since who is seen is often determined by professional decisions rather than consumer decisions.[37] However, the question is important to social workers who, for purposes of planning, must estimate service demand and determine whether people who may benefit from services are actually getting them.

Several studies have attempted to identify the characteristics of people who require social services. One approach, derived from institutional goals, has been to look at people whose stays in the hospital have been excessively long. Altman found that 40 percent of the excessive stays were for psychosocial reasons.[38] Glass found that patients over 80 years old who had to live somewhere new after discharge and who experienced chronic disorientation were most likely to stay in hospitals for social reasons.[39]

Russo et al. tested four referral criteria for their accuracy in identifying the users of a pediatric clinic whom social workers would judge as suitable candidates for services.[40] The criteria used were the age of the patients, the number of children, the existence of social problems, previous use of medical care, and the presence of falling plaster in the home. They compared a group selected according to these criteria with a randomly selected group. Only families who reported social problems or falling plaster were more likely to require services than the control group.

A number of investigators have sought to identify the reasons that hospital patients request or are referred to social workers. Moncure found that 20 percent of the patients discharged from Veterans Administration hospitals were referred for posthospital planning services.[41] Of these, 67 percent returned to their own homes where 19 percent received home care. The remainder were provided help with psychosocial adjustment or financial planning. This is in contrast to the finding of Coulton and Vielhaber. In a study of eighteen nonfederal hospitals, they found that only 42 percent of the patients referred for posthospital planning went to their own homes. However, social workers in large teaching hospitals provided planning services to much larger proportions of the people returning to their own home than did workers in community hospitals.[42]

Lindenberg and Coulton, studying the posthospital care plans made for social service patients, found that 98 percent were to receive medical follow-up, 55 percent psychosocial support, 53 percent personal care, 50 percent nursing care, 49 percent equipment, 42 percent health teaching, and 41 percent homemaker services.[43] Most medical care was to be provided by private physicians, most psychosocial support by the hospital social worker, and most personal care by family and friends.

The lack of community resources for the chronically ill has been documented in several studies. Blaxter found that one year following hospital discharge, most people who had been critically ill had solved their personal care problems, but 18 percent had job problems, 12 percent had money problems, and 19 percent had problems in personal relationships.[44] Donabedian and Rosenfeld reported that three months after discharge, 50 percent of the patients studied had not complied with medical recommendations, and 40 percent reported that they were unable to obtain one or more health-related social services.[45]

Several investigators have attempted to determine why patients were referred to social services.[46] Stoeckle et al., for example, found that 33 percent of the patients seen by social workers in a medical clinic were referred for help with social resources, 17 percent for evalua-

tion, 13 percent for help with personal problems, and 7 percent for work placement.[47] Such studies have frequently concluded that social workers are receiving too few referrals for emotional problems and too many referrals for coordination of concrete resources. This interpretation may reflect a tendency to define research questions from the perspective of what social workers want to do, rather than beginning to look for the incidence and prevalence of various patient problems. Little in the research evidence suggests that emotional problems are more prevalent than problems in obtaining supportive and care services.

There are other similar examples of how decisions about research design and about instruments of data collection affect findings. In a study done in England, the major lack of social resources identified was for night sitters and extended good neighbor services.[48] In contrast, many of the U.S. studies found more patients needing psychosocial counseling or help with emotional problems. Since it is unlikely that the chronically ill in the two countries are vastly different, it seems distinctly possible that the definitions of the research questions have been influenced by different professional traditions of social workers in the two countries.

The Social Worker and Other Professionals. The role of the social worker in the health care organization, particularly as perceived by other professions, has been the subject of a number of studies. A survey of physicians and social workers elicited agreement that social workers should coordinate services, arrange community referrals, and assist in posthospital planning. However, physicians saw the role of social workers in helping patients with emotional problems as less important than did social workers.[49] A recent survey of hospital ad-

ministrators and social work administrators detected a high level of agreement
that social workers should occupy leadership roles within the hospital.[50]

The domain of counseling and helping
patients with emotional problems is one
that many disciplines now want to claim
as their own. Family practice residents
reported a willingness to refer to social
workers most patients who had problems
with community resources, but the residents wanted to handle most emotional
reactions to illness themselves.[51] Similarly, several studies of the role perceptions of nurses and social workers suggest
that each profession sees itself as responsible for counseling, community referrals, and emotional problems. The
biggest source of dissatisfaction for social
workers was what they saw as the intru-
sion of other professionals into their area
of competence.[52]

Teamwork among health care professionals has been the focus of several
studies. An examination of a comprehensive, multidisciplinary health program in
a low-income area revealed that social
workers managed 73 percent of the psychological problems brought to the clinic
and that physicians managed the remainder. Of all the episodes of counseling and
health education, 23 percent were delivered by the social worker, 39 percent by
the nurse.[53]

A provocative study of a health care
team found that the percentage of
patients seen by social workers in the
first year was 74 percent, but that this
declined to 35 percent in the second year.
Patients reported that they would rather
take their interpersonal, childrearing, or
emotional problems to the nurse or physician. The social worker was almost always ranked last as the person to whom
they would go with any type of problem,
even after the secretary. Further inquiries revealed that patients saw referral
to the social worker for counseling as a
sign that "all hope was lost." The nurse
was seen as a part of everyday health care
practice. Relationships with the nurse
had been established while she delivered
"concrete" services and discussed more
neutral topics.[54]

Health teams appear to have some
unique characteristics. A study of alco-
holic treatment teams revealed that
members became increasingly preoccu-
pied with interpersonal relationships
when they faced severe barriers to success in the environment. Although it was
intended that the team members be
equal, the member with most control over
resources—in this case the rehabilitation
counselor—had the most power. Patients
usually identified the rehabilitation counselor, rather than the team, as responsible for their care.[55] Siegal and Zayone
learned that teams were more willing to
make risky decisions than were individual team members. Social workers
were most likely to maintain their individual opinions even when participating
in the team's decision making. The medical member of the team was most influential only when the decision was a clinical one.[56]

With the belief that early contact results in better relationships, several investigators examined interprofessional
contact during professional education. A
survey of MSW programs disclosed that
50 percent had a strong emphasis on interprofessional teamwork in the field curriculum.[57] In another study, social workers reported more nurse–social worker
contacts during training than did
nurses.[58] However, the expected positive
effect of interprofessional contact has not
always been substantiated. Phillips found
that before social workers joined a family
clinic, other professionals believed many
patients could be helped by social workers; the percentage decreased after the
social workers joined the staff.[59] Hookey
compared two group practices and found

the social worker was most successful in the one in which the physicians had worked with social workers in their training.[60]

Services. Various investigators have been interested in describing the patterns of social service delivery in health settings. Approximately 60 percent of the hospitals now have social service departments. This can be compared to less than 20 percent in 1953.[61] Social workers were still scarce, however, in private health care practice: only 3 percent of the group practice settings include a social worker.[62]

Coulton and Vielhaber found that an average of 19 percent of the adult medical and surgical hospital patients were served by social workers; however, in some large teaching hospitals as many as 35 percent of the patients encountered social workers.[63] Stoeckle et al. found that social workers saw only 2 percent of an outpatient clinic's patients.[64] In a pediatric setting, Pfouts found the figure to be 11 percent.[65]

Several studies have attempted to determine how hospital social workers spend their time. Chernesky and Lurie found that 55 percent of the social work time was spent on patient-related activities, 11 percent on administrative tasks, 6 percent for staff development, 4 percent on research, and the rest on other assorted tasks.[66] Ullman et al. found that hospital social workers spent more time in direct service than did social workers in other fields of practice.[67]

A few studies examined social work practice in nursing homes. Austin and Kosberg noted that one-half of the nursing homes they studied had no social services or occupational therapy and that the administrators of one-third of the homes did not believe a plan for meeting the socioemotional needs of patients was necessary.[68] Pearman and Searles also found that only 50 percent of the nursing homes they surveyed had a social worker. However, even when a social worker was present, comprehensive social services were not always available.[69] Thus, the presence of a social worker did not assure that all social services were provided.

Many consider home health services to be a social service function. There is debate about whether home health services should be part of the health care system or the social service delivery system. Now they are delivered in both systems. Morris and Harris concluded that home health services were not available in many locations in Massachusetts and that a well-organized system was required to deliver this complex and growing type of service.[70]

Several investigators have examined some of the processes involved in social work practice in the hospital. Berkman and Rehr conducted a series of early and important studies on the case-finding process. First, through comparison of the characteristics of patients referred to social service with the characteristics of the total patient population, they found that social service patients were more likely to be Jewish and white and to be referred rather late in their hospital stay.[71] They followed this study with a quasi-experiment that compared patients who were referred with those who were identified through screening by social workers. Screening resulted in more patients being seen early in their hospitalization, more private patients and more persons whom the social worker believed needed help with the stress of becoming hospitalized. Patients in the experimental groups had a mean length of stay of ten days less than those referred through regular channels.[72] These studies have had a profound impact on the field; many hospitals now supplement the traditional referral procedure with some mechanism for finding cases.

Summary and Future Directions. In any developing profession, an early task is to categorize objectively what the profession does. What are the tasks and functions that distinguish it as a profession? What are its techniques and who needs its services? The research described in this section on social service delivery seems to be fulfilling this function. It has been documented that the supply of social workers in hospitals, clinics, health planning agencies, and nursing homes is clearly increasing. Somewhere between 10 and 35 percent of the patients in hospitals use social services. Most of them request at least some assistance in arranging supportive and care services. Those over 80 requiring new living arrangements and experiencing disorientation are particularly prone to remain in the hospital needlessly unless social services are promptly available.

Both patients and other professionals tend to see the management and coordination of multiple-care and supportive services as the central function of social work. Patients seem more willing to accept interventions directed at emotional or behavioral problems when they are delivered in conjunction with these other services. However, it is clear that many required social services are unavailable or inaccessible in many communities. Resources for personal care, social contact, structured activities, and home management are particularly lacking. Nursing homes remain seriously underserved by social workers.

Research has had an impact on some aspects of social work practice in health care. This is most clearly seen in the move toward case-finding procedures that do not rely solely on referrals. This occurred subsequent to the research identifying the limitations of the referral process.

These descriptive studies of service delivery suggest several avenues for further research. First, it is interesting that many professionals now prefer to deal directly with the emotional components of patients' illness, a realm in which social workers have long claimed supremacy. Given the beginning evidence that patients are more comfortable receiving counseling as an adjunct to the provision of more neutral services, how can emotional support be most effectively delivered? Are patients more likely to benefit when counseling is provided in conjunction with another service? The answers to these questions require experimental studies that examine patient outcomes under several arrangements.

Second, studies of patients' problems have been biased by the categories the profession has constructed. Social workers are captives of their own categories. Needs are conceptualized in terms of the services that exist, and the services already provided are the ones most likely to be emphasized. That presumably similar patients in different countries are considered to have needs for different services is evidence of the strong biasing effect of the profession's traditional patterns of service. To escape these blinders, the profession needs a taxonomy of needs or problems that is not limited by the extent of present services. It must truly reflect the resources, capacities, or opportunities that the patients lack. Studies will then be capable of revealing needs that require the invention of new services.

Third, there is still no consistent picture of what social workers do. This stems, in part, from the lack of agreed-on terms to describe social work activities. The profession must begin with a dictionary of social work tasks that contains mutually exclusive categories. These tasks must be observable and capable of being combined into clusters of goal-directed activities that constitute services. This capacity to categorize actions and services must exist before social workers can move to detailed evaluative studies in which the independent variable—treatment—is understood.

Effects of Social Services

It is understandable that there is little research evaluating the effectiveness of health-related social work services. Most of the research so far has emphasized descriptions of the psychosocial problems of the physically ill and of what social workers do in health settings. It is first necessary to know what is being done with whom before it is possible to find out whether it works.

Nevertheless, several studies do focus on social work results with patients. Blumberg et al. interviewed thirty former clients of a pediatric social service department and found that 46 percent had not known what to expect from the social worker and 35 percent said they had expected help with concrete resources. Fifty percent recalled receiving emotional support, and 43 percent recalled help in finding resources. Sixty-seven percent said the social worker was helpful and 33 percent felt they received insufficient concrete help.[73]

Berkman and Rehr studied the services contracted for and the goals attained among 172 social service patients in a hospital. They found that two-thirds of social service problems to be dealt with were identified early in treatment. Problems in posthospital care tended to be identified early, and family interaction problems emerged later. Two-thirds of the identified problems were judged to be ameliorated. Successful outcome was least likely when there was a family disturbance or a depression related to prognosis. Problems were not found to vary by medical diagnosis, but the longer the patient's hospital stay, the greater the number of problems identified.[74]

Lindenberg and Coulton examined the results of discharge planning in nine hospitals. One month after discharge, only about 60 percent of the hospital social workers' plans for posthospital personal care and psychosocial counseling had been carried out satisfactorily, even though a plan for obtaining these services had been made by hospital social workers. In a few service categories, satisfactory follow-through was alarmingly low.[75]

Several studies by social workers have focused on the effects of comprehensive home care programs for the chronically ill and disabled. Neilson randomly assigned an experimental group of patients to receive organized posthospital home care and a comparison group to rely on traditional community and family resources. Patients in the experimental group had fewer admissions into long-term care institutions and seemed to display more contentment. No significant differences in mortality were detected.[76]

Merlin described a social work department that arranged and coordinated the provision of at-home oxygen for hospital patients. Since she assumed that without the program these patients would have remained as inpatients, she reported a 99 percent cost saving for this home-based care over hospital care.[77]

An increasing number of small clinical studies are beginning to emerge in the social work and health literature. They focus on the application of specific social work actions with small groups of patients with a particular problem. This is encouraging since such studies can generate promising hypotheses to be tested later on larger groups using experimental designs. At this point, however, only a few of the studies involve systematic data collection designed to minimize observer bias.[78] The majority are primarily anecdotal accounts of experience with unique cases. Some of these studies could have been improved by the application of principles of measurement and single-subject research; others could have been carried out as small, longitudinal surveys. They do indicate, however, that social work practitioners are more frequently asking researchable clinical questions and are motivated to contribute to social work knowledge. These efforts should be greatly enhanced by present attempts to translate research principles into techniques that are consistent with the resources and needs of social work practitioners in health care.

No discussion of the evaluation of health-related social services can be complete without mentioning quality assurance. In the last few years, the literature has been replete with reports on the activities of individual hospitals in this area. The purpose of quality assurance programs is to evaluate the care delivered to patients and to correct any observed deficiencies. A comparative analysis of twenty-seven quality assurance programs revealed that they consisted of one or all of the following components.

• An information system collecting data on patient characteristics, services received, and client outcomes.

• A peer review system examining social work care to determine whether it complies with what is believed to be good care.

• A guaranteed access system assuring that patients who are likely to need services are actually receiving them.[79]

The most prevalent component was the peer review system. Usually focusing on the process of care, these systems used professional peers to set criteria for acceptable practice. Medical records were then reviewed to determine whether there was written evidence that these criteria had been met.

Such systems do not assess the effect of social services on the patient. They assume that good practice will lead to good outcomes. Although this assumption has not yet been tested in social work, the process-outcome relationship has been examined in medical care. This has revealed that what practitioners prescribe as acceptable process does not necessarily lead to acceptable outcomes; conversely, bad practice does not necessarily lead to bad outcomes.

Such findings imply that although peer review systems are efficient and assure compliance with the present state of the art, they must be accompanied by practice research. This research must test hypotheses regarding relationships between process and outcome, and when specified procedures are not found to increase the likelihood of desirable outcomes, their value as criteria should be reassessed.

Summary and Future Directions. It is obvious that the type of evaluative research that will contribute to the social worker's technological competence in health care is just beginning. The few early studies that exist indicate that only approximately 60 percent of the social services required by the chronically ill are being delivered, but it is difficult to know whether this finding is indicative of success or failure. The need is clearly for additional studies of specific social work interventions to suggest hypotheses about the interventions that are most useful for particular problems.

A perplexing problem in evaluating social work services in the health area is measuring patient outcome. Unlike the services provided in mental health settings, the majority of social services in health facilities are not directed toward producing behavioral change in the patient. These services are more likely to have changing the patient's environment as an objective, and research consequently cannot rely on the counting of observable behaviors that has been so useful in single-subject behavioral research. If the goal of services is to arrange a suitable living environment for a disabled person, the need is for tools to determine whether that suitable situation is achieved.

Specification of the independent variable is also crucial in evaluative research. As stated earlier, this is an area that requires much work. Unless the components of the particular service that produced the desired results are known, it will be impossible to replicate that service. Any reliable technology must, of course, be replicable.

Quality assurance programs are spreading rapidly. The peer review component of quality assurance is best suited for a profession in which techniques are well developed and knowledge of cause and effect has been confirmed. In social work, it is seldom possible to state the probability with which certain services lead to desired results. However, it is encouraging that these peer review structures and procedures are being set into place. They will be useful vehicles for assuring that what is known about effective practice is actually being applied. The criteria in use at present are basic, but they reflect the present state of knowledge. It is important that these systems are capable of incorporating new knowledge as it develops.

Finally, the information system components of quality assurance programs are routinely collecting data on patient problems, interventions, and outcomes that could be analyzed to test practice hypotheses. Although at the present time measurement problems limit the usefulness of these systems, the systems have the potential to provide a valuable data base for practice-oriented research.

Development of Social Work Research

Research on social work in health care can be seen as being in an early stage of technological development.[80] The bulk of the studies are descriptive. They describe the requests and problems of consumers, the activities and characteristics of social workers, the social workers' relationships to other professions, and the roles they occupy in the health service delivery system.

A smaller group of studies are analytic. They attempt to discover the nature of the conditions or situations that social workers address. They attempt to account for psychosocial distress or well-being. Although many of these studies have been carried out by other disciplines, a substantial number have involved social workers. Such studies vary greatly in the extent to which they inform social work practice by identifying causal factors in the health and well-being of patients. Most of the time they suggest hypotheses for studies of practice with particular patient groups.

Only a few studies can be considered to be genuinely evaluative. As yet there has been little use of single-subject or experimental designs to test the effects of specific social work actions on patients' functioning or situations. However, the prevalence of anecdotal reports on new programs and techniques suggests that there are opportunities for these types of systematic studies to occur.

The many unanswered questions raised in the preceding pages suggest several immediate strategies for future health-related social work research. It is essential to continue descriptive studies of social service delivery patterns to provide information for management and planning decisions. There is as yet no comprehensive data on the incidence and prevalence of patient problems or services delivered.

There is an urgent need for ways of categorizing and quantifying social work activities that can lead to the computation of unit costs. In the health field, where cost control is paramount, social research must soon yield information about productivity.

Social work research should take the lead in studying the climates of health care organizations. It is necessary to develop measurement procedures capable of assessing the characteristics of situations that affect patient satisfaction and health status and to determine what kinds of environments are most suitable for certain types of patients. Since social workers are frequently responsible for arranging caring environments for patients (in discharge planning, for example), the profession must acquire more precise knowledge about the impact of such services.

If social workers are to participate effectively in efforts to prevent illness and disability, the profession must increasingly study the psychosocial factors that affect health. It is necessary to identify those factors that are accessible to social intervention and that can be changed or controlled if they are shown to be detrimental to health.

Additional evaluative studies are needed to build social work practice technology. This will include many small-scale studies of particular techniques used with specific groups of patients. Both positive and negative findings should be reported. As the understanding of an approach builds, it can be subjected to more rigorous, experimental research. It is critical that these studies contain detailed and replicable specification of the independent or treatment variables. In addition, social work researchers must expand the scope of outcome indicators to include measures of environmental change as well as behavioral change.

Finally, social workers should assume leadership in planning and carrying out empirical studies. When research questions are conceptualized by other profes-sionals or by researchers from outside the applied social sciences, findings will not have direct implications for social work practice. Any research is somewhat biased by the conceptual framework of the investigator, so it is understandable that social workers have often found it difficult to apply the findings of studies conducted by non-social workers.

Equipping social workers to conduct research requires that schools of social work make better use of instruction in research methodology. Practitioners are in the best position to apply principles of single-subject and clinical research and, therefore, must learn these techniques. Planners and administrators are more likely to have use for survey and operations research and quasi-experimental methods. The health care field has historically been oriented toward medical research. Since social factors are also salient, social workers must have the tools that will allow social work research to become more prominent in the health care field.

The call for social workers to conceive and carry out more empirical research in the field of health care is not new, and a sizeable body of well-validated information has been compiled since Gordon and Bartlett issued such a plea in the late 1950s.[81] Research on health-related social work is now passing through a descriptive phase, and this work must continue as researchers move toward testing and evaluating practice techniques. Pressures for accountability and productivity will keep the profession moving rapidly along all these avenues as social work continues to expand its contribution in the field of health care.

NOTES AND REFERENCES

1. Health Resources Administration, *Health Resources Statistics*, Publications No.

75–1509 (Washington, D.C.: Government Printing Office, 1974).

2. Eileen Wolff, *Technical Notes* (Washington, D.C.: U.S. Department of Health, Education & Welfare, 1978).

3. Conversation with Sallie Rosen, Executive Director, Society for Hospital Social Work Directors, Chicago, Illinois, 1978.

4. Robert Finney, Rita Pessin, and Larry Mathesis, "Prospects for Social Workers in Health Planning," *Health and Social Work*, 1 (August 1976), pp. 7–26.

5. See, for example, Henry S. Maas, ed., *Five Fields of Social Service: Reviews of Research* and *Research in the Social Sciences: A Five-Year Review* (New York: National Association of Social Workers, 1966 and 1971, respectively); and Sidney E. Zimbalist, *Historic Themes and Landmarks in Social Welfare Research* (New York: Harper & Row, 1977).

6. This is consistent with the boundaries adopted by Zimbalist, op. cit., p. 12.

7. See, for example, Andrew Twaddle, "Health Decisions and Sick Role Variations," *Journal of Health and Social Behavior*, 10 (June 1969), pp. 105–115; David Mechanic and Edmund Volkart, "Stress, Illness Behavior and the Sick Role," *American Sociological Review*, 26 (February 1961), pp. 51–58; and Derek Phillips, "Self-Reliance and the Inclination to Adopt the Sick Role," *Social Forces*, 43 (May 1965), pp. 555–563.

8. Stephen Cole and Robert Lejunae, "Illness and the Legitimation of Failure," *American Sociological Review*, 37 (June 1972), pp. 347–356.

9. See, for example, Stanley Croog, "Ethnic Origins, Educational Level and Responses to a Health Questionnaire," *Human Organization*, 20 (Spring 1961), pp. 65–69; David Coburn and Clyde Pope, "Socioeconomic Status and Preventive Health Behavior," *Journal of Health and Social Behavior*, 15 (June 1964), pp. 67–68; and Edward Suchman, "Sociomedical Variations among Ethnic Groups," *American Journal of Sociology*, 70 (November 1964), pp. 319–413.

10. See, for example, Stephen Kegeles, "A Field Experiment Attempt to Change Beliefs and Behavior of Women in an Urban Ghetto," *Journal of Health and Social Behavior*, 80

(September 1965), pp. 115–121; and Don Haefner and John Kirscht, "Motivational and Behavioral Affects of Modifying Health Beliefs," *Public Health Reports*, 85 (May 1970), pp. 478–487.

11. Avery Weisman and William Worden, *Coping and Vulnerability in Cancer Patients* (Boston: Massachusetts General Hospital, 1977).

12. Harris Chaklin and Martha Warfield, "Stigma Management and Amputee Rehabilitation," *Rehabilitation Literature*, 34 (December 1973), pp. 162–166.

13. David Kaplan, Rose Grobstein, and Aaron Smith, "Predicting the Impact of Severe Illness in Families," *Health and Social Work*, 3 (August 1976), pp. 72–82.

14. Phillip Starr, "Use of Research in Social Work Practice," *Social Work in Health Care*, 2 (Spring 1977), pp. 305–309.

15. See, for example, Melvin Stern, Linda Pascole, and James McLoone, "Psychosocial Adaptation Following an Acute Myocardial Infarction," *Journal of Chronic Diseases*, 29 (August 1976), pp. 513–526; Janis Gogan et al., "Impact of Childhood Cancer on Siblings," *Health and Social Work*, 2 (February 1977), pp. 42–58; Sheila Joel and Susanne Wieder, "Factors Involved in Adaptation to the Stress of Hemodialysis," *Smith College Studies in Social Work*, 43 (June 1973), pp. 193–205; Juanita Turk, "Impact of Cystic Fibrosis on Family Functioning," *Pediatrics*, 34 (July 1964), pp. 67–71; June Jackson and Herbert Delgado, "Sex Counseling for Those with Spinal Cord Injuries," *Social Casework*, 55 (December 1974), pp. 622–627; Ronald Koenig, "Fatal Illness: A Survey of Social Service Needs," *Social Work*, 13 (October 1968), pp. 85–90; and Lynn Kiely, Richard Sterne and Carl Witkop, "Psychosocial Factors in Low Incidence Genetic Disease: The Case of Osteogenesis Imperfecta," *Social Work in Health Care*, 1 (Summer 1976), pp. 409–420.

16. Sara Braham et al., "Evaluation of the Social Needs of the Non-Hospitalized Chronically Ill Persons," *Journal of Chronic Diseases*, 28 (August 1975), pp. 401–419.

17. Olive Stone and Edith Shapero, "Post-Hospital Changes in Role Systems of Patients," *Social Service Review*, 42 (September 1968), pp. 314–325.

18. Angela Finlayson, "Social Networks as Coping Resources," *Social Science in Medicine*, 10 (January 1976), pp. 97–103.

19. *See*, for example, the report on the National Health Interview Survey in *Public Health Reports*, 89 (December 1974), pp. 504–523.

20. Lawrence Hinkle and Harold Wolff, "Ecologie Investigations of the Relationships between Illness, Life Experiences and the Social Environment," *Annals of Internal Medicine*, 49 (December 1958), pp. 1373–1388.

21. *See*, for example, Barbara S. and Bruce P. Dohrenwend, *Stressful Life Events: Their Nature and Effects* (New York: John Wiley & Sons, 1974); and Richard Rahe et al., "Social Stress and Illness Onset," *Journal of Psychosomatic Research*, 8 (January 1964), pp. 35–44.

22. Kathy Bergin, "Social and Psychological Factors in Congestive Heart Failure," *Social Work*, 14 (January 1969), pp. 68–76.

23. *See*, for example, William Richardson, "Poverty, Illness and the Use of Health Services in the U.S.," *Hospitals*, 43 (July 1969), pp. 34–42; and Bonnie Bullough, "Poverty, Ethnic Identity and Preventive Health Care," *Journal of Health and Social Behavior*, 13 (December 1972), pp. 347–354.

24. *See*, for example, Runyan Deere and James Hoffmeister, "Health Attitudes and Practices in Arkansas," *Health Education Monographs*, 3 (Spring 1975), pp. 100–108; and Dorothy D. Watts, "Factors Related to Acceptance of Modern Medicine," *American Journal of Public Health*, 56 (July 1966), pp. 1205–1210.

25. *See*, for example, Robert M. Gary, Joseph P. Kessler, and Philip M. Moody, "Effects of Social Class and Friends' Expectations on Oral Polio Vaccination Participation," *American Journal of Public Health*, 56 (December 1966), pp. 2028–2033; and Reid Geersten et al., "An Examination of Suchman's Views on Social Factors in Health Care Utilization," *Journal of Health and Social Behavior*, 16 (June 1975), pp. 226–237.

26. *See*, for example, Gerald Sparer and Arne Anderson, "Utilization and Cost Experience in Four Prepaid Plans," *New England Journal of Medicine*, 289 (July 1973), pp. 67–72; and Seymour Bellin and H. Jack Geiger, "The Impact of a Neighborhood Health Center on Patients' Behavior and Attitudes Relating to Health Care: A Study of a Low Income Housing Project," *Medical Care*, 10 (May–June 1972), pp. 224–239.

27. Elizabeth Watkins, "Low Income Negro Mothers: Their Decision to Seek Prenatal Care," *American Journal of Public Health*, 58 (April 1968), pp. 655–667.

28. Mary Sivigar, Donald Quinean, and Sherry Wexler, "Abortion Applicants: Characteristic Distinguishing Remaining Pregnant and Those Having Abortion," *American Journal of Public Health*, 67 (February 1977), pp. 142–147.

29. Alma Young, Barbara Berkman, and Helen Rehr, "Women Who Seek Abortions: A Study," *Social Work*, 18 (May 1973), pp. 60–65.

30. *See*, for example, Marshal H. Becker et al., "Compliance with a Medical Regimen for Asthma: A List of the Health Relief Model," *Public Health Reports*, 93 (May–June 1978), pp. 268–277; Susan Steckel and Mary Ann Swain, "Contracting with Patients to Improve Compliance," *Hospitals*, 51 (December 1977), pp. 81–84; and Rona Levy, Phillip Weinstein, and Peter Milgram, "Behavioral Guidelines for Plaque Control Programs," *Dental Hygiene*, 51 (January 1976), pp. 13–18.

31. Ray Elling, Ruth Wittenmore, and Morris Green, "Patient Participation in a Pediatric Program," *Journal of Health and Human Behavior*, 1 (March 1960), pp. 183–189.

32. Barbara Felton, *Person-Environment Fit in Three Homes for the Aged*. Unpublished doctoral dissertation, School of Social Work, University of Michigan, Ann Arbor, 1975.

33. Eva Kahana, "Matching Environments to the Needs of the Aged: A Conceptual Scheme," in Jaber Gubrium, ed., *Late Life: Communities and Environmental Policies* (Springfield, Ill.: Charles C Thomas Publisher, 1974), pp. 201–204.

34. Eldon Killian, "Effects of Geriatric Transfers on Mortality Rates," *Social Work*, 15 (January 1970), pp. 19–26.

35. Jerome Berloff and Mieko Korpor,

"The Health Team Model and Medical Care Utilization," *Journal of the American Medical Association*, 219 (January 1972), pp. 359–366.

36. Michael Murphy, "The Development of a Community Orientation Scale," *American Journal of Public Health*, 65 (December 1975), pp. 1293–1297.

37. Seymour Bellin, H. J. Geiger, and Count Gibson, "The Impact of Ambulatory Health Care Services on the Demand for Hospital Beds," *New England Journal of Medicine*, 280 (April 1969), pp. 808–812.

38. Isadore Altman, "Some Factors Affecting Hospital Lengths of Stay," *Hospitals*, 39 (July 1965), pp. 68–73.

39. Roger Glass et al., "The 4 Score: An Index for Predicting Non-Medical Hospital Days," *American Journal of Public Health*, 67 (August 1977), pp. 751–755.

40. Robert M. Russo et al., "Detecting, Referring Families Needing Services," *Hospitals*, 48 (December 1974), pp. 57–59.

41. Claribel Moncure, "Clinical Social Work Planning with 5000 General Medical and Surgical Patients for Their Hospital Discharge," *Journal of Chronic Diseases*, 11 (February 1960), pp. 176–186.

42. Claudia Coulton and David Vielhaber, "Patterns of Social Work Practice in Planning for Post-Hospital Care" (Cleveland: Northeast Ohio Society for Hospital Social Work Directors, 1977). (Mimeographed.)

43. Ruth Ellen Lindenberg and Claudia Coulton, "Planning for Posthospital Care: A Follow-up Study." To be published in *Health and Social Work*, February 1980.

44. Mildred Blaxter, *The Meaning of Disability* (London: Heinemann Educational Books, 1976).

45. Avedis Donabedian and Leonard S. Rosenfeld, "Follow-up Study of Chronically Ill Patients Discharged from Hospitals," *Journal of Chronic Diseases*, 17 (September 1964), pp. 847–862.

46. *See*, for example, Martha Gentry, "Early Detection and Treatment: Social Worker and Pediatrician in Private Practice," *Social Work in Health Care*, 3 (Fall 1977), pp. 49–59; and Eleanor Soroker, "An Analysis of Pediatric Outpatient Care," *Health and Social Work*, 2 (May 1977), pp. 90–103.

47. John Stoeckle, Ruth Settler, and Gerald Davidson, "Social Work in a Medical Clinic: The Nature and Course of Referrals to the Social Worker," *American Journal of Public Health*, 56 (September 1966), pp. 1570–1579.

48. Matilda Goldberg and June Neill, *Social Work in General Practice* (London, England: George Allen & Unwin, 1972).

49. Katherine M. and Marvin Olsen, "Role of Expectations and Perceptions for Social Workers in Medical Settings," *Social Work*, 12 (July 1967), pp. 71–78.

50. Shirley Wattenberg, Michael Orr, and Thomas O'Rourke, "Comparison of Opinions of Social Work Administrators and Hospital Administrators toward Leadership Tasks," *Social Work in Health Care*, 2 (Spring 1977), pp. 285–294.

51. Ann Frangos and Donna Chase, "Attitudes of Family Practice Residents toward Collaboration with Social Workers in Their Future Practices," *Social Work in Health Care*, 2 (Fall 1976), pp. 65–76.

52. Constance Dunbar, Louise Miner, and Jane Tripleet, "Social Workers Look at Public Health Nursing," *Nursing Outlook*, 5 (February 1957), pp. 70–72; Joan Mullaney, Ruth Fox, and Mary Lestan, "Clinical Nurse Specialist and Social Worker: Clarifying the Roles," *Nursing Outlook*, 22 (November 1974), pp. 712–718; and Sally Robinson, "Is There a Difference?" *Nursing Outlook*, 15 (November 1967), pp. 34–36.

53. Kenneth Rogers, Mary Mally, and Florence Marcus, "A General Medical Practice Using Non-Physician Personnel," *Journal of the American Medical Association*, 206 (November 1968), pp. 1753–1757.

54. Eliot Freidson, *Patients Views of Medical Practice* (New York: Russell Sage Foundation, 1961).

55. Lincoln Fry and Jon Miller, "The Impact of Interdisciplinary Teams on Organizational Relationships," *The Sociological Quarterly*, 15 (Summer 1974), pp. 417–431.

56. Sheldon Siegal and Robert Zayone, "Group Risk Taking in Professional Decisions," *Sociometry*, 30 (December 1967), pp. 339–349.

57. Rosalie Kane, "Interprofessional Edu-

cation and Social Work: A Survey," *Social Work in Health Care*, 2 (Winter 1976–1977), pp. 229–238.

58. Cindy Williams et al., "Social Work and Nursing in Hospital Settings: A Study of Interprofessional Experiences," *Social Work in Health Care*, 3 (Spring 1978), pp. 311–322.

59. William Phillips, "Attitudes toward Social Work in a Family Medicine Clinic: A Before and After Survey," *Social Work in Health Care*, 3 (Fall 1977), pp. 61–76.

60. Peter Hookey, "The Establishment of Social Worker Participation in Rural Primary Health Care," *Social Work in Health Care*, 3 (Fall 1977), pp. 87–99.

61. Maryland Pennell and James Cooney, "Social Service Departments in Hospitals—1954 and 1964," *Hospitals*, 41 (March 1967), pp. 88–100.

62. Hookey, op. cit.

63. Coulton and Vielhaber, op. cit.

64. Stoeckle et al., op. cit.

65. James Pfouts and Brandon McDaniel, "Medical Handmaidens or Professional Colleagues: A Survey of Social Work Practice in the Pediatrics Departments of Twenty-Eight Teaching Hospitals," *Social Work in Health Care*, 2 (Spring 1977), pp. 275–283.

66. Rosalyn Chernesky and Abraham Lurie, "The Functional Analysis Study: A First Step in Quality Assurance," *Social Work in Health Care*, 1 (Winter 1975–76), pp. 213–223.

67. Alice Ullmann et al., "Activities, Satisfaction and Problems of Social Workers in Hospital Settings," *Social Service Review*, 45 (March 1971), pp. 17–29.

68. Michael Austin and Jordan Kosberg, "Nursing Home Decision Makers and the Social Service Needs of Residents," *Social Work in Health Care*, 1 (Summer 1976), pp. 447–455.

69. Lee Pearman and Jean Searles, "Unmet Social Services Needs in Skilled Nursing Facilities," *Social Work in Health Care*, 1 (Summer 1976), pp. 457–470.

70. Robert Morris and Elizabeth Harris, "Home Health Services in Massachusetts, 1971: Their Role in Care of the Long-Term

Sick," *American Journal of Public Health*, 62 (August 1972), pp. 1088–1093.

71. *See* Barbara Gordon and Helen Rehr, "Selectivity Biases in Delivery of Hospital Social Services," *Social Service Review*, 43 (March 1969), pp. 35–41; and Barbara Berkman and Rehr, "Unanticipated Consequences of the Case-Finding System in Hospital Social Service," *Social Work*, 15 (April 1970), pp. 63–68.

72. Barbara Berkman and Helen Rehr, "Early Social Service Case-Finding for Hospitalized Patients: An Experiment," *Social Service Review*, 47 (June 1973), pp. 256–265.

73. Deborah Blumberg, Audrey Ely, and Anita Kerbeshian, "Clients' Evaluation of Medical Social Services," *Social Work*, 20 (January 1975), pp. 45–47.

74. Barbara Berkman and Helen Rehr, "Social Work Undertakes Its Own Audit," *Social Work in Health Care*, 3 (Spring 1978), pp. 273–286.

75. Lindenberg and Coulton, op. cit.

76. Margaret Nielson et al., "Older Persons after Hospitalization: A Controlled Study," *American Journal of Public Health*, 62 (August 1972), pp. 1094–1100.

77. Debrah Merlen, "Home Care Project for Indigent Allows Dignified Care, Cuts Cost," *Hospitals*, 49 (October 1975), pp. 77–78.

78. *See*, for example, Katherine O'Connor, "Treatment for Adults with Psychosomatic Symptoms," *Health and Social Work*, 2 (November 1977), pp. 90–110; and William Farley, Margie Edwards, and Rex Skidmore, "A New Program for Hyperactive Children," *Health and Social Work*, 2 (August 1977), pp. 68–85.

79. Claudia Coulton, *Social Work Quality Assurance Programs: A Comparative Analysis* (New York: National Association of Social Workers, 1979).

80. Edwin Thomas, "Mousetraps, Developmental Research and Social Work Education," *Social Service Review*, 52 (September 1978), pp. 468–483.

81. William Gordon and Harriet Bartlett, "Generalizations in Medical Social Work: Preliminary Findings," *Social Work*, 4 (July 1959), pp. 72–76.

Social Services for Older Persons: A Review of Research

ABRAHAM MONK AND ROSE DOBROF

IN THE STORY "The Machine That Won the War," Asimov tells about three men sitting around their Multivac computer after they had won the war against the Denebians. While pondering the victory, each felt a compulsion to confess. First the chief programmer admitted that the information he fed into the machine became less and less reliable and that he had ended up inventing the data. The computer technician then acknowledged that Multivac was not working right in the first place and that he therefore adjusted the output according to his whim. Finally, the policy analyst and planner confessed that he never paid much attention to the computer material anyway. Asked the obvious question about how then he made his decisions, he reached into his pocket, saying,

"Multivac is not the first computer, friends, nor the best known, nor the one that can most efficiently lift the load of decision from the shoulders of the execu-tive. A machine did win the war . . . at least a very simple computing device did; one that I used everytime I had a particularly hard decision to make."

With a faint smile of reminiscence he flipped the coin he held.[1]

The planning of services for the aged often seems to rely on similar decision-making technologies. Missing has been the reciprocity that one might expect between gerontological researchers and policymakers: the knowledge generated by the researchers seldom guides policy formation, and, conversely, the experi-ence derived from implementing pro-grams is seldom used to test, refine, and expand the basic scientific premises. Lowy found a considerable time lag be-tween the completion of studies and their incorporation into programs.[2] Political pressures, clients' demands, and pres-sure from activists prompt policymakers to advocate adopting goals that neither reasonable evidence nor scientific analysis gives much hope of achievement. Morris and Binstock found that planners are subject to pressure for quick and visible results and that they are motivated by organizational survival rather than careful consideration of their clients' needs.[3]

Asimov's indictment of prevailing decision-making technologies should not be taken too literally, however. Even when flipping a coin, policymakers are choosing among discrete alternatives.

Policy Framework

Services for the aged did not emerge as a critical public issue until early in the twentieth century. Until then life expectancy was comparatively low. The individual rarely outlived the span of his or her work life, and only a small segment of the population ever reached age 65. Filial responsibility was effectively and universally assured on behalf of aging parents, but the uprooted, indigent, or lonely elderly who could not rely on relatives for support shared with the disabled and mentally retarded a virtual second-class citizenship. From the moment they appealed to society for assistance, these elderly were deprived of their right to vote or keep any property. The provision of custodial care in the almshouses was hardly concerned with rehabilitation or the preservation of human rights; nor did it discern the service requirements of each category of need. Rather than attending to the needs of older persons, states and localities aimed to discourage reliance on public support. Homes for the aged were usually established under sectarian or ethnic auspices, and their purpose was to rescue groups of deserving old people from the degradation of the almshouses. These homes were small in size and few in number, however, and their existence largely reflected the humanitarianism of their founders rather than the judgments of social planners.

When life expectancy began to increase significantly and filial responsiveness began, in many instances, to conflict with the capacity of families to provide for dependent children, the public reluctantly assumed responsibility for a large number of destitute older persons. The Social Security Act of 1935 marked the beginning of a strategy of income maintenance meant to gradually replace the local provision of custodial care and relief. It was expected that social security benefits would offer the means for purchasing services and living arrangements. Manney contends that the American system of social services reflects a deliberate decision by policymakers to deal with the aged through income maintenance programs and to reserve for the young such social services as counseling, recreation, job training, and education, which are "conspicuously unavailable to the old."[4] It was taken for granted that institutional or intensive care would be required only for the severely incapacitated and that they would constitute a manageable minority of exceptional cases.

In the 1960s, Title XVIII amendments to the Social Security Act signaled an orientation toward acute care rather than long-term care. This policy reversal ignored the obvious epidemiological fact that, as mortality rates decline, morbidity rates are bound to increase. As people live longer and their chronic conditions multiply, they come to require a vast array of specialized services on a continuous basis.

To fill out this historical perspective, it is necessary to mention a number of recent developments in the response of society and social service professionals to the needs of the elderly.

• In setting up the old age assistance programs mandated under the Social Security Act, the vast majority of the states sustained the expectation of filial responsibility. These provisions remained in effect until 1974 when state programs were replaced by the Supplemental Security Income Program.

• Services were created as expedient reactions to the critical upsurge of specific needs. They were not properly coordinated or articulated into an intelligible, coherent model. Multiple sources of sponsorship and assorted eligibility and financial requirements have made the service network an intimidating labyrinth that easily discourages even the most enterprising and resilient applicants. Only in the early 1970s did official policy turn toward the establishment of a coordinated and comprehensive delivery system at the local level. The 1973 Comprehensive Service Amendments to the Older Americans Act of 1965 sought to make the Area Agencies on Aging of Title III a powerful coordinating instrument. Unfortunately, most cities or counties lack the comprehensive range of services that area agencies are supposed to coordinate.

• The 1972 amendments to the Social Security Act mandated a search for alternatives to institutionalization and provided that day care services, including personal care and supervision, be established by the Department of Health, Education, and Welfare on an experimental basis.[5] This search for alternatives to institutionalization does not imply the wholesale nullification of long-term institutional services. There is general recognition that a coherent model must include long-term care, not as an exceptional component, but as part of a continuum stretching from community-based services for the well aged to institutional long-term services for those in need of skilled attention around the clock. The aim is to achieve a better match between individual needs and services and to find ways to deliver intensive services at less cost.

• In the late 1970s, concern over the adequacy of service resources led the Federal Council on the Aging to identify an especially vulnerable group, the frail elderly, as the target for a substantial infusion of supportive services. The notion of frailty does not imply a clinical syndrome, but a statistical indicator of high risk. Because the group aged 75 and older tends to have a higher degree of frailty and dependence, a social policy addressed to this group needs to encourage and facilitate independent living in accustomed environments. This requires that primary support networks be coordinated with the formal service system and that the elderly be encouraged to engage in self-help.

Focuses of Research

Service-oriented research in social gerontology has responded to these trends by emphasizing four specific avenues of inquiry: (1) the high-risk or frail elderly, (2) the interfacing of primary support networks and formal service systems, (3) the development and operation of a comprehensive and effective service system, and (4) the development of successful deterrents to long-term institutionalization.

Further examination shows that these four focuses of inquiry have guided service-oriented research into two major domains. The first monitors the changing demographic profile of aging populations and subpopulations; it sensitively registers the complex social and ecological arrangements leading to a higher sense of well-being and life satisfaction. An understanding of the social concomitants of a high quality of life is a prerequisite for reliable social planning.

The second major thrust of service-oriented research assesses the specific needs of the aged. It looks at what services they require, what the most effective interventions are, and how these services can be delivered in the most effective and efficient way. Once a service has been provided, this domain of research also determines how to measure outcomes and how the service system might better respond to the high-risk category of frail elderly.

Subsidiary concerns of service-oriented research have been the testing of basic normative assumptions. Is it better, for example, to favor age integration as a model intergenerational pattern? Should older persons exercise self-determination and take primary leadership in matters concerning their lives? Are services rendered in the normal community habitat preferable to institutional segregation?

This review is meant to be comprehensive in addressing the major trends of service-oriented research, but it makes no claim of exhaustiveness. Rather, it is selective in highlighting developments and methodological concerns. The review also includes contributions from disciplines other than social work.

Methodological Concerns

Before addressing the four major avenues of research, however, it will be helpful to identify certain methodological concerns that directly affect research on services to the aged.

• New federal and state programs for the aged, like services in other categorical areas, often begin as time-limited demonstrations. They are put into effect for small, incidental samples, and their ex post facto evaluations tend to lack scientific rigor. Representative samples of aged populations are not easy to obtain, however. Aged participants in research are usually well-functioning individuals.

• Longitudinal samples invariably fail to meet the criterion of representativeness because survival is itself selective. The changes that occur in the composition of a cohort as a result of the incapacity or death of members are selective rather than random.

• Since individual differences increase with time, experiential variables accrue with age. This creates a biased effect, which is difficult to control in longitudinal designs.

• Gerontological research designs aimed at drawing conclusions by comparing different age cohorts at the same point in time may be committing what Sherwood calls the cross-sectional fallacy.[6] She argues that findings from such studies point to differences between groups rather than within groups. Members of the same cohort have gone through similar life experiences and have been affected by the same historical events.

• Information is separately collected from specific services—health, legal, counseling, nutrition, housing, and so on—but not across services for the same population. Each service measures a different type of outcome, and each defines the client's needs differently. Taber and Flynn caution that "comprehensive policy planning cannot be predicated on micro effects observed on one sector of the total service."[7]

• The lack of comparative data is a matter of serious concern. Community case studies of programs, even those that use standardized instruments of assessment, do not properly control for local idiosyncrasies of service delivery. Rarely does one encounter two communities with service networks similar enough to have confidence about comparisons between them.

The Frail Elderly

Demographic trends indicate that the aged, as a group, are becoming both more numerous and older. Palmore pointed out that between 1960 and 1970 the group over 75 grew at a rate three times as great as the 65–74 cohort. "Since older age is associated with higher rates of illness and disability," Palmore noted, "the increased age of the older population would be expected to increase illness and disability rates."[8] It may therefore be anticipated that the demands on the service network will increase as this oldest and highest-risk cohort grows. Planners are particularly concerned that it will become increasingly difficult to draw the line between intensive but justified utilization of services and abusive utilization. Furthermore, the packaging of alternatives to institutionalization is still in its experimental stage. In studying this high-risk cohort, researchers' attention has largely been directed at (1) the measurement of need, (2) the extent of need, (3) client preferences for service, and (4) indicators of a population at risk.

Measurement of Need. Needs associated with health and functional competence for independent living tend to be measured either through outside assessments of ability or through self-ratings. Although clinical examinations offer more accurate information than self-ratings, considerations of cost and time often make such examinations unfeasible. In aging, moreover, wellness does not imply an absence of chronicity; and conversely, crippling as many disabilities may be, some older persons manage to maintain a high level of personal self-sufficiency. Lawton identifies levels of competence that are function related: life maintenance, functional health, perception and cognition, physical self-maintenance, instrumental self-maintenance, effectance (which includes motivational behaviors like hobbies and recreation that are self-initiated and go beyond physical and instrumental self-

maintenance), and social role performance.[9]

Measurement instruments are usually designed to determine functional levels. Among the instruments frequently used in clinical practice and population surveys are those developed by Kutner, Fanshel, Togo, and Langner; Thompson and Streib; Maddox; Shanas; Rosow and Breslau; Lowenthal; Katz; Lawton and Brody; and Rosencranz and Pihlblad.[10] These instruments scrutinize behaviors by direct observation in natural situations, and they may be used separately or in combination with personal interviews and self-ratings. The latter are extensively used despite reservations about their validity. Some respondents, it is claimed, do not know the conditions that are affecting them; others deny their illnesses or disabilities; and still others hypochondriacally rate themselves worse than is warranted. Shanas observed that among bedfast or housebound people, more than a third did not think their health was poor, and 16 percent felt they enjoyed good health.[11] Irelan and Motley found that 75 percent of a sample of self-employed men and women nearing retirement considered their health to be as good or better than that of others their own age.[12] Busse vindicated the value of self-ratings: he found that self-evaluations are 65 to 70 percent consistent with the results of medical examinations, although people 70 and older tended to overrate their health.[13] This finding is consistent with an earlier conclusion by Suchman, Phillips, and Streib.[14]

The trend in recent years is to resort to more inclusive instruments. Cantor's Index of Vulnerability, which incorporates demographic, environmental, and social-interaction variables, has both diagnostic and prognostic applications and is used as part of a general survey questionnaire.[15] The most comprehensive instrument is the OARS Multidimensional Functional Assessment Strategy developed by the staff of the Older Americans Resources and Services program at Duke University.[16] It is defined as a "present state assessment technique for individuals and/or populations," and it measures the respondent's functional level in each of the following dimensions: social resources, economic resources, mental health, physical health, and capacity for self-care or activities of daily living. The OARS questionnaire gathers both subjective and objective information in a way that the information in each of the five dimensions can be synthesized or compressed into a single summary functional rating. The questionnaire also seeks information about the range of services that aging individuals might need and permits definition of an "appropriate service package for individuals or populations under review." Pfeiffer, the questionnaire's editor, claims that the OARS technique has four specific applications: (1) population surveys for planning purposes, (2) clinical assessment, (3) admission screening or referral, and (4) evaluation of service interventions.

Although the OARS questionnaire offers comprehensiveness and universality of application, it has received a lukewarm reception among social work practitioners. Some argue that it is too inflexible and time-consuming an instrument and that it underscores present performance and capacity at the expense of potential performance. Finally, the OARS questionnaire cannot act as a substitute for a thorough psychosocial scrutiny. Its merits outweigh these deficiencies, however, and, when properly used, this assessment instrument is a powerful adjunct of practice.

Extent of Need. The extent of the need for community-based services is not easy to ascertain. The Levinson Gerontological Policy Institute estimated that 13.8 percent of the noninstitutionalized aged require some form of help in the home and personal care services.[17] This figure is higher than the 8 percent found by Shanas and associates in their nationwide probability study.[18] Dunlop of the Urban Institute claimed that one out of every four older persons have chronic conditions that require some form of systematic, continued care.[19] This represents over 5 million people, 2.6 million of whom diagnostically belong in sheltered environments—congregate living facilities, boarding homes, or long-term facilities with skilled nursing services. The remainder are in need of supportive services in the home. In the absence of such environments or home services, the individual's health may deteriorate and make institutionalization inevitable.

Shanas compared data obtained from a 1975 national sample with her 1962 survey and found that the proportions of noninstitutionalized elderly who were ambulatory and those who were homebound had not changed over the thirteen-year period. Access to medical care increased, but the degree of reported impairment remained stable.[20] Later studies by Kovar and LaVor concluded that one out of every seven aged persons 65 to 74 and one out of four 75 or older were sufficiently impaired to warrant the provision of home care and home support services.[21] This represents nearly 3.5 million people, a figure that exceeds by 40 percent the 2.4 million reported by the Urban Institute.

Assessments of mental impairment among persons 60 and over who live in urban environments ranged between 7 and 10 percent, according to Blenkner, Bloom, and Nielsen; only a minimal fraction of this cohort was thought to be receiving adequate treatment.[22] In 1978, Donahue denounced the deinstitutionalization of patients from mental hospitals into the community, arguing that it was done in a summary fashion for reasons of fiscal expediency. Most hospitals did not keep records of their discharged aged, but Donahue contended that the evidence suggested that the majority wound up in nursing homes and that a substantial segment drifted into marginal boarding houses and single-occupancy welfare hotels in deteriorating neighborhoods and subsequently lost touch with social and health support systems.[23]

In contrast, referrals of older persons to mental hospitals may be unjustified in the majority of cases. Markson, Levitz, and Gognalons-Caillard reviewed the records of 348 elderly referrals to two mental hospitals and concluded that the needs of 77 percent could have been met in the community.[24] The U.S. Department of Health, Education, and Welfare estimated that from 25 to 40 percent of the institutionalized elderly, and perhaps a higher proportion of the elderly in mental institutions, were inappropriately placed because of a lack of home and community support services.[25] Interestingly, in 1972, although home support services had already received a strong emphasis in the reordering of social priorities, only 2.4 percent of the aged estimated to require such services were actually receiving their benefits.[26]

Client Preferences. Older persons dread the prospect of institutionalization or relocation to a strange environment. Bell found that, given a choice, 85 percent of the physically impaired elderly in and out of institutions preferred to remain in their homes.[27] In an evaluation of protective service projects, Gold discovered that the service most commonly requested by those elderly clients unable to care for themselves was homemaker service.[28] Cryns and Monk conducted a study among an urban sample from upper New York State measuring the relative

need for thirteen community-based services and the attitudes related to each service need.[29] The most desired services were in the instrumental category of environmental reinforcement, such as transportation and home maintenance services. Ego supportive services, such as counseling and casework, ranked lowest. The authors also found that "rootedness to place" among the elderly of blue-collar backgrounds was so pronounced that they did not want to move even when their environment had deteriorated and no longer offered minimal guarantees of safety.

Population-at-Risk Indicators. The most vulnerable aged, those who qualify for home support services, have salient common attributes. Tobin, Davidson, and Sack identified the at-risk population as having a preponderance of females in their mid-to-upper seventies, unmarried (either widowed, divorced, separated, or never married), living alone, poor, and incapable of taking care of themselves.[30] Cryns and Monk found that those with the greatest need for services tended to be renters, in poor health, with low incomes, low activities of daily living (ADL) scores, and a high subjective sense of immobility.[31] Blenkner, Bloom, and Nielsen reported that men, nonwhites, the foreign born, and married persons were underrepresented in their protective services demonstration project.[32]

Predictors of vulnerability, if properly identified and isolated, will be a powerful resource for planning gerontological services. It must be borne in mind, however, that dependencies resulting from varying levels of jeopardy are normally expected in the aged, but the dilemma confronting the service provider is how to respond to those limitations without at the same time contributing to an increase in the state of dependency. Kleban, Brody, and Lawton described the phenomenon of excess disability, a behavioral expression of incapacity that exceeds the actual functional limitation.[33] It occurs when the individual anticipates the social expectation of dependence and adopts the role with overzealousness and exaggeration.

Primary Support Networks

An examination of the range of services the frail elderly need to remain in the community must begin by taking into account the availability and effectiveness of primary support networks. The family remains the major provider of social support for the older person. The stereotype of the lonely or abandoned older person has not been confirmed by research. Shanas found that 84 percent of older people of every social class live less than one hour away from at least one of their adult offspring.[34] There are many face-to-face meetings in addition to telephoning, letter writing, expressions of affection, and exchanges of services and financial assistance. Families do more for their elderly relatives than they are given credit for; the family, rather than formal service systems, provides most of the home health services for incapacitated or homebound relatives.

The optimistic assumption, however, that relatives or kin are universally capable of taking care of older members of their families and that institutional long-term care can therefore be done away with is naive. Such an assumption overlooks the mean age of the institutionalized population, which is 82. Most of these elderly are widows or women who never married. Nearly half of them have lost all their close relatives, and many widows have even outlived their own children.[35] Resorting to institutional care, as Brody found, does not necessarily constitute evidence of filial or

kin neglect. She added that there is no such a thing as a wholesale dumping of older relatives into nursing homes and that applying to an institution is a measure of last resort in almost all instances, after all other avenues of help have been exhausted.[36] Moreover, Dobrof found that even after the institutionalization of the aged person, the majority of families continued to maintain both affective and instrumental ties to these relatives. They visited regularly, brought special food treats and small necessities, and gave gifts on birthdays and holidays.[37] Although older people strongly prefer to remain close to their children, research also bears witness to the preference of the overwhelming majority of the aged to maintain their own households and live there as long as possible. Moving in with a child is usually resorted to only in extreme situations and often as a temporary, not a permanent, arrangement.[38] Troll points out that although one-third of all elderly who have children live with one of them, these households tend to consist of two, rather than three generations.[39] It is often the postparental, middle-aged couples who bring in their aged parents to live with them.

The expectation that primary support networks—children or grandchildren—successfully attend to their ailing elderly relatives was investigated by Sussman, Vanderwyst, and Williams.[40] The researchers studied the topic from the view of possible policy incentives, such as cash allotments, tax rebates, home health care, and homemaking services that would foster or facilitate a process of multigenerational living. Prior to World War II, three-generational households were common, but this was partly a consequence of such circumstances as the Great Depression and housing shortages. The researchers hypothesized that with the continued increase in life expectancy, higher costs of nursing home care, and the prohibitive cost of new housing, interest in three-generational housing might rekindle.

The survey the researchers conducted in Cleveland to test that hypothesis revealed that although 86 percent of the elderly interviewed were favorably inclined toward living with their children, the majority, 76 percent, also stated their preference to continue living separately, in their own home. They felt that only the older individual who can no longer attend to his or her own needs should move in with relatives. A sample of young and middle-aged heads of households saw merits in the program, particularly if it were supported by tax or cash incentives and medical and home services. About 60 percent were in favor and 33 percent said no, but for only 19 percent was the negative response an unequivocal one, that is, that they would not accept an elderly relative, under any circumstances.

Close analysis of the answers of the middle-aged and young respondents who had expressed a willingness to accept an older person into their households revealed an interesting attitudinal disposition: they expressed willingness to take in female elderly relatives, but displayed a strong exception to accepting males, even if they were active, healthy, and self-sufficient. Older women were perceived as a nurturing buffer between the second and third generations; they can absorb tensions and share the chores of the family unit. Old men were regarded as consumers rather than providers of familial services, often in competition with the young offspring.

It has been widely assumed that primary support networks or extended families are more prevalent and effective among black and Hispanic minority communities. Cantor studied the experience of urban elderly residing in poor, high-risk, and deteriorating neighborhoods; her aim was to isolate the effects of ethnic identification on the aging process.[41] She found that the Hispanic elderly were worse off economically than any other group, but that they enjoyed more closely knit family lives. The black elderly faced many of the same problems of finances and discrimination as their Hispanic counterparts, but they lacked the compensations of extended family support. Fewer blacks in old age were still married and living with a spouse; more were living alone, and they experienced less supportive assistance on the part of their offspring. The white elderly in the study displayed greater conflicts than any other group. Role losses, economic demotions, and social discontinuities were more extreme and traumatic for them. Although they were better off economically than their Hispanic and black peers, they were more reluctant to apply for or accept services to which they were entitled. Cantor concluded that problems of isolation from relatives and the incidence of living alone were increasing for the three ethnic groups, although at different rates.

Social work practice has been influenced by Parsons' formulation of the theory that the psychodynamic focus on the socialization of the child is the foremost function of the isolated nuclear family. Neither Parsons nor Freud had a role for the postparental middle-aged parent, and they were even less prepared to find a place for the aging grandparents. Blenkner claimed that this theoretical framework guided social work practitioners into helping to free adult children from the parental tie instead of encouraging them to accept the concerns of reciprocal kinship.[42] Similarly, Leichter and Mitchell, in a study of the kinship values and interactions of caseworkers and clients, found that although kinship involvement and responsibility are extensive in urban society, casework intervention was designed to restrict or redefine rather than to expand relationships with kin, particularly those with parents.[43] Caseworkers apparently uphold the notion that the nuclear family should operate as an independent unit, without interference from close relatives or kin.

If one is to take Blenkner's formulation and the Leichter and Mitchell study as accurate reflections of social work practice during the 1960s, one must note that the pendulum swung in the opposite direction in the 1970s. The importance of the extended family in the lives of the majority of older people was rediscovered by many authors, and experimental projects demonstrating various approaches to social work practice with the relatives of older people were undertaken. It is probable that there is considerable unevenness in this area of practice. Some agencies claim to pay respectful attention both to the family relationships of older clients and to the role of grandparents in the family systems of younger people, although more agencies espouse these values than practice them. In other agencies, work with the families of older clients is so much a part of daily practice that it is not regarded as special.[44].

Some practitioners and researchers are concerned that the rediscovery of the family may have some untoward consequences: the capacity of the family to provide care—particularly of seriously impaired older people—may be overestimated. The three-generation household may be idealized, and the assumption on the part of professionals that families prefer and are able to care for their own may stand as an obstacle to the development of services, particularly in economically deprived, minority neighborhoods.

Long-Term Care Facilities

There is every reason to believe that institutional care will continue to be the arrangement of necessity for severely incapacitated and seriously impaired older people. This group is a minority within the aged cohort, although not so small a group as is popularly believed. Kastenbaum and Candy called attention to what they aptly labeled "the 4 percent fallacy."[45] They found that although, on any given day, 4 percent of those 65 and older in the United States—nearly one million people—were domiciled in long-term care facilities, this 4 percent understates the total percentage—estimated at 20 percent—of older people likely to spend some time at the end of their lives in long-term care facilities.

Social work practitioners are frequently caught between the traditional anti-institutional bias of the profession and the reality of some of their clients' need for the care provided in nursing homes and other long-term care facilities. Research has consequently highlighted (1) the quality control problems of institutions, (2) the high risk of mortality that accompanies institutionalization, (3) the effects of institutionalization on the patient's career, and (4) the cost-benefit comparisons of institutionalization with alternative forms of care. Researchers analyzed the effect of such variables as size, individuation, privacy, and staff-patient ratios to arrive at a model of service that is less damaging to the psychological integrity of patients.[46] Bennett and Nahemow studied the socialization patterns in five residential settings, ranging from a psychiatric state hospital to a housing project, and found that positive forms of interaction increased in inverse relation to the degree of institutional "totality."[47] Goldfarb scrutinized the profile of the applicants for institutional care and found the existence of a self-selection bias, with highly dependent individuals more likely to resort to institutional care.[48]

Research on the impact of relocating

elderly patients points to hastened physical deterioration, higher mortality rates in the initial months following institutionalization, and depressive reactions and low morale.[49] The negative effects of relocation are reduced when the move is voluntary, when it does not accompany the loss of a spouse or loved one through death, and when the individual has been thoroughly prepared to handle the transition.[50] Pablo monitored the impact of intrainstitutional relocation on the mortality and morbidity of movers and nonmovers over a period of thirty months.[51] The mortality data confirmed relocation as a negative phenomenon. Intrainstitutional transfer, although less traumatic than transfers from home to an institution, could nevertheless induce sufficient stress to jeopardize survival. Males were more susceptible to stress, but the hypothesis that there were age effects in relocation—that the older the patient, the higher the risk of dying after relocation—was not supported by data. Although relocation had negative effects, the overall mortality was reduced when the patients were prepared for relocation by caseworkers who obtained the patients' agreement with the transfer and, through careful planning, minimized the disruption of routine.

Tobin and Lieberman examined the process by which old people become institutionalized and explored the four stages of this process: the time preceding the decision to seek institutional care; the period following that decision, when the individual is awaiting entrance into the institution; the first two months after entering the home; and one year after living in the institution.[52] The study revealed that the greatest psychological damage occurs before entrance into the institution; that passivity heightens the aged person's vulnerability to the effects of environmental discontinuity; and that hopelessness and dependency, once they are entrenched, become nearly irreversible.

A system of ancillary community-based services is clearly necessary if premature or unnecessary institutionalization is to be avoided. Tobin, Hammerman, and Rector; Lawton; and Barney identify eight overall categories of such services: counseling, activities, vocational rehabilitation, day care, noninstitutional residential care, medical diagnosis, health care, and income maintenance.[53] Barney, in her analysis of the Detroit Well-Being Service for Aging, underscores certain features of service delivery that appear essential if the services offered are to be effective in preventing institutionalization. She recommends information, problem-solving, and referral through individual counseling provided by a "widely dispersed network of lone operating counselors."[54]

Alternatives to Institutionalization

The range of alternatives to institutionalization, or "parallel services" as Shore suggests they be called, has been placed by Tobin and Lieberman on a structural continuum that encompasses services for the well elderly, services for preventing premature institutionalization, and services for those whose high level of disability may necessitate institutional placement.[55] Research on the effectiveness and efficiency of those categories of service began to emerge only in the mid-1970s, and the discussion here is confined to just three of these services—foster care, day care, and home care.

Foster Care. Foster care for older persons has received little systematic attention. Kahana and Coe noted that "in spite of the benefits and potential feasibility of this approach, . . . research on the subject is almost nonexistent."[56] Newman and Sherman interviewed caretakers of one hundred adult foster homes, looking at the extent to which four aspects of familial behavior—affection, social interaction, ritual, and minimization of distance—were present in these homes.[57] Although data on home use indicated some social distance, 75 percent of the residents appeared well integrated in their surrogate families. Newman and Sherman concluded that the program represents a promising component in the service system. In addition to providing a home for the elderly, it gave a great deal of personal satisfaction and a meaningful role to the caretakers, who were in their fifties. Operational problems did occur, such as lack of training and lack of caretakers' participation in the selection of their residents, but these are easily solvable.

Adult Day Care. Using an iterative technique of model development, Weissert discerned two distinct models of adult day care.[58] The first places a heavy emphasis on health services and enrolls participants needing intensive rehabilitative care. The second model is designed for less impaired participants and, in its staffing patterns, emphasizes nursing supervision over therapy. The latter model also uses more nonprofessionals. The strength of day care programs, according to this study, is the match between the capabilities of the health care staff and the needs of the participants. Most programs, however, lack measurable admission criteria, written plans for care, utilization review mechanisms, and adequate transportation programs. One surprising finding was that the cost of adult day care is higher, on the average, than nursing home care. As Monk pointed out, this is not consistent with previous studies, although the Weissert study had pointed out that transportation

to and from day care programs weighs heavily in the final costs.[59] Monk found that day care programs lodged in nursing homes or multiservice facilities develop staffing problems and encounter tensions between their two clienteles.[60]

Day care programs for older people can be an important element in the parallel or alternative service system for the impaired or incapacitated. In the light of the reports of their high operational costs, however, it seems clear that the case for these programs must be made on the basis of careful documentation of the value of community-based rehabilitation services. The claim that the costs of these programs are low has not been warranted.

Home Care. "Home care" is a catch-all label that includes home health care, homemaker services, and home health aide services. Thus far, although it is considered a critical element in a comprehensive community-based service system, home care has been assigned a low priority by local, state, and federal authorities. There are signs, however, that all levels of government are becoming increasingly interested in expanding these programs. The President's Commission on Mental Health, for example, concluded that "home care must become an essential component of the continuum of mental and physical health care of the elderly."[61]

If the commission's recommendation is heeded and additional funds for home care programs are provided, certain research findings merit serious attention. The need for thorough systems of quality control, including in-service training and ongoing professional supervision of the line staff, was documented in several studies.[62] Friedman, Kaye, and Farago, in their study of a publicly funded home care program for older people in New York City, documented the untoward

consequences of the absence of appropriate quality controls, including case management and supervision.[63] They found
evidence of client exploitation and even
blackmail, with painful delays in the reassessment of need and the modification
of service plans. There were disparities
between client expectations about the
range of services and the actual job descriptions of the workers. The clients
often expected that the workers would
provide personal services, socialization,
and the like, and these unfulfilled expectations generated tension and anger in
the client-worker relationship. Finally,
there were "no-show" workers on the
payroll, an obvious indication of the absence of quality control and one that is
grist for newspaper headlines and a
threat to official and public support for
the program.

Impact studies of home care programs
have usually used reductions of institutionalization, improvements in the
client's quality of life, and increases in
levels of competence and life satisfaction
as their criteria of success. Studies by
Blenkner, Bloom, and Nielsen and Breslau and Haug found that institutionalization rates actually increased among service recipients when they were compared
to control groups.[64] The first of those
studies found improvements in the
clients' environmental surroundings, but
no significant impact on physical and
mental competence or on the degree of
life satisfaction. Other studies contradict
these findings and report greater gains
among beneficiaries of home care services.[65] Noelker and Harel also concluded that with the expected exception
of the most disabled cases, institutional
placement can be prevented through
home care services for all its beneficiaries.[66]

Research on home care, like that on
adult day care programs and other service categories, remains inadequate and
unsystematic. Seldom do studies address
themselves to considerations of both effectiveness and efficiency. Outcome
variables are ill defined, and rarely is
there a clear focus on intervening organizational planning factors. Too often,
cost effectiveness seems to be the over-
riding concern of researchers. What is
required are comparative studies of
functionally comparable samples,
matched on key variables and utilizing
the same or analogous investigative instruments. In the meantime, the available studies are sketchy and case bound.
As a consequence, their potential for
generalizability and their usefulness in
policy formulation are limited.

Comprehensive
Community Services

The Older Americans Act of 1964
signaled the beginning of an active and
persistent federal policy of service development on behalf of the aged. Subsequent amendments to the OAA were
aimed at achieving an operational decentralization of services and at filling gaps
in programs at the local level. The first
objective led to the creation of over 3,500
Title III Area Agencies on Aging (AAAs)
and nutrition programs. This is an impressive network, but there are justified
doubts whether it can function in a coordinated and efficient manner. Hudson
claims that the AAAs are thrown into an
impossible situation: they are expected to
perform an administrative and monitoring
task while at the same time developing
services that are needed but not otherwise available.[67] The linkage function requires the power to sanction and a certain
leverage that AAAs do not possess. The
developmental function in turn may put
them in conflict with the entrenched
interests of existing agencies. Armour,
Estes, and Noble similarly found that

AAAs have a problematic structure and conflicting objectives.[68] These researchers single out two major concerns: there are no clear guidelines for determining the relative weights of AAAs' intervention strategies—planning and coordination versus direct service provision—and there is a tendency to increase services in response to direct pressure from local constituencies, but to neglect quality controls and services to assure access.

AAAs are self-contained planning units with responsibility for outlining their priorities. With the exception of the few largest and better staffed, the AAAs lack the research capability to determine those priorities. Even at the federal level, the yearly reauthorizations of the Older Americans Act set new priorities in expediential rather than scientific ways. Over the last years two major normative directions have emerged: AAAs must create comprehensive service networks, but such networks must give substantial weight to effective alternatives to institutionalization.

The first of these directions entails a hypothetical model of services sketchily outlined in the Older Americans Act. This model has not been sufficiently tested, however, to confirm its comprehensiveness and effectiveness. A mere inventory of services, even if conceptually coherent, does not become a viable network until it successfully withstands the test of client acceptability, steady demand, affordability, accessibility, and adaptation to clients' changing preferences. Furthermore, models or inventories of services, no matter how comprehensive, do not necessarily resolve the instrumental and operational aspects of their delivery. Should services be scattered in a way that facilitates accessibility, or should they be concentrated in large, one-stop geriatric multipurpose centers better able to achieve continuity of service? Should services be age specific or age integrated?

Planners of services are left, as in Asimov's tale, with little research evidence to guide them. The question about whether services should be age specific or age integrated is a pertinent illustration of this. Age-integrated service programs are often faulted for neglecting or bypassing the elderly in favor of younger clients. The low percentage of older people (4 percent) who seek the services of Community Mental Health Centers (CMHCs) or the fact that in 1971 only 3 percent of all admissions to outpatient psychiatric clinics were 65 or older are typical of the evidence adduced to support this negative appraisal of age-integrated services. A report by the Special Senate Committee on Aging revealed that few staff members of Community Mental Health Centers showed any genuine interest in serving older people and that most CMHC directors recommended age-segregated mental health services staffed by professionals with specialized preparation for work with this age group.[69]

Age-segregated services seem to have their own set of problems. Kahana and Kahana claim that age segregation in the service system contributes to a perpetuation of negative stereotypes about old people and the aging process.[70] Wagner reports that the elderly resist becoming engaged in programs exclusively for the elderly.[71]

Hansen et al. examined the patterns of participation in multiservice centers for the aged.[72] They looked at four groups: actual users, nonusers who resort to a nutrition site, former users or dropouts, and those who never use the services. Little difference was found among the four groups in terms of demographic characteristics, distance from the center, and social interaction with children. There were differences concerning their health attributes, however. The dropouts had the highest depression scores, and the users were less depressed and more active. The indications of this study are that the well aged used this service best and that those who apparently needed it the most were not reached. This may apply to age-integrated services too. Participation and utilization of services by the aged may involve a host of motivational and functional considerations that transcend the debate about whether age-integrated or age-specific services are more effective. Given the contradictory research findings, this debate is not yet closed. More studies on the processes of setting priorities for alternative models of service delivery and on the relative merits of coordination and decentralization are necessary to arrive at an empirically validated and viable comprehensive model of services.

Theoretical Foundations

The theories of intrinsic disengagement and activity interaction dominated gerontological work during the 1960s and early 1970s. Although these theories were antithetical, social workers found both useful as foundations for practice. Lowy observed that caseworkers were more ready to adhere to the disengagement theory because it fit their decremental vision of aging and legitimated the prescription of decreased rates of social involvement and even passive withdrawal.[73] Group workers sought instead to underscore the positive relationship between activities, role performance, and life satisfaction. Their programs were designed according to activity theory and the premise that old persons are forced into a "roleless" role, that, given the chance, the elderly tend to remain as committed and involved as they were in their middle years.

Planners and policymakers grav-

itate—if not purposefully, at least by temperament—toward an exchange theory. They strive for a better fit between primary support networks and formalized services. They also seek to redress the progressive loss of societal power that afflicts the aged. Emerson identified four possible balancing strategies: (1) withdrawal (akin to disengagement), (2) network extension, (3) statusgiving, and (4) coalition formation.[74] The last three have been actively pursued or at least advocated by gerontological social workers. Network extension is the province of the community organizer, who aims to create self-help, social action, and lobbying organizations that the aged operate on their own behalf. Coalition formation—intergenerational or with other underprivileged groups—seeks to overcome the progressive segregation and even isolation that threaten the aged in an age-homogenous society. Statusgiving includes the creation of opportunities, both functional and symbolic, to enhance the battered image of the aged.

The disengagement theory has lost its initial appeal, and the polemic ardor of the activity theoreticians has also faded away. Social work was drafted into the fashionable gerontological bandwagons of the 1960s, but soon gave them up in favor of a more cautious empiricism. The gap left by the disengagement theory has not yet been filled, and the applications of the exchange theory remain limited. It is conceivable that a genuine gerontological theory will evolve from practice experience. In the meantime, however, social workers draw from a multitude of sources and forge a multiplicity of conceptual equations. The state of the art remains eclectic and open.

Future Perspectives

It seems likely that the two major domains of service-oriented research that have been identified here—the monitoring of changes in the demographic characteristics of the elderly and the assessment of service needs—will continue to be important areas of inquiry in the coming decade. The call by Neugarten and others for recognition of the over 65 cohort as consisting of two distinct generations of older people has been heeded by gerontologists.[75] There have been few efforts to study the relationships between these two generations, however, and little investigation of the impact of these generational differences on service delivery and social work practice has been reported. For example, there is overwhelming evidence of the importance of children as care givers. When the children are themselves young members of the aged cohort, however, it is possible that their own age may adversely affect their ability to play this role.

In Dobrof's 1976 study of the family relationships of institutionalized aged, the median age in her sample was 84, and the median age of her subjects' children was over 50.[76] She found that among the critical events leading to the decision to seek admission to a long-term care facility were age-associated changes in the family situation of the children—the retirement of a son or son-in-law and the decision to migrate to a warmer climate; the age-associated incapacity of the care-giving child; or the death of a key member of the first descendent generation, the son-in-law, for instance, followed by the daughter's decision to move.

The special social service needs of families in which the first and second generations are both old require careful assessment. It is important that priorities be assigned both to the charting of this demographic trend and to the identification of the accompanying service needs.

If Lowy's time lag is to be avoided, researchers will have to give attention to anticipated changes in the characteristics of future cohorts of the elderly. To illustrate, the group now in their 50s—born in the years between the end of World War I and the beginning of the Depression—is different from the current cohort in certain important ways. Men in this group are likely to have served in the armed forces, typically in World War II, but also in Korea; the percentage who have had at least some college increases dramatically, partially as a consequence of the G.I. Bill of Rights; there will be a much higher percentage of women who have been in the labor force for a significant portion of their adult lives; and the percentage of foreign born in this cohort will be lower than in previous groups.

Important research questions emerge from these and other demographic characteristics of the next generations of older people. There has, for example, been scant attention given to women in retirement. Typically, the crises of the later years have been retirement for men and widowhood for women. With the marked increase of working women, the knowledge base of the future will need to include special attention to the retirement process of women and to their adjustment to the loss of their status as workers. The change in the mandatory retirement age from 65 to 70 also creates an area of interest. At this writing, a major task is to estimate the number of workers between the ages of 65 and 70 who can be expected to remain in the labor force and to assess the potential impact of this change in certain sectors—in institutions of higher learning, for example. How the change will affect the preretirement planning of upcoming generations of older people, whether the seventieth birthday will become for them the milestone birthday that the sixty-fifth has been since passage of the Social Security Act, and how the change will affect geographic mobility are among the questions that merit attention.

The decline in the percentage of foreign born individuals in the older population leads to questions about the impact of ethnicity on service delivery and utilization. Black, Hispanic, Asian, and Native American aged receive particular attention under the present policies of the Administration on Aging, and this pattern seems likely to continue. This requires support for research aimed at increasing knowledge about the life experience of members of these cohorts—about particularities in their aging processes, the structure and function of the informal support systems within these groups, and ethnic differentials in the accessibility and utilization of formal support systems. It will be important also to identify and monitor intracohort differences. Cantor's work indicates the power of class differentials within the three ethnic groups she studied and the importance of the interrelationship between class and ethnicity.[77] Also in need of research are questions about distinctions within ethnic and religious subgroups of the white majority. What, for example, is the status of the older person in the family? How are the functions and task assignments of family members defined? How do groups differ in their utilization of formal organizations?

Formal and Informal Support Systems. As was mentioned earlier, the interface between the formal and informal support systems of older people is presently one of the major focuses of service-oriented research. This may continue to be an area of substantial concern. It is related both to the study of the changing demographic characteristics of the aged cohort and to the efforts to refine the technology for assessing needs. Clearly, the attempts to define the components of a comprehensive and effective formal service system and to develop community services for high-risk elderly

require continued study of the informal support networks of older people.

In addition to the research areas already identified, such as the ability of older children to perform the care-giving tasks, there are other lines of inquiry that require study. Litwak and Szelenyi saw important functional and structural differences among the types of primary groups that constitute the informal support system of many older people, that is, families, neighbors, and friends.[78] In her inner-city studies, Cantor found more evidence of interchangeability among these groups than Litwak and Szelenyi did.[79] This remains an important subject for service-oriented research. If Cantor's findings are replicated in other studies and it is found that, under certain circumstances or with professional and agency help, groups of friends and neighbors are able to perform familial functions, such findings would have clear import to service providers. Then the support of surrogate families for familyless older people might well become a service strategy, with tax and cash incentives available to the nonfamily groups as well as to families. Conversely, if further studies find that the structural differences among these types of primary groups seriously limit or preclude significant interchangeability, then different policy and service issues will present themselves. Are there tasks that customarily belong to the family which can be assigned to a formal organization? And what kinds of organizational adaptations and staff training would be required to guarantee effective performance of these tasks?

Mutual Aid Groups. There is increasing interest among mental health and other helping professionals in a special genre of support systems, the formal mutual help group. Most such groups are composed of people who share a problem or predicament.[80] Alcoholics Anonymous or Parents without Partners are prototypic examples of such groups. A survey of the literature, particularly the works of Gartner and Reissman and of Caplan and Killilea, reveals the potential value of mutual aid and self-help groups.[81]

Researchers in this field distinguish between the indigenous support systems—families, neighbors, and friends—and those that are established by or for people who share "a common problem or predicament" and who "band together for mutual support and constructive action toward shared goals."[82] In the field of aging, such groups may be composed of older people in a particular geographic area.[83] They may also be composed of older people facing a particular problem, widowhood or retirement, for example. Senior Citizens' and Golden Age Clubs are frequently mutual aid groups for their members, and at least some local chapters of the American Association of Retired Persons perform a similar function in the lives of their members.

Of interest also are the mutal aid and social action groups established to provide support for family members coping with special age-associated problems. Safford's work with groups of relatives of mentally impaired older people is one example.[84] Another is the Community Service Society's Natural Support Program described by Zimmer, Gross-Andrew, and Frankfamer.[85]

Killilea concludes her extensive review of the literature on mutual help organizations with a series of recommendations for future research, and although aging received relatively little attention in her article or its bibliography, her suggestions are useful:

> The most productive work will be accomplished by the accumulation of evidence from extensive case studies of specific groups. . . . Surveys of different kinds of

mutual help organizations . . . are needed, . . . [as are] historical studies which would provide us with information about the intellectual traditions, the social and political forces which impinge on specific persons with needs, who take significant action culminating in the development of a particular helping service.[86]

It is to be hoped that the interest in mutual aid groups for the aging will insure that the lines of inquiry suggested by Killilea are pursued.

Final Notes

Given the continuing demographic changes in the age composition of the over-65 cohort, it is likely that the frail elderly will continue to claim the attention of researchers, planners, and practitioners. Of particular importance will be the work on measurement instruments—those having to do with assessing the service needs of the individual and those designed to measure the extent of the service needs in a catchment area.

Federal initiatives—including those of the Administration on Aging and the Health Care Financing Administration—offer the potential of more systematic analysis of the array and location of the services required by the frail elderly than has been achieved to date. It is worth repeating that the need is for attention to effectiveness as well as efficiency. In a society in which good management is a highly regarded virtue, it sometimes may seem that social workers must be like Janus. One head must be turned toward efficiency, lest support for programs be lost for reasons of mismanagement. The other head must face effectiveness, lest the program survive but be of no real service to older people.

Sufficient concern has been expressed in this article about the quality of some of the current research, about the continued evidence of Lowy's time lag between the completion of studies and the incorporation of relevant findings into the design and operation of programs, and about the frequency with which decisions are made on grounds of expediency. Nonetheless, the progress made in the last several decades in providing services for the aging and the increasing numbers of well-educated and highly committed researchers coming into the field of aging justify optimism about the work that will be done in the years to come.

NOTES AND REFERENCES

1. Issac Asimov, "The Machine That Won the War," in *Nightfall and Other Stories* (Garden City, N.Y.: Doubleday & Co., 1969), pp. 326–327.

2. Louis Lowy, "The Role of Social Gerontology in the Development of Services for Older People," and "A Social Work Practice Perspective in Relation to Theoretical Models and Research in Gerontology," both in Donald P. Kent, Robert Kastenbaum, and Sylvia Sherwood, eds., *Research, Planning and Action for the Elderly* (New York: Behavioral Publications, 1972), pp. 20–36 and 538–544, respectively.

3. Robert Morris and Robert H. Binstock, *Feasible Planning for Social Change* (New York: Columbia University Press, 1966), pp. 94–127.

4. James D. Manney, *Aging in American Society* (Ann Arbor, Mich.: Institute of Gerontology, 1975), p. 99.

5. P.L. 92–603, Sec. 222.

6. Sylvia Sherwood, "Social Science and Action Research," in Kent, Kastenbaum, and Sherwood, op. cit., pp. 70–96.

7. Merlin Taber and Marilyn Flynn, "Social Policy and Social Provision for the Elderly in the 1970's," *The Gerontologist*, 11 (Winter 1971), pp. 51–54.

8. Erdman Palmore, "The Future Status of the Aged," *The Gerontologist*, 16 (August 1976), p. 297.

9. M. Powell Lawton, "Assessing the Competence of Older People," in Kent, Kastenbaum, and Sherwood, eds., op. cit., pp. 122–143.

10. Bernard Kutner, David Fanshel, Alice M. Togo, and Thomas S. Langner, *Five Hundred over Sixty: A Community Survey on Aging* (New York: Russell Sage Foundation, 1956); Wayne E. Thompson and Gordon F. Streib, "Situational Determinants: Health and Economic Deprivation in Retirement," *Journal of Social Issues*, 14 (March 1958), pp. 18–34; George L. Maddox, "Self-Assessment of Health Status: A Longitudinal Study of Selected Elderly Subjects," *Journal of Chronic Diseases*, 17 (May 1964), pp. 449–460; Ethel Shanas, *The Health of Older People* (Cambridge, Mass.: Harvard University Press, 1962); Irving Rosow and Naomi Breslau, "A Guttman Health Scale for the Aged," *Journal of Gerontology*, 21 (October 1966), pp. 556–559; Marjorie F. Lowenthal, *Lives in Distress* (New York: Basic Books, 1964); S. Katz et al., "Studies of Illness in the Aging—The Index of ADL," *Journal of the American Medical Association*, 185 (1963), pp. 94–99; M. Powell Lawton and Elaine Brody, "Physical Self-Maintenance," in Kent, Kastenbaum, and Sherwood, eds., op. cit., pp. 131–133; and Howard A. Rosencranz and C. Terence Pihlblad, "Measuring the Health of the Elderly," *Journal of Gerontology*, 25 (April 1970), pp. 129–133.

11. Ethel Shanas, "The Health Status of the Aged, 1962 and 1975: Comparisons of Two National Surveys." Paper presented at the Twenty-Ninth Annual Meeting of the Gerontological Society, New York, N.Y., October 1976.

12. Lola M. Irelan and Dena K. Motley, "Health on the Threshold of Retirement." Paper presented at the Twenty-Fourth Annual Meeting of the Gerontological Society, Houston, Tex., October 1971.

13. Ewald W. Busse, "Social Factors in Influencing Care and Health of the Elderly," in John C. McKinney and Frank T. De Vyver, eds., *Aging and Social Policy* (New York: Appleton-Century-Crofts, 1966), pp. 126–141.

14. Edward A. Suchman, Bernard S. Phillips, and Gordon F. Streib, "An Analysis of the Validity of Health Questionnaires," *Social Forces*, 36 (March 1958), pp. 223–232.

15. Marjorie Cantor, "Extent and Corre-

lates of Mental Health Vulnerability among an Inner-City Elderly Population." Paper presented at the Twenty-Seventh Annual Meeting of the Gerontological Society, Portland, Ore., October 1974.

16. Eric Pfeiffer, ed., *Multidimensional Functional Assessment: The OARS Methodology–A Manual* (Durham, N.C.: Center for the Study of Aging and Human Development, Duke University, 1975).

17. Robert Morris, "Development of Parallel Services for the Elderly Disabled," *The Gerontologist*, 14 (February 1974), pp. 14–19.

18. Ethel Shanas et al., *Old People in Three Industrial Societies* (New York: Atherton Press, 1968), p. 45.

19. Burton D. Dunlop, "Long-Term Care: Need Versus Utilization," as quoted in Subcommittee on Long-Term Care, Special Committee on Aging, U.S. Senate, *Nursing Home Care in the United States: Failure in Public Policy* (Washington, D.C.: U.S. Government Printing Office, 1974), p. 59.

20. Shanas, "The Health Status of the Aged, 1962 and 1975," op. cit. p. 6.

21. Mary G. Kovar, "Health of the Elderly and Use of Health Services," *Public Health Reports*, 92 (January–February 1977), pp. 9–19; and Jean J. LaVor, "Long-Term Care: A Challenge to Service Systems" (rev. ed.; Washington, D.C.: Office of the Assistant Secretary for Planning and Evaluation, U. S. Department of Health, Education & Welfare, 1977).

22. Margaret Blenkner, Martin Bloom, and Margaret Nielsen, "A Research and Demonstration Project of Protective Services," *Social Casework*, 52 (October 1971), pp. 483–499.

23. Wilma T. Donahue, "What about Our Responsibility Toward the Abandoned Elderly?" *The Gerontologist*, 18 (April 1978), p. 102.

24. Elizabeth W. Markson, Gary S. Levitz, and Maryvonne Gognalons-Caillard, "The Elderly and the Community: Reidentifying Unmet Needs," *Journal of Gerontology*, 28 (October 1973), pp. 503–509.

25. U.S. Department of Health, Education, and Welfare, "Home Health Care: Report of

Regional Public Hearings," Publication No. 76–135 (Washington, D.C.: U.S. Government Printing Office, 1976).

26. Robert Morris and Elizabeth Harris, "Home Health Services in Massachusetts, 1971: Their Role in Care of the Long-Term Sick," *American Journal of Public Health*, 62 (August 1972), pp. 1088–1093.

27. William G. Bell, "Community Care for the Elderly: An Alternative to Institutionalization," *The Gerontologist*, 13 (Autumn 1973), pp. 349–354.

28. Jean Gold, "Comparison of Protective Service Projects," *The Gerontologist*, 12 (Autumn 1972), p. 85.

29. Arthur G. Cryns and Abraham Monk, "The Awareness of Need for Social Services among the Aged: An Area Study." Paper presented at the Twenty-Eighth Annual Meeting of the Gerontological Society, Louisville, Ky. October 1975.

30. Sheldon S. Tobin, Stephen M. Davidson, and Ann Sack, *Effective Social Services for Older Americans* (Ann Arbor, Mich.: Institute of Gerontology, 1976).

31. Cryns and Monk, op. cit.

32. Blenkner, Bloom, and Nielsen, op. cit.

33. Morton Kleban, Elaine Brody, and M. Powell Lawton, "Personality Traits in the Mentally Impaired Elderly and Their Relationship to Improvements in Current Functioning," *The Gerontologist*, 11 (Summer 1971), pp. 134–140.

34. Shanas et al., *Old People in Three Industrial Societies*, pp. 226–257.

35. Leonard E. Gottesman and Evelyn Hutchison, "Characteristics of the Institutionalized Aged," in Elaine M. Brody, ed., *A Social Work Guide for Long-Term Facilities*, report prepared for the National Institute of Mental Health (Washington, D.C.: U.S. Government Printing Office, 1974), pp. 63–65.

36. Brody, ed., op. cit., p. 73; and Elaine M. Brody, "Aging," *Encyclopedia of Social Work*, Vol. 1 (Washington, D.C.: National Association of Social Workers, 1977), p. 72.

37. Rose Dobrof, "The Care of the Aged: A Shared Function." Unpublished doctoral dissertation, Columbia University School of Social Work, 1976.

38. Lillian E. Troll, Sheila J. Miller, and Robert C. Atchley, *Families in Later Life* (Belmont, Calif.: Wadsworth Publishing Co., 1979), pp. 83–106.

39. Lillian E. Troll, "The Family in Later Life: A Decade Review," *Journal of Marriage and the Family*, 33 (May 1971), pp. 263–282.

40. Marvin Sussman, Donna Vanderwyst, and Gordon K. Williams, "Will You Still Need Me, Will You Still Love Me When I'm 64?" Paper presented at the Twenty-Ninth Annual Meeting of the Gerontological Society, New York, N.Y., October 1976.

41. Marjorie Cantor, "The Elderly in the Inner City: Some Implications of the Effect of Culture on Life-Styles." Paper presented at the Institute on Gerontology and Graduate Education for Social Work, Fordham University, New York, N.Y. March 1973. (Mimeographed.)

42. Margaret Blenkner, "Social Work and Family Relationships in Later Life with Some Thoughts on Filial Maturity," in Ethel Shanas and Gordon F. Streib, eds., *Social Structure and the Family: Generational Relations* (Englewood Cliffs, N.J.: Prentice-Hall, 1965), pp. 46–59.

43. Hope J. Leichter and William E. Mitchell, *Kinship and Casework* (New York: Russell Sage Foundation, 1967), pp. 194–208.

44. Rose Dobrof and Eugene Litwak, *Maintenance of Family Ties of Long-Term Care Patients* (Rockville, Md.: National Institute of Mental Health, 1977), pp. 32–42.

45. Robert Kastenbaum and Sandra Candy, "The Four Percent Fallacy: A Methodological and Empirical Critique of Extended Care Population Statistics," *International Journal of Aging and Human Development*, 4 (Winter 1973), pp. 15–21.

46. Allen M. Pincus, "The Definition and Measurement of the Institutional Environment in Homes for the Aged," *The Gerontologist*, 8 (Autumn 1968), pp. 207–210; and Jordan Kosberg and Sheldon Tobin, "Variability among Nursing Homes," *The Gerontologist*, 12 (Autumn 1972), pp. 214–219.

47. Ruth Bennett and Lucille Nahemow, "Socialization and Social Adjustment in Five Residential Settings for the Aged," in Kent, Kastenbaum, and Sherwood, eds., op. cit., pp. 514–524.

48. Alvin Goldfarb, "The Psychodynamics of Dependency and the Search for Aid," in Richard A. Kalish, ed., *The Dependencies of Old People* (Ann Arbor, Mich.: Institute of Gerontology, 1969), pp. 1–14.

49. C. Knight Aldrich and Ethel Mendkoff, "Relocation of the Aged and Disabled: A Mortality Study," *Journal of the American Geriatrics Society*, 11 (March 1963), pp. 185–194; Oswaldo Camargo and George H. Preston, "What Happens to Patients Who Are Hospitalized for the First Time When Over Sixty-Five?" *American Journal of Psychiatry*, 102 (September 1945), pp. 168–173; J. R. Whittier and D. Williams, "The Coincidence of Constancy of Mortality Figures for Aged Psychotic Patients Admitted to State Hospitals," *Journal of Nervous and Mental Disease*, 124 (December 1956), pp. 618–620; E. E. Nicholson, *Planning New Institutional Facilities for Long-Term Care* (New York: G. P. Putnam's Sons, 1956); Eldon C. Killian, "Effects of Geriatric Transfers on Mortality Rates," *Social Work*, 15 (January 1970), pp. 19–26; and Elliot Markus, Margaret Blenkner, and Thomas Downs, "Some Factors and Their Association with Post-Relocation Mortality among Institutionalized Aged Persons," *Journal of Gerontology*, 27 (July 1972), pp. 376–382.

50. Frances F. Carp, "Effects of Improved Housing on the Lives of Older People," in Bernice Neugarten, ed., *Middle Age and Aging* (Chicago: University of Chicago Press, 1968), pp. 409–416; Morton Lieberman, Sheldon Tobin, and D. Slover, "The Effects of Relocation on Long-Term Geriatric Patients," Project 17–1328, Final Report, Illinois Department of Health and Committee on Human Development (Chicago: University of Chicago, 1971); and Evelyn H. Ogren and Margaret W. Linn, "Male Nursing Home Patients: Relocation and Mortality," *Journal of the American Geriatric Society*, 19 (March 1971), pp. 229–239.

51. Renato Y. Pablo, "Intra-institutional Relocation: Its Impact on Long-Term Care Patients," *The Gerontologist*, 17 (October 1977), pp. 426–435.

52. Sheldon Tobin and Morton Lieberman, *Last Home for the Aged* (San Francisco: Jossey-Bass, 1976).

53. Sheldon Tobin, Jerome Hammerman, and Vicki Rector, "Preferred Disposition of Institutionalized Aged," *The Gerontologist*, 12

(Summer 1972), pp. 129–133; M. Powell Lawton, "Assessment, Integration and Environments for Older People," *The Gerontologist*, 10 (Spring 1972), pp. 38–46; and Jane L. Barney, "The Prerogative of Choice in Long-Term Care," *The Gerontologist*, 17 (August 1977), pp. 309–314.

54. Barney, op. cit., p. 314.

55. Herbert Shore, "Alternatives to Institutional Care: Fact or Fancy," *Journal of Long-Term Care Administration*, 2 (September 1973), pp. 23–35; and Tobin and Lieberman, op. cit., p. 226.

56. Eva Kahana and Rodney Coe, "Alternatives in Long Term Care," in Sylvia Sherwood, ed., *Long Term Care* (New York: Spectrum Publications, 1975), pp. 511–560.

57. Evelyn S. Newman and Susan R. Sherman, "A Survey of Caretakers in Adult Foster Homes," *The Gerontologist*, 17 (October 1977), pp. 436–439.

58. William G. Weissert, "Two Models of Geriatric Day Care, *The Gerontologist*, 16 (October 1976), pp. 420–427.

59. Abraham Monk, "Day Care Programs for the Aged: Trends and Planning Issues," *Perspectives on Aging*, 4 (May–June 1975), pp. 23–26; and Weissert, op. cit.

60. Monk, op. cit.

61. President's Commission on Mental Health, *Task Panel Reports*, Vol. 3 (Washington, D.C.: U.S. Government Printing Office, 1978), appendix.

62. Kurt G. Kerz, "Community Resources and Services to Help Independent Living," *The Gerontologist*, 11 (Spring 1971), pp. 59–66; Brahna Trager, "Homemaker Services for the Aged and the Chronically Ill," in *Readings in Homemaker Services* (New York: National Council for Homemaker Services, 1969), pp. 36–42; Eugene B. Shinn and Nancy Day Robinson, "Trends in Homemaker–Home Health Aide Services," *Abstracts for Social Workers*, 10 (Fall 1974), pp. 3–8; and Florence Moore, "New Issues for In-Home Services," *Public Welfare*, 35 (Spring 1977), pp. 26–37.

63. Susan Friedman, Lenard Kaye, and Sharon Farago, "Maximizing the Quality of Home Care Services for the Elderly." Paper presented at the Thirtieth Annual Meeting of the Gerontological Society, San Francisco, Calif., November 1977.

64. Blenkner, Bloom, and Nielsen, op. cit.; and Naomi Breslau and Marie R. Haug, "The Elderly Aid and the Elderly: Senior Friends Project," *Social Security Bulletin*, 35 (November–December 1972), pp. 9–15.

65. U.S. Department of Health, Education, and Welfare, Social and Rehabilitation Service, Community Services Administration, *Report of the National Protective Services Project for Older Adults* (Washington, D.C.: U.S. Government Printing Office, 1971); Philip W. Brickner et al., "Home Maintenance for the Home-Bound Aged: A Pilot Program in New York City," *The Gerontologist*, 16 (February 1976), pp. 25–29; and Barney, op. cit.

66. Linda Noelker and Zev Harel, "Aged Excluded from Home Health Care: An Interorganizational Solution," *The Gerontologist*, 18 (February 1978), pp. 37–41.

67. Robert Hudson, "Rational Planning and Organizational Imperatives: Prospects for Area Planning in Aging," *Annals of the American Academy of Policital and Social Science*, 415 (September 1974), pp. 41–54.

68. Philip K. Armour, C. L. Estes, and Maureen M. Noble, "Problems in the Design and Implementation of a National Policy on Aging: A Study of Title III of The Older Americans Act," in Howard W. Freeman, ed., *Policy Studies Review Annual* (Beverly Hills, Ca.: Sage Publications, 1978), pp. 616–639.

69. Special Committee on Aging, United States Senate, *Mental Health Care and the Elderly: Shortcomings in Public Policy* (Washington, D.C.: U.S. Government Printing Office, 1971).

70. Eva Kahana and Boaz Kahana, "Therapeutic Potential of Age Integration," *Archives of General Psychiatry*, 23 (July 1970), pp. 20–29.

71. S. Wagner, "Challenge for Tomorrow: A Report on Research Findings of a Study of Senior Group Programs." Paper presented at a meeting of the Western Gerontological Society, San Francisco, Calif., April 1975.

72. Anne M. Hansen et al., "Correlates of Senior Center Participation," *The Gerontologist*, 18 (April 1978), pp. 193–200.

73. Lowy, op. cit.

74. Richard M. Emerson, "Exchange Theory, Parts 1 and 2," in Joseph Berger, Morris Zelditch, and Bo Anderson, eds., *Sociological Theories in Progress*, Vol. 2 (Boston: Houghton Mifflin Co., 1972), pp. 38–87.

75. Bernice L. Neugarten, "The Future and the Young-Old," *The Gerontologist*, 15 (February 1975), pp. 4–10.

76. Dobrof, "The Care of the Aged: A Shared Function."

77. Cantor, "The Elderly in the Inner City: Some Implications of the Effect of Culture on Life-Styles."

78. Eugene Litwak and Ivan Szelenyi, "Primary Group Structures and Their Functions: Kin, Neighbors, and Friends," *American Sociological Review*, 34 (August 1969), pp. 465–481.

79. Cantor, "The Elderly in the Inner City: Some Implications of the Effect of Culture on Life-Styles," p. 6.

80. Marie Killilea, "Mutual Help Organizations: Interpretations in the Literature," in Gerald Caplan and Killilea, eds., *Support Systems and Mutual Help: Multidisciplinary Explorations* (New York: Grune & Stratton, 1976), pp. 37–95.

81. Alan Gartner and Frank Reissman, *Self-Help in the Human Services* (San Francisco: Jossey-Bass, 1977); and Caplan and Killilea, op. cit.

82. Killilea, op. cit., p. 38.

83. Arlie Russell Hochschild, *The Unexpected Community* (Englewood Cliffs, N.J.: Prentice-Hall, 1973), pp. 1–15.

84. Florence Safford, *Developing a Training Program for Families of the Mentally Impaired Aged* (New York: Isabella Geriatric Center, 1977).

85. Anna H. Zimmer, Susannah Gross-Andrew, and Dwight Frankfamer, "Incentives to Families Caring for Disabled Elderly: Research and Demonstration Project to Strengthen the Natural Supports System." Paper presented at the Thirtieth Annual Scientific Meeting of the Gerontological Society, San Francisco, Calif., November 1977.

86. Killilea, op. cit., pp. 78–79.

Development, Dissemination, and Utilization of Youth Research

RONALD A. FELDMAN

OVER THE YEARS there have been raging, and sometimes rancorous, debates about what social work is and what social work ought to be.[1] But nowhere is the vast discrepancy between what is and what ought to be more evident and more distressing than in social work services for youths. Ideally, social work ought to serve large numbers of youths with a high degree of proficiency. Presumably, social work services for youths should be both preventive and rehabilitative. These services should be based on the systematic and intelligent application of scientific knowledge. Moreover, evidence of the effectiveness of social work should be a product of the valid and reliable implementation of scientific methods.

It can be stated forthrightly at the outset of this discussion that a coherent and identifiable social work knowledge base about youths and adolescents is virtually nonexistent. Yet social workers annually serve hundreds of thousands, if not millions, of youths. Since the inception of social work, youths have constituted one of the profession's main consumer populations.[2] Social work thus serves a large client population, namely, youths, with little scientific knowledge about their biological, sociological, and psychological attributes or experiences. In so doing, social work jeopardizes the integrity and legitimacy of its identity as a profession.

The remainder of this article is devoted to the documentation of the foregoing contentions and to recommendations about the generation, dissemination, and utilization of social work knowledge concerning youths. It addresses the following questions, among others: What forms of youth development research have emerged from social work and the social sciences? In particular, what have been the substantive focuses, methodological attributes, and overall qualities of this research? What steps are necessary to facilitate the dissemination and utilization of youth development research by social work educators and practitioners? The article concludes with a broad set of recommendations concerning the future involvement of social work in youth development research and in the dissemination and utilization of research-based knowledge for practice and policy purposes. Although these recommendations could be innumerable, the main focus is on a limited number of recommendations that are of overarching significance for the social work profession.

Many definitions of "youth" and "adolescence" have been set forth.[3] Most use chronological criteria, but some utilize more biological and sociological referents.[4] For the purpose of this discussion "youth" will comprise a relatively broad age span, varying roughly from 10 through 24 years. "Adolescence" is more narrowly defined, ranging from approximately 12 through 18 years.

Youth Development and Social Work

The data about various problems of youths are highly visible and well documented. Most authorities agree that the youths of today are vulnerable to many factors that influenced their forebears only on a minor scale, if at all. These include earlier biological maturation; prolonged adolescence in the form of deferred entry into the labor force; widespread family deterioration, measured by divorce rates and by incidences of working mothers and unwed mothers; increased influence of the peer group, as found in educational choices, occupational aspirations, drug and alcohol use, delinquent activities, and other forms of behavior; rapid social change, exemplified by increasing geographic mobility and changing sex roles; sus-

tained bombardment by the mass media; and continuous exposure to threats of industrial pollution, ecological disaster, and even nuclear annihilation. These factors and others—including changes in voting laws, juvenile justice systems, and other institutions that affect youths— have contributed to the high incidence of sociobehavioral problems among contemporary youths.[5]

The United States Senate Judiciary Committee reported that crime by young offenders "increased alarmingly" throughout the years between 1960 and 1974.[6] Violent crimes by persons under 18 jumped 254.1 percent. Property crimes such as burglary, larceny, and auto theft increased 133 percent. Persons under 25 years of age accounted for nearly 60 percent of all crimes of violence and for slightly over 80 percent of all property crimes committed each year. The director of the Center for Studies of Crime and Delinquency predicts that one out of nine youths, and one out of six male youngsters, will probably be referred to a juvenile court for a delinquent act committed prior to his eighteenth birthday.[7] These estimates of rising juvenile delinquency are conservative, moreover, and tend to increase sevenfold in self-report data obtained from youths.[8]

A seminal longitudinal study by Wolfgang, Figlio, and Sellin has shown that delinquent behavior is not a transient problem that merely emerges and vanishes during the course of youth development. Rather, they found that 66 percent of all adult offenders in a cohort of subjects from Philadelphia, Pennsylvania, had been arrested under age 18. Among those with at least one arrest under age 18, the probability of being arrested between 18 and 26 years of age is 0.436. This is three and one-half times greater than the probability of adult arrest among those with no records as juveniles.[9] Similar longitudinal trends have been found for a variety of antisocial and delinquent behaviors.[10]

Systematic surveys show that violence in public schools is also a pervasive problem. Data obtained from school administrators reveal serious problems (that is, approximately seven incidents during a one-month period) in 26 percent of the urban schools.[11] Estimates concerning the costs of school crime range upward from $200 million a year. About 2.4 million secondary school students (11 percent of the population) have something stolen from them in a typical month, and each month about 1.3 percent (282,000) report being attacked. Some 5,200 secondary school teachers are physically attacked every month, 1,000 of whom are injured seriously enough to require medical attention.[12]

Other youth problems also occur in large, if not startling, numbers. About 10 percent of teenagers are "heavy drinkers" who imbibe at least once a week and consume a minimum of four drinks each time.[13] Over 50 percent of the high school students report that they have been drunk during the previous year, and 10 percent state that their drinking has gotten them in trouble with the police.[14] Survey studies of adolescent drug abuse reveal high incidences of heroin and cocaine addiction.[15] Teenage pregnancy also is a serious social work concern.[16] It is conservatively estimated that half of all female dropouts from secondary schools are pregnant when they leave school.[17] Research demonstrates that bearing a child while in secondary school has dramatic adverse effects on both the completion of school and on later economic and occupational success.[18]

Somewhat less visible, but of substantial concern to social workers, are problems such as teenage prostitution, both male and female; intrafamilial violence by teenagers; and adolescent suicide, which is now the fourth most common cause of death among youths between 15 and 19 years of age; and youths' fear of school.[19] Rubel reports that 33 percent of junior high school students consistently avoid certain places in their schools, such as restrooms or a hallway, out of fear of being assaulted. Even more dramatic, 7 percent of large-city junior high students report that they are "afraid most of the time," and 8 percent say that they "stay home at least one day in a month out of fear."[20]

What has been the social work response to such challenges? Obviously, large numbers of social workers devote their entire careers to the problems of youths. They are employed by juvenile courts, correctional institutions, residential and outpatient treatment centers, drug and alcohol abuse agencies, public schools, teenage pregnancy and marriage counseling clinics, and many other types of service organizations. Many youth-oriented social workers are affiliated with nationwide "socializing" organizations, such as the YMCA, YWCA, YM & YWHA, Boy Scouts, Girl Scouts, Campfire Girls, Boys' Clubs of America, Girls' Clubs of America, and B'nai Brith Youth Organizations.[21] In addition, some social workers have been instrumental in shaping national policies for children and youths. They have testified before congressional subcommittees, served on presidential task forces, and assisted prestigious study groups, such as those sponsored by the Assembly of Behavioral and Social Sciences.

Unfortunately, however, the merits of social work programs for youths have been investigated only on a sporadic and inconsistent basis. Following comprehensive reviews of delinquency prevention efforts and other programs, some scholars have urged the cessation of social casework, social group work, and other forms of psychosocial intervention among youths.[22] The available data do not convincingly demonstrate, however, that social workers are less effective than other types of helping agents, such as psychologists, psychiatrists, and guidance counselors. Three phenomena could account for the purported failures, and each of them must be considered if social work is to increase its effectiveness in preventing and remediating youth problems.

First, the knowledge base concerning youths may be deficient in certain critical respects. Second, even when suitable knowledge about youth development is available, practitioners and policymakers may be unaware of its importance, or even of its existence. Third, although they may be acquainted with the requisite knowledge, some practitioners may find themselves unable to utilize or implement it efficiently. These potential deficiencies prompt an examination of the three interrelated processes of knowledge production, knowledge dissemination, and knowledge utilization—all of which directly affect social work efforts to deal with youth problems.

Volumes could be devoted to a comprehensive review of youth development research in social work and the social sciences. The present discussion will be limited to a broad overview. Clearly, the preponderance of research concerning youths has emanated from the biomedical sciences, from the disciplines of psychology, sociology, and social psychology, and, to a lesser extent, from political science and economics. Additional research concerning youth development also has been generated by criminal justice specialists, counseling professionals, and others. Social work research, in contrast, has been slow to develop. Yet, as social work doctoral programs proliferated during the past two decades, there was a concerted effort to borrow and adapt knowledge from the social sciences for practice and policy purposes.[23] This discussion will focus first, therefore, on social science contributions to social work knowledge about youths.

Youth Research in the Social Sciences

Social work has probably borrowed more heavily from psychology than from any other social science, and within psychology, the largest and most influential body of research about children and youths has emanated from the subfield of developmental psychology. Among the topics examined by developmental psychologists are subjects' changes along biological and cognitive dimensions; their various social roles as son, daughter, peer, pupil, and so forth; and selected facets of psychosocial functioning, such as detachment, autonomy, intimacy, sexuality, achievement, and identity formation. Yet, in surveying research about adolescence, it is pertinent to recall the lament of one eminent scholar that

> a list of the twenty-five leading developmental psychologists today selected on the basis of almost any criterion would not include one whose reputation was established primarily on the basis of scholarship in the adolescence area.[24]

Hill also declared that there

> is no set of national centers of excellence in the adolescence area . . . not even one. . . . It is doubtful whether more than 5 percent of the pages in the discipline's two leading journals have been devoted to adolescence.[25]

Despite this regrettable state of affairs, a number of theoretical formulations concerning youth have been elaborated by social scientists. These formulations tend to organize various knowledge bases into a general theory of human development that includes the adolescent period.[26] Such formulations offer the distinct advantages of coherence, cogency, and parsimony. Furthermore, they sometimes are amenable to imaginative theoretical refinements and to empirical research concerning one or more facets of the general theory.[27] As a result, many of these formulations have been readily assimilated into the literature of social work.

Although such frameworks are sometimes of use for the diagnosis of youth problems, they seldom provide discrete practice interventions or policy guidelines. This is largely a result of their being phrased in "universalistic" terms that actually pertain primarily to middle-class populations. They are consequently of relatively little value to the many social workers who deal with minority youths and clients from lower socioeconomic strata. Some scholars contend that the treatises of Piaget and Erikson have been so influential that they have exerted a stultifying effect on alternative formulations that could be of value in understanding adolescence—a pheonomenon that is little different from the profound influence Freudian theory exerted on social work for many years.

Like psychologists, some of the sociologists and social psychologists who study adolescence focus on such broadly defined processes as socialization.[28] In doing so, however, they tend to expand their research interests to include social desiderata such as peer group influences, social class, ethnic background, family structure, and kinship patterns.[29] In addition, their work includes sophisticated analyses of intergenerational differences among youths and thoughtful investigations of youth and adolescence within discrete socioecological contexts.[30] Other work by sociologists and social psychologists examines youth and adolescence in relation to the total life span.[31] Although, as will be discussed later, these lines of research are essential for future efforts aimed at policy formulation, the few social scientists who are expert in such areas have seemed reluc-

tant or unable to apply their work directly to policy formulation. Perhaps such challenges will be more readily accepted by social workers with an immediate interest in linking research and policy.

One framework that crosscuts the youth research of many disciplines is role theory. It is employed frequently by psychologists and sociologists, and it links the knowledge bases of these disciplines with social psychology.[32] Role theory has also been the subject of relevant social work research.[33] Although most role studies are essentially descriptive, they lend themselves readily to a variety of social work interests, including the examination of client attributes, behaviors, and self-conceptions. In addition, role concepts can contribute to the diagnosis of common client problems, such as role conflicts, role ambiguities, and role overloads, and to the elaboration of rudimentary intervention procedures for resolving or eliminating these problems.[34] Such phenomena are typically interpreted within the context of relevant social networks, including clients' work, friendship, and neighborhood groups. Cross-disciplinary frameworks like role theory are indispensable for understanding youth behavior. Furthermore, they provide the unique perspective of interaction that makes social work distinctive and potentially more productive than other helping professions.

The social sciences contain a substantial literature on youth that could be of value to social work. This body of knowledge has exerted only a negligible impact on the profession, however, because few social workers are systematically engaged in translating and synthesizing it. This is attributable to an institutionalized reward system that barely recognizes the potential benefits of such activity and to job constraints that are severely delimiting. In those rare circumstances that enable talented professionals to incorporate such skills into their practice repertoires, there are few incentives or opportunities for them to exchange the resultant information with colleagues or to introduce it to the mainstream of the social work literature. With proper recognition of the importance of such activities, and with concomitant reward systems for individuals who are so engaged, it is likely that the social work profession could take a quantum leap forward in its ability to benefit from the vast body of knowledge already available in the social sciences. This potentiality applies not only to knowlege about youth development, but to all other areas of social work interest. In part, however, such a capability depends also on factors that are external to the profession, including the availability of outside funding.

Federally Sponsored Youth Research

For many years the federal government has played an important role in shaping social science research on youths and adolescents. The most comprehensive overview of childhood and adolescence research sponsored by federal agencies is prepared annually by the Social Research Group of George Washington University in conjunction with the government's Interagency Panel for Research and Development on Adolescence. Representatives on the panel are from a broad span of federal agencies: ACTION, the Department of Commerce, the Department of Housing and Urban Development, the Department of Justice, the Department of Labor, the National Science Foundation, the Office of Management and Budget, and the Department of Health, Education and Welfare. The panel also includes representatives from numerous offices within the Department of Health, Education and Welfare: the Office of the Assistant Secretary for Planning and Evaluation, the Office of Human Development Services, the Office of Planning, Research, and Evaluation, the Administration for Children, Youth and Families, the Administration for Public Service, the Rehabilitation Services Administration, the Bureau of Community Health Services, the National Institute of Mental Health, the National Institute of Neurological and Communicative Disorders and Strokes, the National Institute on Drug Abuse, the National Institute on Alcohol Abuse and Alcoholism, the National Center for Education Statistics, the Office of Education, and the National Institute of Education.

In the latest report of the Social Research Group, Berkeley reveals that the agencies participating in the panel sponsored 4,998 research projects on children and youths during fiscal year 1977 at a total expenditure of $474 million.[35] Of this total, 3,440 of the projects, accounting for $323.1 million, included adolescents. Only 1,334 of the projects focused exclusively on youths who were 10 years of age or older. About $14 million more was spent during 1977 on children and youth research than in 1976, an increase of approximately 3 percent. Over half the research projects were funded by the Office of Education.

During the past few years the proportion of the $474 million allocated to basic research has remained stable at 7.9 percent. The proportion spent on applied research, defined as having results that are directly applicable, declined to 33.1 percent, and that for demonstrations and utilizations, defined as attempting to promote the use of research findings or innovative practices, increased to 38.6 percent. Only 7.4 percent of the funds were spent on evaluation research, 5.3 percent on support and utilization, 4.0 percent on policy research, and 3.8 percent on social accounting.

It is possible to array federal research funding patterns along several dimensions. For example, in 1977, of the studies focusing on adolescents with special characteristics, the greatest proportion of funds was allocated to bilingual subjects (27.0 percent), the physically handicapped (11.5 percent), drug users (8.3 percent), and delinquents (7.5 percent). It should be noted that Social Research Group classification categories and funding patterns are not mutually exclusive and many of the research projects fit two or more categories. Lesser proportions of money were spent on subjects with the following characteristics: aural handicaps, deafness, visual handicaps, blindness, neurological handicaps, brain damage, hyperkinesis, cerebral palsy, orthopedic handicaps, communicative disorders, multiple handicaps, the combination of deafness and blindness, mental retardation. learning disabilities, at-risk conditions, physical illness, emotional illness, and children who were runaways, school dropouts, abused or neglected, academically slow, gifted, adolescent parents, or educationally disadvantaged.

Under the category of adolescent developmental processes, about 38 percent of 1977 funds was allocated to cognitive development, largely to cognitive performance and language development; 37 percent to social-emotional development, mostly for processes of self-perception, motivation, emotional development, and interpersonal relations; and about 11 percent for physical development. Classification by adolescents' social and physical environments indicates an emphasis on economic environments, employment, and laws and policies that affect youths. An encouraging note was the growing interest in ecological studies of adolescents, accounting for 3.6 percent of the funds allocated to basic research on children.

Categorization by types of relevant people in the adolescents' environments reveals that the greatest amount of funds was spent on educational personnel, 40.6 percent. Only 0.5 percent was spent on social workers, and even less was spent on psychologists (0.1 percent). Other relevant constituencies were as follows: community members (4.1 percent), vocational counselors (1.1 percent), youth workers (0.4 percent), welfare personnel (2.0 percent), police (0.4 percent), health personnel (2.0 percent), community workers (0.7 percent), volunteers (1.7 percent), and policymakers (1.9 percent). Only 0.4 percent was allocated to peer research.

Classification by research on intervention programs produced the startling finding that nearly 74 percent of the funds in this category went to educational services. About 12 percent was spent on welfare services and 11 percent on health services. In the area of welfare, most moneys were allocated for employment programs, advocacy services, child abuse services, and delinquency treatment. Funds devoted to treatment for adolescents emphasized counseling (21.1 percent), diagnostic procedures (13.4 percent), career counseling (12.9 percent), and referral services (6.6 percent). Negligible moneys were spent on peer counseling (0.4 percent).

An assessment of research sites reveals that the bulk of research funds was for schools (49.3 percent), with lesser amounts directed toward adoptive homes (0.2 percent), foster homes (0.2 percent), group care centers (1.9 percent), hospitals (2.4 percent), medical clinics (3.6 percent), work places (6.3 percent), residential institutions (3.2 percent), and sheltered workshops (0.5 percent).

In terms of research design, the greatest proportion of funds was awarded to pretest-posttest studies (44.5 percent) and surveys (18.5 percent). Much less was spent on longitudinal studies (10.9 percent), experimental investigation (8.1 percent), multidisciplinary research (4.0 percent), and cross-cultural research (0.5 percent). Categorization by types of research measure revealed that funds were allocated as follows: named measures (36.2 percent), unnamed measures (29.3 percent), questionnaires (23.1 percent), interviews (20.3 percent), and observations (9.3 percent).

These general trends point, by and large, to an underemphasis on the types of adolescent research that would be of primary interest to social workers. It should also be noted that even the comprehensive efforts of the Interagency Panel and the Social Research Group are sadly lacking in some respects. For instance, in over 70 percent of the research projects reviewed, the sex of the subjects was not reported. Race and ethnic identity were unavailable for more than half the projects. The socioeconomic status of subjects was unavailable for over 70 percent of the projects. The subjects' location of residence also was rarely available. Although these variables undoubtedly are investigated in many of the funded studies, it is essential to incorporate them systematically into emergent data bases to permit a more refined assessment of funding patterns and potential policy directions.

Consequences of Professional Isolation

With funds provided by the Ford Foundation, Lipsitz conducted a comprehensive independent assessment of social science research on youths. Unlike the assessment of the Social Research Group, her evaluation concentrated specifically on studies of preadolescents, that is, youngsters ranging from 12 through 15 years of age. The title of her book, *Growing Up*

Forgotten, succinctly summarizes her findings. Lipsitz's review encompassed biological, socioemotional, and cognitive research, as well as studies conducted about schools, service institutions (including youth-serving agencies), juvenile justice systems, and family networks. Lipsitz asserted that she was

startled by the extent to which this age group is underserved. . . . What is discussed over and over again is how much is not known about this time of life, and yet how critical most researchers feel early adolescence is to the health and productive functioning of the individual throughout the rest of the life span. Also documented is how few researchers are devoting themselves to answering the many unanswered questions about early adolescence. Even more serious is how few are asking, in reference to early adolescence, the questions that are prerequisite to developmental research. Despite the critical importance of this age group, the intellectual and economic resources of the research community are not being fully allocated to its study. In fact, where this age group is concerned, there appears to be no research community at present.[36]

In a poignant observation, Lipsitz added that

isolation is a pervasive theme in [the] investigation of programs and research for young adolescents—the isolation that young people feel within themselves, the isolation of the age group from other groups, of one institution in relation to another, of each research discipline from others, and of researchers within disciplines from their colleagues who speak different methodological languages.[37]

Lipsitz's observations are especially disturbing in view of longitudinal research that documents a relationship between preadolescent behavior problems and subsequent difficulties in adulthood.[38] An understanding of such problems is not fostered by narrowly defined career incentives, increasing specialization, and rigid disciplinary boundaries, which produce and perpetuate homogeneous research agendas. Also, the major social science research organizations have been slow to direct their attention to youths and even slower to consider the policy or practice implications of their work for this age group. This is unfortunate because the social sciences would benefit from a mutually facilitative relationship with the helping professions. Such a relationship would enable both bodies to strengthen their credibility, public acceptance, and financial support.

Among the consequences of professional insulation and isolation are a plethora of conceptual and methodological problems. These, too, require attention if social science knowledge is to become more useful for social work. Key barriers to effective research on adolescence include the "tendency to perceive the period as discontinuous from the remainder of the life cycle," "the tendency to view adolescents as homogeneous or, at best, a little-differentiated lot," and "the tendency to view the nature of adolescence as endogenously programmed and the typical behavior of individual adolescents as determined by intrapsychic forces."[39] Much of the research about youths tends to be cross-sectional and to use instruments that are inadequate for measuring social and emotional growth. The naive use of multiple-variable assessment often carries with it violations of important assumptions that undergird the experimental investigation of adolescence. Hence, additional research with a primary focus on methodology is necessary to advance scientific knowledge about adolescence. This will require, among other things, close attention to a landmark study by Hobbs that comprehensively catalogued the problems wrought by inadequate systems of classifying children and youths.[40] The sophisticated taxonomies and implicit labels of such systems frequently generate or exacerbate youth problems. Some investigators have even advocated that all such systems be dismantled.[41] It would seem fruitful, however, to redefine them in behaviorally specific and operationally discrete terms, thus rendering them more useful for social work diagnosis and intervention.[42]

Constructs and referents used in youth research—*Sturm und Drang*, for example—are often difficult to apply in social work practice. Similarly, far too many studies of youths are conducted in laboratory environments. Despite the rigorous experimental standards applied in such studies, the results seldom are readily generalizable to practice settings. In contrast, few field studies of youths introduce basic experimental conditions, such as nontreatment control groups and the random assignment of subjects. At the same time, effective policy formulation has been deterred by the dearth of comprehensive longitudinal data about youths. Little is known about the relationship between youth development and preadolescent and postadolescent behavior or about the concurrent influences of contextual and ecological determinants, such as families, peer groups, and neighborhoods.

These problems and others are obviously subject to remediation by professionals who have a keen interest in bringing social science knowledge to bear on societal problems. The major difficulties lie not so much in reconceptualizing future research, as in reordering research priorities and attending to the interrelated concerns of synthesizing, translating, disseminating, and adapting social science knowledge for practice and policy purposes. In many instances, promising research agendas have foundered merely because social scientists from a sufficiently broad variety of disciplines have not been brought together on a day-to-day basis. Research on a major youth problem of interest to many observers, namely, the difficult transition from adolescence to responsible adulthood, is but one of many topics that have suffered from this kind of deficiency.[43].

An effective program to prepare youths for such a transition must be informed by many different knowledge bases. Thus, long-term projections about employment trends must be drawn from economics and from other disciplines that study human capital.[44] Sociology offers life-span studies that link adolescent and adult work experiences.[45] It can also provide an acquaintance with the family, peer group, and educational factors that shape the processes of career and status attainment.[46] Furthermore, it offers insight into how neighborhood and community contexts can strengthen or weaken parental influences.[47] And if research is to be launched in the ponderous bureaucratic structures that provide the context for much of social work practice, more than a passing acquaintance with the organizational literature would be of value. From psychology it is pertinent to gain a more sophisticated understanding of parenting skills that can prepare youths for employment.[48]

Upon whom, then, does the burden of integrating these disparate knowledge bases fall? Simply put, those who need such knowledge are most likely to bear the primary burden—and social workers are in need of the knowledge if they are to create more effective programs for youths.

Youth Research in Social Work

There are nationally recognized social work experts in such research areas as child welfare, foster care, group care of children, and family policy, but only a portion of their work focuses on youth populations. More immediately relevant to youth is social work research on such topics as correctional institutions for youths, group work intervention, and programs related primarily to delinquent behavior. Some of these studies provide survey-type statistical overviews.[49] Others emphasize post hoc comparisons of treatment effectiveness.[50] Rarely do they examine intricate longitudinal processes: nor do they lead to direct practice prescriptions. To some extent, however, these modes of research have resulted in significant policy recommendations for children and youths.

Only a portion of the better youth research by social workers finds its way into the most widely disseminated journals of the profession. Instead, it tends to be published in book form, which is sometimes a product of the broad scope of the research, or in social science journals. The latter phenomenon is of interest to the extent that it represents researchers' preconceptions about the most interested and appropriate audiences for their work or about the need to demonstrate their scholarly competencies for colleagues in related disciplines. Although this approach is frowned on in some circles, it would seem advisable for the profession's journals to encourage social work researchers to revise and adapt portions of work they have published elsewhere in an attempt to make it of direct interest to social work readers.

To gain a more accurate assessment of youth research published in social work journals, the author conducted a computer scan of journal publications concerning "adolescents," "youths," and "teenagers" that appeared during the fifteen-year period 1963–78. The journals reviewed were *Social Work, Social Casework, Social Service Review,* and *American Journal of Orthopsychiatry.* During the fifteen years, less than a score of publications appeared in the first three journals, and not all of these were research based. Nearly three times as many publications appeared in the fourth journal during the same period, but only a few of the authors were social workers. This suggests that there are few, if any, social workers who consistently publish research about youths, adolescents, or teenagers in the profession's major journals.

Where, then, does the social work practitioner seek research-based information about youths and adolescents? One possible source might be *Social Work Research and Abstracts* (formerly *Abstracts for Social Workers*). Its subject index denotes publications concerning "adolescents," "child development," "children," "delinquents," "teenagers," and "youths." Unfortunately, *Abstracts* provides no central heading for publications about youths or adolescents. The most germane classifications are those that pertain to "crime and delinquency," "schools," and "family and child welfare." Although *Abstracts* separately lists publications dealing with "aging and the aged," it is not possible for readers to readily locate under a single heading all the publications regarding youths and adolescents that have been abstracted.

Far more disturbing, however, is the fact that many of the major youth research journals are not even reviewed for *Abstracts*. Particularly glaring omissions include *Adolescence, Journal of Youth and Adolescence, Children and Youth Services Review, Youth and Society,* and *Child and Youth Services.*[51] Although a young publication, *Child and Youth Services* is the most concise and comprehensive source of abstracted research information about youths. *Social Work Research and Abstracts* should expand its review of youth research articles and include major books that might be of interest to social work practitioners and researchers.

Only a handful of youth study centers sponsor research programs that are even partially oriented toward social work interests. Among the most notable are the Center for Youth Development and Research at the University of Minnesota, the Center for the Study of Youth Development at Boys Town, Nebraska, and the Youth Studies Center at the University of Southern California. The first two organizations were headed by social workers during their formative years; the third has been more closely identified with the discipline of sociology. The Center for Youth Development and Research conducts a highly informative series of surveys, entitled the Minnesota Youth Poll, which examines youths' opinions about activities ranging from politics to work and leisure.[52] In addition, it prepares and disseminates curricula and materials concerning work with youths.[53] The Boys Town Center focuses on research concerning such topics as educational and career attainment, transition through secondary schools, life-span development, adolescent maltreatment, parental training, group rehabilitation programs for youths, and peer group integration. A separate division of the Boys Town Center disseminates research-based knowledge to selected consumer populations, including youth workers, social science professionals, research scholars, legislators, parents, and youths. Both print and audiovisual media are used for these purposes. The Youth Studies Center emphasizes research and publishes reports on delinquent behavior, peer group influence, and programs to divert youths from the juvenile justice system.

By any criterion, the activities of these centers and others represent only a minor contribution toward the creation of a scientific knowledge base about youths and their problems. Furthermore, only a portion of their work is directed specifically toward social work concerns. Unlike many organizations, however, their main research emphases are on field studies and practical social problems; also, they are especially interested in the effective dissemination of youth research.

In conjunction with her work at the Center for Youth Development and Research, Konopka has nicely summarized some of the key obstacles to normal youth development, thereby implying a potential research agenda for social work.[54] Among the basic obstacles are some highly visible social problems, such as poor nutrition, inadequate housing, poverty, and discriminatory practices. Among the obstacles to development that afflict youth in particular are the tendency of adults to treat youths in an overly subordinate fashion, thus producing a loss of self-respect; society's tendency to view adolescence as a preparatory phase in development; the prolonged economic dependence of youths; limited outlets for experimentation by youths; popular acceptance of the notion of a generation gap; confused societal values about adolescent sexuality; the dominance of youth organizations by adults; the denial of equal participation to youths, and inconsistent laws pertaining to youths. To this list one can add a number of fundamental research questions that are still subject to highly variable interpretations, such as whether a generation gap truly exists in modern society and whether youths experience a profound identity crisis during adolescence.[55] Hill raises the questions of whether adolescents typically encounter a period of *Sturm und Drang* and whether it is possible to operationalize such a conception.[56]

Even this brief overview of research on adolescence reveals several distinct trends. It is possible, therefore, to recommend how social work research can take these trends into account. However, such efforts must also be coordinated with the interrelated challenges of research dissemination and utilization.

Dissemination and Utilization of Youth Research

The dissemination and utilization of research-based knowledge constitutes two distinctly different enterprises, and each requires far more attention from social work than it has received until now. As noted earlier, a basic premise of this review is that there exists a substantial body of youth research that can be of benefit to social work so long as it is effectively disseminated and implemented. However, it is unrealistic to expect other professions or disciplines to undertake this task for social work.

The effective dissemination of research-based knowledge about youths represents an exceptionally complex challenge. Even those government agencies that are designed to expedite dissemination tend to experience difficulties in gaining access to dependable information. As Lipsitz comments,

> If the agencies created for the express purpose of gathering and reporting this information have considerable problems, then the individual "research consumer," with poorer access, is understandably frustrated. The coordination and dissemination problems invariably overwhelm the "research consumer" interested in early adolescence.[57]

In social work, the graduate schools and professional associations are the two main bodies that have resources sufficient for the effective dissemination of knowledge. However, few schools of social work offer discrete specializations or concentrations in the youth service area or in youth policy. Although many social work students engage in field practicums in youth service agencies, few educational curricula are oriented specifically toward this type of work. Furthermore, there are no social work doctoral programs with a strong focus on youth. At best, some offer individual students an opportunity to construct their own doctoral curricula within an interdisciplinary framework. However, such a capability is useful to the concerns addressed here only if youth-oriented courses are available from the social science departments of the university. Although this interdisciplinary approach may provide a superior educational experience for some students with a research interest in youths, it offers little as a coherent educational format that can be followed by large numbers of research trainees. Schools of social work have also done little to create research institutes that focus either on youth studies or on knowledge dissemination processes. Scientific knowledge in either area could play an inestimable role in training students for practice as well as for research. Schools of social work have sponsored a veritable explosion of research-oriented journals during the past decade, but none of them focuses specifically on youths or on children or families.[58]

Similarly, although the professional associations of social work have played a major role in disseminating research-based knowledge through their respective journals and conferences, the abstracting system operating under the profession's aegis can, as noted earlier, be substantially improved to facilitate the retrieval of research-based knowledge about youths and adolescents. The profession's journals have done little to encourage or publicize youth research—by sponsoring special youth research issues, for example, or by preparing joint issues with one or more youth research journals. Furthermore, the professional associations have been slow to invite research colleagues from the social sciences to participate in their conferences, although not nearly as slow as the latter have been to

invite social work researchers to their professional gatherings. One noteworthy exception is the recent addition of social work youth researchers to the Committee for Interdisciplinary Affairs of the Society for Research in Child Development.

The mere dissemination of research-based knowledge is not sufficient for meaningful implementation. In addition to communicating knowledge so that practitioners and policy experts are aware of its existence, it is important to assure that limited portions of the knowledge base can be tested on a trial basis.[59] To be maximally applicable for social work, the real-world referents of the knowledge base must be readily identifiable, accessible, and manipulable, and all this must be possible at a reasonable cost.[60] Furthermore, there must be intermittent monitoring to assure that the knowledge is actually implemented and to identify accurately those instances when implementation has been incomplete or inadequate.[61] This requires an organization that is effectively oriented toward research and quality control. Obviously, these prerequisites for knowledge utilization are not restricted to youth research; they apply to most areas of social work. Nonetheless, unless these prerequisites are satisfied, essential links in the feedback and reinforcement systems for youth researchers and practitioners are weakened, and the likelihood of adequate youth research in the future is jeopardized.

Recommendations for Youth Research

Recommendations concerning social work and youth research must address two major considerations, namely, methodological concerns and substantive research topics. Since the latter can be developed only within the limits of appropriate research design, methodology must be considered first.

Research Methodology. The review of the literature clearly indicates that the bulk of youth research is performed in experimental laboratories, is cross-sectional, and is devoid of significance for long-term predictions. There have been only a handful of longitudinal research programs with a strong emphasis on youths.[62] Most of these, such as the program sponsored by the Institute for Human Development at the University of California at Berkeley are, at best, tangentially associated with the work of research scholars at schools of social work.

In the absence of longitudinal data bases, it is impossible to comprehend the main developmental processes that antecede either normal or abnormal youth development. Furthermore, the long-term implications of variations in youth development lose meaning if they are divorced from subsequent effects on early, middle, or late adulthood. It is recommended, then, that one or more schools of social work assume major responsibility for the initiation of a longitudinal research program that examines subjects throughout their full course of life. To be of maximum predictive utility, the data base should draw on subjects from various sociodemographic circumstances. Since longitudinal research is exceptionally expensive, however, and because it calls for skilled manpower that may be scarce in social work, an effort by a consortium of disciplines seems especially advisable. Phenomena that are of special concern to social work should be included, such as peer, sibling, and parental relationships and the antecedents, correlates, and consequences of deviant or maladaptive behaviors.

Despite their immense complexity, the most fertile longitudinal studies take cog-

nizance of subjects' social surroundings. Factors such as youths' peer groups, schools, and neighborhoods and the formal organizations to which youths belong are important determinants of their behavior. As a result, to be of diagnostic and interventive value for social work, forthcoming studies of youths should increasingly examine the subjects in their natural ecological contexts.[63] This requires the exposure of social work doctoral students to research methodologies that arise primarily from sociology and ecological psychology.[64] Moreover, because a plethora of factors influence adolescent development, it is essential to design studies that are multivariate and that examine the interactive relationships among complex sets of variables. It follows, therefore, that youth researchers should be well versed in advanced statistical analysis and the use of computers for research.

It should be recalled that many studies of youth behavior, particularly those that examine the efficacy of treatment programs, have been criticized for design deficiencies. To avert such deficiencies, forthcoming youth research programs should reemphasize random assignment of subjects, control and comparison groups, baseline periods, and thorough follow-up investigations. For both practice and policy purposes, renewed efforts should also be made to examine variables that not only have content validity, but that will be of high predictive and variable potency. In addition, the operational referents of these variables must be readily identifiable and accessible and should be manipulable at a reasonable cost.

Social work researchers should design studies that are truly interdisciplinary. For at least two decades, ritualistic homage has been paid to the need for interdisciplinary research in social work. It is obvious that sound practice and policy formulation must draw on a variety of disciplines, but although seminal work of an interdisciplinary nature has evolved in certain areas, there are few instances of bona fide interdisciplinary youth research that includes social workers.[65] To foster such efforts, social work training programs at all levels should facilitate student exposure to the offerings of the various social sciences, particularly as they pertain to research-based knowledge about youths.

Substantive Research Topics. In view of the dearth of prior youth research, it could be argued justifiably that more study is needed in all areas. Nonetheless, several priorities are readily apparent for social work, and they can be set forth in a series of eight recommendations.

1. To formulate viable social policies for youths it is essential to develop an adequate data base. Therefore, it is recommended that a series of social indicators for youths be established by one or more segments of the social work profession. Such indicators have been conceptualized and created in a number of realms, but none has been devised specifically for youths or for social work. Data should be gathered on topics that bear directly on social policy and in a fashion that permits valid comparisons among different cohorts of subjects over a period of years. Information should be drawn from discrete demographic clusters, such as urban areas, rural areas, and neighborhoods of varying structure or composition. Such reference points are bound to be more useful for policy formulation than those that are based solely on broad national samples.[66]

2. To attain normal adulthood, youths must negotiate a difficult transition from adolescence. The report, *Transition to Adulthood*, prepared by the Panel on Youth identified this challenge to be one of the most critical and complex that confronts young people living in contemporary America.[67] Nevertheless, few research programs have systematically investigated how youths become responsible workers, procreators, parents, and citizens. It is recommended that social work researchers play an active role in designing transition-to-adulthood studies. The intricacies of such research are likely to require strong interdisciplinary efforts, with experts versed in educational and career attainment, life-span development, economic analysis, parent training, and so forth. Social workers should be particularly interested in orienting such studies toward meaningful practice and policy concerns.

3. The dearth of research on youths from minority groups is especially limiting for social work. With few exceptions, the available data about such youths are derived from large-scale surveys or from studies about narrowly defined topics, such as delinquent behavior, that provide few insights about subcultural processes.[68] The paucity of significant field studies about such youths is undoubtedly attributable in part to the current shortage of minority researchers in social work. Hence, in addition to increasing the emphasis on field studies of minority youths, schools of social work should make vigorous efforts to recruit minority doctoral students with research interests in youth behavior.

4. Closely related to the preceding recommendation is the need for a more sophisticated understanding of peer group influences on youths. It is assumed that, during adolescence, youngsters become increasingly susceptible to peer influence and that parental influence wanes. This is likely the case for certain forms of behavior, such as marijuana use and juvenile delinquency.[69] It evidently is not so, however, for political beliefs, educational planning, and other attitudinal

and behavioral areas.[70] It is essential, then, to learn more about the various processes of peer group influence and to compare this influence with that of parents and other reference groups. More important, it is necessary to study how peer groups can exert prosocial influences on youths. Such knowledge is essential if social work programs are to achieve greater potency and relevance for youths.

5. For many years social workers have sought to refine their techniques for changing behavior, and such efforts have included a number of programs that attempted to impart effective parenting skills to those who rear children and youths. A great many of these programs remain untested, and many have assumed the form of fads or social movements.[71] Social work researchers need to test these programs and to develop any new ones that may be necessary. In doing so, the researchers should draw extensively on the related work being done by psychologists, sociologists, educators, and others. The research must differentiate the competencies needed for various phases of the life span and identify ways to equip parents to meet each substantive challenge. This requires research characterized by greater creativity and experimental rigor than has been the case thus far.

6. Another area of youth research that requires serious attention is the creation and revitalization of service delivery programs for youths. It is well known that many of the organizations which traditionally serve youths have experienced serious declines.[72] Their programs have become rigidly institutionalized, and the constituencies that they previously served no longer need or value their ministrations. As is often the case, however, these organizations' resources permit self-perpetuation even though they no longer provide effective services. A major research effort should focus on the revitalization of such organizations.[73] At the same time, schools of social work should develop special curricula on youth services and establish working linkages with other organizations that share similar interests, such as extension units of state universities and private youth service agencies.

7. Social work researchers should play a leading role in the establishment and evaluation of a prototypical youth service corps in the United States. This would be consonant with currently emerging interests within segments of the Department of Health, Education, and Welfare, with recommendations of the Panel on Youth of the President's Science Advisory Committee, and with the innovative programs created by such organizations as the National Commission for Resources on Youth and the National Youth Alternatives Project.[74] Although substantial federal funding has already been earmarked for disadvantaged youth populations, little attention has been paid to programs that simultaneously inculcate prosocial attitudes and values, develop basic skills, permit meaningful community service, facilitate career development, and temporarily remove youths from oppressive environments. Such programs would also have the salutary effect of creating an experienced pool of potential recruitees for the helping professions. Unfortunately, the United States lags far behind many countries that already have established viable youth service programs, including England, Ireland, Keyna, the Philippines, Thailand, Ethiopia, Chile, Poland, Lebanon, and Yugoslavia.[75]

8. Related to the foregoing item is the critical need to improve research on the social service organizations that provide residential care for youths. Residential organizations have been among the most impervious to research and change.[76]

Although social work researchers such as Vinter, Sarri, Wolins, Pappenfort, Fanshel, Kahn, Kadushin, and others have performed significant studies of correctional institutions, group homes, foster homes, and related forms of residential care, the bulk of such research has been descriptive. It is now necessary to devise field experiments that demonstrate how these various forms of institutional care can be refined to benefit children and youths. Associated with this challenge is the need for researchers to develop measures of cost-effectiveness that can be useful to social service administrators and policy formulators.

The foregoing represent only a few of the possible priorities for social workers who are interested in youth research. They have been selected primarily because they address many different forms of youth problems and because they represent overarching problems and knowledge requirements for social work. Valid and reliable knowledge concerning these items might contribute to the prevention or remediation of a whole host of youth problems, such as those relating to delinquency, drug and alcohol abuse, and teenage pregnancy. Although the recommendations are oriented toward youths, adolescence constitutes only one phase of a continuous life span, and many aspects of the proposed research could apply as well to other types of populations. Many of the gaps in the knowledge of youth development also exist for other age groups.

Few of the recommendations set forth here are original. Rather, they reflect needs that have been recognized increasingly by informed observers.[77] The challenge that lies before social work rests not so much in developing awareness as in reordering priorities, providing research resources, and developing appropriate mechanisms of implementation and coordination. These concerns lead naturally to a consideration of the role of social work schools and professional associations in the dissemination and utilization of research-based knowledge about youths.

Recommendations for Dissemination and Utilization

Implicit in the foregoing discussion are a number of recommendations concerning the dissemination and utilization of youth research. For example, a comprehensive social indicator series, along with more limited regional surveys, should result in quarterly or semiannual newsletters and reports to youth service organizations. A steady flow of research-based information to such organizations not only would strengthen their service delivery, but might also lead to the creation of an identifiable network of service organizations that share a common interest in research-based knowledge about youths. The staff training officers of major youth service organizations would willingly serve as active partners in such an enterprise.

As suggested earlier, *Social Work Research and Abstracts* should designate a special section for publications about youths and adolescents, and it should regularly abstract and report on items from the major youth research journals. At least one issue of a major social work journal should be devoted to research studies concerning youths and social work; such an effort should invite contributions from allied disciplines and professions. Furthermore, the editorial boards of the major social work journals should seek additional representation from experts in research on youth and adolescence, and the next edition of the *Encyclopedia of Social Work* should devote a separate section to research on youth and adolescence. If adequate funds could be acquired, a comprehensive handbook on youth and social work would be desirable. The major professional associations should strengthen their efforts toward the synthesis and dissemination of research about youth and adolescence by designing pertinent workshops. Professional conferences should highlight the importance of the subject through keynote addresses and other means.

To enhance the utilization of available knowledge, each school of social work should offer at least one research-based course on youth development. One or two schools should also establish prototypical youth service curriculum on an experimental basis. Such courses could draw on such materials as the *Youthworker Bibliography* and on relevant work generated by various youth service organizations and extension schools.[78]

Graduate training should prepare youth workers to collect and analyze empirical data about their clients. This service-research linkage would provide a valuable data base for youth researchers and enable practitioners to assess their own work more consistently and rigorously.[79] Both researchers and practitioners would then be in a better position to carry out either formative or summative evaluations of programs.[80] Even more important, such endeavors could provide the framework for longitudinal studies of the interrelationships between social intervention and youth development. They would enable practitioners and researchers to become better acquainted with each other's needs and potential contributions. At the same time, researchers and practitioners would be able to explore many of their conceptions with one another prior to implementation.

To enhance training for youth research, social work doctoral programs should develop stronger linkages with university departments that offer relevant courses. They should also provide computer and field experiences that are essential for sophisticated research on youth and adolescents. In addition, larger numbers of minority students should be recruited to such doctoral programs.

An experimental postgraduate training program should be designed for social work dissemination specialists who wish to synthesize, translate, and popularize research-based knowledge and at the same time protect its scientific rigor and integrity. Graduates would be akin to trained science writers. Such programs could be based on collaborative efforts between schools of social work and journalism. Social work students at the master's level should be exposed to innovative courses that enable them to be effective consumers of research. Such courses should transcend elementary statistics and introduce students to the similarities, commonalities, and complementarities among the interrelated worlds of practice and research.

Social work researchers should attempt to develop working linkages with youth research and policy centers on their respective campuses and elsewhere throughout the nation.[81] These linkages can be of mutual benefit for both social workers and allied professionals. The knowledge base of youth researchers in social work would be strengthened immeasurably. In turn, social workers would sharpen the practice and policy focuses of such centers and could expedite the dissemination, utilization, and evaluation of the research findings.

Summary

This article has reviewed major problems besetting contemporary youths, including high rates of juvenile delinquency, school vandalism, teenage pregnancy, drug and alcohol abuse, prostitution, and adolescent suicide. It cites evidence indicating that many forms of maladaptive behavior in youths bear a determinate relationship to deviance in adulthood and discusses key influences that heighten the vulnerability of contemporary youths, including earlier biological maturation, prolonged adolescence, widespread family deterioration, increased influence of the peer group, rapid social change, sustained bombardment by the mass media, and continuous exposure to threats of industrial pollution and ecological disaster.

The article discusses recent patterns of federal funding for research on youths and adolescents and cites data indicating that the existing research about youths is highly limited both quantitatively and qualitatively. Compounding this deficiency is the likelihood that few social work practitioners and policymakers are aware of the research on youth that does exist. Much research-based knowledge about youths, moreover, is in a form that does not lend itself to ready utilization or implementation by social workers.

The vast bulk of youth research is characterized by critical deficiencies. Paramount among these are (1) the inadequacy of the measurement instruments, (2) the naive use of multiple-variable assessments, (3) the inadequate taxonomies for describing youth behavior and the socioenvironmental factors that influence it, and (4) the use of concepts and referents that are difficult to apply in youth work. Furthermore, much youth research is characterized by an excessive emphasis on laboratory studies that are of little direct value for policy formulation or practice.

Most field studies about youths are nonexperimental. They tend to neglect random assignment of subjects, baseline periods, and the use of nontreatment control groups. There are few longitudinal studies of youths and few investigations with either a life-span orientation or an ecological perspective. Also, many social workers who are engaged in youth research publish their most scholarly contributions in journals that seldom are read by social work practitioners. A brief survey reveals that few social workers consistently publish reports of youth research in the profession's leading journals. Likewise, *Social Work Research and Abstracts* does little to meet the needs of social workers who are concerned about youths: it provides no major classificatory designation for studies about youths or adolescents, and it omits reviews of studies published in most of the leading youth research journals. Consequently, the article sets forth three general sets of recommendations about youth research in social work. These pertain, respectively, to the methodology of youth research, the substantive focuses of youth research, and the dissemination and utilization of youth research.

The article suggests the following measures to strengthen the methodology of social work research on youth:

1. One or more schools of social work should establish a major longitudinal research program about youths.

2. The research should be characterized by strong ecological and life-span orientations.

3. It should examine key sociodemographic determinants of youth development and should focus on phenomena that are of special concern to social workers, such as relationships with peers, teachers, and parents or, similarly, the antecedents, correlates, and consequences of maladaptive youth behaviors.

4. Bona fide interdisciplinary studies should examine youths in their natural ecological contexts, such as schools, peer groups, and the family, rather than in experimental laboratories.

5. Such studies should introduce appropriate forms of random assignment,

baseline periods, control and comparison groups, and follow-up investigations.

6. Forthcoming youth research should be based increasingly on informed multivariate and interactive analyses.

7. Researchers should examine variables that are characterized by high predictive and variable potency.

8. The referent features of such variables should be identifiable, accessible, and manipulable at a reasonable cost.

The article suggests substantive topics for social work research about youths:

1. Practitioners and policymakers need research-based social indicators for youths.

2. Related investigations should focus on the transition of youths to adulthood and on the circumstances and developmental needs of minority youths.

3. The processes of peer-group influence should be examined, including the potentiality for peers to exert positive and prosocial influences on one another.

4. Investigators should examine the efficacy of intervention programs for troubled youths, the functioning of youth service and child care institutions, the formation and revitalization of youth service organizations, and the designs and evaluation of a prototypical youth service corps.

Such research emphases necessarily require certain alterations in the recruitment and training of social work researchers and in the construction of interdisciplinary research teams. To accommodate a renewed emphasis on youth research, the social work profession will need to reorder certain of its priorities, reallocate research resources, and design better mechanisms for the coordination of research and the dissemination of knowledge.

Social workers also must synthesize, translate, disseminate, and adapt social science knowledge about youths. Youth researchers from allied professions should be regular participants at social work conferences, and they should be welcome contributors to the profession's journals. Social work researchers should be encouraged to revise and refine their work so that it will be more useful to youth workers in the field. Social work journals should sponsor or cosponsor special issues about youths. Similarly, the editors of *Social Work Research and Abstracts* should consider the advisability of creating a separate section for abstracts of youth research and, more important, of reviewing major youth research journals that have been neglected thus far. Analogous matters should be considered by the editors of the Encyclopedia of Social Work.

The article also recommends that schools of social work strive to enhance the dissemination and utilization of youth-based research. To the extent possible, they should create institutes of applied youth research and design curriculums on research-based youth work. Furthermore, they should establish a prototypical training program for professionals who are interested in synthesizing, translating, and disseminating youth research for social work practitioners and policymakers.

NOTES AND REFERENCES

1. *See*, for example, Scott Briar, "Effective Social Work Intervention in Direct Practice: Implications for Education," in Briar et al., eds., *Facing the Challenge* (New York: Council on Social Work Education, 1973), pp. 17–30; Briar and Henry Miller, *Problems and Issues in Social Casework* (New York: Columbia University Press, 1971); and Arnold Gurin and David Williams, "Social Work Education," in Everet C. Hughes et al., eds., *Evaluation for the Professions of Medicine, Law, Theology, and Social Welfare* (New York: McGraw-Hill Book Co., 1973), pp. 201–248; and Carol H. Meyers, *Social Work Practice: A*

Response to the Urban Crisis (New York: Free Press, 1970). *See also* Edwin J. Thomas, "Social Casework and Social Group Work: The Behavioral Modification Approach," pp. 1309–1321, Emanuel Tropp, "Social Group Work: The Developmental Approach," pp. 1321–1328, William Schwartz, "Social Group Work: The Interactionist Approach," pp. 1328–1338, and Paul H. Glasser and Charles D. Garvin, "Social Group Work: The Organizational and Environmental Approach," pp. 1338–1350, *Encyclopedia of Social Work*, Vol. 2 (Washington, D.C.: National Association of Social Workers, 1977).

2. Catherine P. Papell, "Youth Service Agencies," *Encyclopedia of Social Work*, pp. 1598–1608; and William Schwartz, "Neighborhood Centers and Group Work," in Henry S. Maas, ed., *Research in the Social Services: A Five-Year Review* (New York: National Association of Social Workers, 1971), pp. 130–191.

3. *See* Joan Lipsitz, *Growing Up Forgotten* (Lexington, Mass.: D.C. Heath & Co., 1976), pp. 3–55.

4. Gisela Konopka, "Requirements for Health Development of Adolescent Youth" (St. Paul, Minn.: Center for Youth Development and Research, May 1973). (Mimeographed.)

5. *See* Miriam McClosky, *Youth into Adult: Nine Selected Youth Programs* (New York: National Commission on Resources for Youth, 1974).

6. United States Senate Committee on the Judiciary Juvenile Delinquency Subcommittee, *School Violence and Vandalism: The Nature, Extent, and Cost of Violence and Vandalism in Our Nation's Schools: Hearings, April 16 and June 19, 1975* (Washington, D.C.: U.S. Government Printing Office, 1976).

7. Saleem Shah, "Juvenile Delinquency: A National Perspective," in J. L. Khanna, ed., *New Treatment Approaches to Juvenile Delinquency* (Springfield, Ill.: Charles C Thomas, Publisher, 1975), pp. 3–23.

8. Jay R. Williams and Martin Gold, "From Delinquent Behavior to Official Delinquency," *Social Problems*, 20 (Fall 1972), pp. 209–229; A. L. Paddock, *Incidence and Types of Delinquency of Middle-Class Youth: The Effect of Selected Sociocultural, Socialization,* *and Personality Factors* (Ann Arbor, Mich.: University Microfilm, 1975); and Arnold Caplan and Michel LeBlanc, "Measuring Delinquency: The Homogenous-Heterogeneous Issue" (Montreal, Quebec, Canada: Université de Montreal Groupe de Recherche sur L'Adaptation Juvenile, 1976). (Mimeographed.)

9. Marvin E. Wolfgang, Robert M. Figlio, and Thorsten Sellin, *Delinquency in a Birth Cohort* (Chicago: University of Chicago Press, 1972), pp. 244–255.

10. D. Farrington and D. West, "A Comparison between Early Delinquents and Young Aggressives," *British Journal of Criminology*, 11 (October 1971), pp. 341–358; Dorothy P. Cantwell, "Hyperactivity and Antisocial Behavior," *Journal of Child Psychiatry*, 17 (Spring 1978), pp. 252–262; Daniel Koenigsburg, David Balla, and Dorothy Lewis, "Juvenile Delinquency, Adult Criminality, and Adult Psychiatric Treatment: An Epidemiological Study," *Child Psychiatry and Human Development*, 7 (Spring 1977), pp. 141–146; Charles E. Goshen, *Society and the Youthful Offender* (Springfield, Ill.: Charles C Thomas, Publisher, 1974); Lee N. Robins, *Deviant Children Grown Up* (Baltimore: Williams and Wilkins, 1966), and "Antisocial Behavior Disturbances of Childhood: Prevalence, Prognosis and Prospects," in Elwyn J. Anthony and Cyrille Koupernik, eds., *The Child in His Family: Children at Psychiatric Risk* (New York: John Wiley & Sons, 1974), pp. 447–460.

11. Robert J. Rubel, "Analysis and Critique of H.E.W.'s Safe School Study Report to the Congress," *Crime and Delinquency*, 24 (July 1978), pp. 257–265.

12. Ibid.

13. Thomas F. A. Plaut, "Addiction: Alcohol," *Encyclopedia of Social Work*, pp. 22–30.

14. *See also* Marion L. Radosevich et al., "The Sociology of Adolescent Drug and Drinking Behavior: A Review of the State of the Field," *Working Papers of the Boys Town Center for the Study of Youth Development*, 2 (June 1978), pp. 1–62.

15. Lloyd Johnston and Jerald G. Bachman, *Monitoring the Future: A Research and Reporting Series on the Drug Use and Lifestyles of American Youth* (Ann Arbor, Mich: Institute for Social Research, 1974).

16. Frank R. Furstenberg, Jr., *Unplanned Parenthood: The Social Consequences of Teenage Childbearing* (New York: Free Press, 1976).

17. *Request for Proposals: Youth Policy Studies* (Washington, D.C. National Institute of Education, 1978), p. 2.

18. Kathy A. Moore et al., *The Consequences of Early Childbearing: An Analysis of Selected Parental Outcomes Using Results from the National Longitudinal Survey of Young Women* (Washington, D.C.: Urban Institute, 1977).

19. On teenage violence within the family, *see* Lawrence Adelson, "The Battering Child," *Journal of the American Medical Association*, 222 (1972), pp. 159–161; Robert L. Jenkins et al., "Interrupting the Family Cycle of Violence," *Journal of the Iowa Medical Society*, 60 (Spring 1970), pp. 85–89; and James M. Sorrels, "Kids Who Kill," *Crime and Delinquency*, 23 (July 1977), pp. 312–320. For discussions of suicide among adolescents, *see* Lipsitz, op. cit., pp. 138–139; and R. D. Ron et al., Adolescents Who Attempt Suicide," *Journal of Pediatrics*, 90 (Fall 1977), pp. 636–638.

20. Rubel, op. cit.

21. Papell, op. cit.; and Schwartz, "Neighborhood Centers and Group Work."

22. *See* Dennis A. Romig, *Justice for Our Children: An Examination of Juvenile Delinquent Rehabilitation Programs* (Lexington, Mass.: Lexington Books, 1978); Douglas Lipton, Robert Martinson, and Judith Wilks, *The Effectiveness of Correctional Treatment: A Survey of Treatment Evaluation Studies* (New York: Praeger Publishers, 1975); William E. Wright and Michael C. Dixon, "Community Prevention and Treatment of Juvenile Delinquency: A Review of Evaluation Studies," *Journal of Research in Crime and Delinquency*, 14 (January 1977), pp. 35–67; and Edwin M. Schur, *Radical Nonintervention: Rethinking the Delinquency Problem* (New York: Harper & Row, 1971).

23. David G. French, "The Behavioral Sciences and the Professions," *Public Health Reports*, 71 (May 1956), pp. 504–510.

24. John P. Hill, "Some Perspectives on Adolescence in American Society" (Ithaca, N.Y.: Cornell University Department of Human Development and Family Studies, 1973), p. 87. (Mimeographed.)

25. Ibid.

26. Jean Piaget, *The Moral Judgment of the Child* (New York: Free Press, 1948) and "Intellectual Evolution from Adolescence to Adulthood," *Human Development*, 15 (1972), pp. 1–12; and Erik Erikson, *Childhood and Society* (New York: W. W. Norton & Co., 1963).

27. For examples of successful theoretical refinements of general theories of development, *see* Helen E. Gruber and John J. Voneche, *The Essential Piaget* (New York: Basic Books, 1977); and Lawrence Kohlberg and Robert Kramer, "Continuities and Discontinuities in Childhood and Adult Moral Development," *Human Development*, 12 (1969), pp. 93–120. For examples of empirical research relating to facets of a general theory, *see* Morton P. Birnbaum, "Anxiety and Moral Judgment in Early Adolescence," *Journal of Genetic Psychology*, 120 (March 1972), pp. 13–26; Sholom H. Schwartz et al., "Some Personality Correlates of Conduct in Two Situations of Moral Conflict," *Journal of Personality*, 37 (March 1969), pp. 41–57; Robert L. Selman, "Taking Another Perspective: Role-Taking Development in Early Childhood," *Child Development*, 42 (December 1971), pp. 1721–1734; and Elliot Turiel, "An Experimental Test of the Sequentiality of Developmental Stages in the Child's Moral Judgments," *Journal of Personality and Social Psychology*, 3 (June 1966), pp. 611–618.

28. John A. Clausen, "American Research on the Family and Socialization," *Children Today*, 7 (March–April 1978), pp. 7–10 and 46; Orville G. Brim, "Socialization through the Life Cycle," in Orville G. Brim, Jr., and Stanton Wheeler, *Socialization After Childhood* (New York: John Wiley & Sons, 1966), pp. 1–50; and James S. Coleman, "The Ways of Socialization," *The Center Magazine*, 9 (May–June 1976), pp. 3–10.

29. *See*, for example, Ronald A. Feldman, "Social Power and Integrative Behavior in Adolescent Peer Groups," *Journal of Group Process*, 6 (1976), pp. 169–193; Feldman et al., "Prosocial and Antisocial Boys Together," *Social Work*, 18 (September 1973), pp. 26–36; Glen H. Elder, Jr., *Children of the Great Depression* (Chicago: University of Chicago Press, 1974); Ronald L. Taylor, "Psychosocial

Development among Black Children and Youth: A Reexamination," *American Journal of Orthopsychiatry*, 46 (January 1976), pp. 4–10; and Marvin B. Sussman, "The Capacity of U.S. Families in the 1970's to Provide an Appropriate Child-Rearing Environment: A Review Paper" (Cleveland, Ohio: Case Western Reserve University, Department of Sociology, June 1973) (mimeographed); and "The Family Today: Is It An Endangered Species?" *Children Today*, 7 (March–April 1978), pp. 32–37 and 45.

30. *See*, for example, Vern L. Bengtson, "Generation and Family Effects in Value Socialization," *American Sociological Review*, 40 (June 1975), pp. 358–371; Bengtson and Neal E. Cutler, "Generations and Intergenerational Relations," in Robert Binstock and Ethel Shanas, eds., *Handbook of Aging and the Social Sciences* (New York: Van Nostrand Reinhold Co., 1976), pp. 1–91; Bengtson and R. S. Laufer, "Youth, Generations, and Social Change, Part II," *Journal of Social Issues*, 30 (1974), pp. 1–205; Bengtson and Jerald M. Starr, "Contrast and Consensus: A Generational Analysis of Youth in the 1970's," in Robert J. Havighurst, ed., *Seventy-Fourth Yearbook of the National Society for the Study of Education, Part I* (Chicago: University of Chicago Press, 1975), pp. 224–266; and Orville G. Brim Jr., "Macro-Structural Influences on Child Development and the Need for Childhood Social Indicators," *American Journal of Orthopsychiatry*, 45 (July 1975), pp. 516–524.

31. Glen H. Elder, Jr., "Adolescence in the Life Cycle," in Sigmund E. Dragastin and Elder, eds., *Adolescence in the Life Cycle: Psychological Change and Social Context* (Washington, D.C.: Hemisphere Publishing Co., 1975), pp. 1–22; and Arthur R. Rowe and Charles R. Tittle, "Life Cycle Changes and Criminal Propensity," *Sociological Quarterly*, 18 (Spring 1977), pp. 223–236.

32. *See* Urie Bronfenbrenner, *Two Worlds of Childhood: U.S. and U.S.S.R.* (New York: Russell Sage Foundation, 1970); Brim, "Socialization through the Life Cycle," op. cit.; and Paul Secord and Carl W. Backman, *Problems of Social Psychology* (New York: McGraw-Hill Book Co., 1974).

33. *See* William P. Lentz, "Delinquency as a Stable Role," *Social Work*, 11 (October 1966), pp. 66–70; and Bruce Biddle, and Edwin J. Thomas, *Role Theory* (New York: McGraw-Hill Book Co., 1966).

34. Edwin J. Thomas and Ronald A. Feldman, "Concepts of Role Theory," in Thomas, ed., *Behavioral Science for Social Workers* (Glencoe, Ill.: Free Press, 1967), pp. 17–50.

35. Muriel Berkeley, *Toward Interagency Coordination: FY '77 Federal Research and Development on Adolescence* (Washington, D.C.: George Washington University Social Research Group, 1978).

36. Lipsitz, op. cit., p. xv.

37. Ibid., p. 8.

38. For a convincing demonstration that the mean age of onset for chronic criminal offenders is about 12 and that "the earlier the offender commits his first offense, the greater number of offenses he will have committed by the end of his seventeenth year," *see* Wolfgang, Figlio, and Sellin, op. cit., p. 103.

39. Hill, op. cit., p. 3.

40. Nicholas Hobbs, *Issues in the Classification of Children* (San Francisco: Jossey-Bass, 1975).

41. Schur, op. cit.

42. Ronald A. Feldman, "Legal Lexicon, Social Labeling and Juvenile Rehabilitation," *Journal of Offender Rehabilitation*, 2 (Fall 1977), pp. 19–30.

43. James S. Coleman, "The Ways of Socialization," op. cit., and *Relationships in Adolescence* (London, England: Routledge & Kegan Paul, 1974); and Panel on Youth of the President's Science Advisory Committee, *Youth: Transition to Adulthood* (Chicago: University of Chicago Press, 1974).

44. Susan E. Berryman, "Youth Unemployment and Career Education: Reasonable Expectations," *Public Policy*, 26 (Winter 1978), pp. 29–69; and Susan J. Carroll and Anthony H. Pascal, *Youth and Work: Toward a Model of Lifetime Economic Prospects* (Santa Monica, Calif.: Rand Corporation, 1969).

45. Elder, op. cit.

46. Archibald O. Haller and Charles E. Butterworth, "Peer Influences on Levels of Occupational and Educational Aspirations," *Social Forces*, 38 (May 1960), pp. 289–295; and Haller and James Woelfel, "Significant Others and Their Expectations: Concepts and Instruments to Measure Interpersonal Influ-

ence on Status Aspirations," *Rural Sociology*, 37 (December 1972), pp. 591–622.

47. Eugene Litwak and Henry J. Meyer, *School, Family, and Neighborhood* (New York: Columbia University Press, 1974).

48. Elery L. Phillips et al., "The Achievement Place Model: A Community-Based, Family-Style Behavior Modification Program for Pre-Delinquents," in J. L. Khanna, ed., *New Treatment Approaches to Juvenile Delinquency* (Springfield, Ill.: Charles C Thomas, Publisher, 1975), pp. 34–81; and Gerald R. Patterson and Gerald Brodsky, "Behavior Modification for a Child with Multiple Problem Behaviors," *Journal of Child Psychology and Psychiatry*, 7 (December 1966), pp. 277–295.

49. *See* Robert D. Vinter, George Downs, and John Hall, *Juvenile Corrections in the States: Residential Programs and Deinstitutionalization: A Preliminary Report* (Ann Arbor, Mich.: National Assessment of Juvenile Corrections, 1975); and Vinter, *Time Out: A National Study of Juvenile Correctional Programs* (Ann Arbor, Mich.: National Assessment of Juvenile Corrections, 1976).

50. Paul Lerman, *Community Treatment and Social Control* (Chicago: University of Chicago Press, 1975).

51. Less serious omissions include *Criminal Justice and Behavior; Small Group Behavior; Journal of Clinical Child Psychology; Professional Psychology; Public Policy; International Journal of Social Economics; Journal of Child Psychiatry; Child Care, Health, and Development;* and *Journal of Research in Crime and Delinquency.*

52. Diane Hedin, *Minnesota Youth Poll: Youth's Views on Work* (St. Paul, Minn.: Center for Youth Development and Research, 1977).

53. Gisela Konopka, Robert Teeter, and Frank Berdie, *Youthwork Bibliography* (St. Paul, Minn.: Center for Youth Development and Research, 1978).

54. Gisela Konopka, *Requirements for Healthy Development of Adolescent Youth* (St. Paul, Minn.: Center for Youth Development and Research, 1973).

55. For discussions of the so-called generation gap, *see* Bengston, op. cit.; and Bengston and Cutler, op. cit. For discussions of whether adolescents experience profound identity crises, *see* James C. Coleman, "Current Contradictions in Adolescent Theory," *Journal of Youth and Adolescence*, 7 (March 1978), pp. 1–11.

56. Hill, op. cit.

57. Lipsitz, op. cit., p. 61.

58. John F. Else, "Social Work Journals: Purposes and Trends," *Social Work*, 23 (July 1978), pp. 267–273.

59. Everett Rogers, *Diffusion of Innovations* (New York: Free Press, 1962).

60. Edwin J. Thomas, "Selecting Knowledge from Behavioral Science," in Thomas, ed., *Behavioral Science for Social Workers*, pp. 417–424.

61. Ronald A. Feldman and Timothy E. Caplinger, "Social Work Experience and Client Behavioral Change: A Multivariate Analysis of Process and Outcome," *Journal of Social Service Research*, 1 (Fall 1977), pp. 5–34.

62. Jerald G. Bachman et al., *Adolescence to Adulthood: Change and Stability in the Lives of Young Men* (Ann Arbor, Mich.: Institute for Social Research, 1976); and Daniel Offer, David Marcus, and Judith L. Offer, "A Longitudinal Study of Normal Adolescent Boys," *American Journal of Psychiatry*, 126 (January 1970), pp. 917–924.

63. *See,* for example, Mihaly Csikszentmihalyi, Reed Larson, and Suzanne Prescott, "The Ecology of Adolescent Activity and Experience," *Journal of Youth and Adolescence*, 6 (September 1977), pp. 281–294.

64. For discussions of research methodologies arising from sociology, *see* Clausen, op. cit.; and Laura Langbein and Allan J. Lichtman, *Ecological Inference* (Beverly Hills, Calif.: Sage Publications, 1978). For discussions of methodologies that derive from ecological psychology, *see* Paul V. Gump, "Ecological Psychology and Children," in E. Mavis Hetherington, ed., *Review of Child Development Research*, Vol. 5 (Chicago: University of Chicago Press, 1975), pp. 75–125; and Robert G. Barker and Paul Schoggen, *Qualities of Community Life: Methods of Measuring Environment and Behavior Applied to an American and English Town* (San Francisco: Jossey-Bass, 1973).

65. For an example of interdisciplinary youth research that includes social workers, *see* Ross D. Parke and Charles W. Collmer, "Child Abuse: An Interdisciplinary Analysis," in Hetherington, op. cit., pp. 509–590.

66. For discussions of the prototypical social indicator program for children and families that was initiated by the Foundation for Child Development, *see* Brim, "Macro-Structural Influences on Child Development and the Need for Childhood Social Indicators"; and Sheila B. Kamerman, *Developing a Family Impact Statement* (New York: Foundation for Child Development, 1976). For a discussion of the Foundation of Child Development's proposal for a national observatory for children and families, *see* Nicholas Zill and Orville G. Brim, *Toward a National Observatory of Child Development* (New York: Foundation for Child Development, 1977) (mimeographed). For discussions of similar proposals for monitoring nationwide youth and adolescent attitudes and behaviors and of the interest these proposals have stirred in such bodies as the United States Congress, *see Adolescence in the Year 2000: Summary Record and Conclusions* (Amsterdam, Netherlands: Jeugdprofiel 2000, 1975) (mimeographed); Eleanor E. Sheldon and Ross D. Parke, "Social Indicators," *Science*, 188 (May 1975), pp. 693–699; Parke and Diane Seidman, "Social Indicators and Social Reporting," *Annals of the American Academy of Political and Social Science*, 435 (January 1978), pp. 1–22; and Elmer B. Staats, "Social Indicators and Congressional Needs for Information," *Annals of the American Academy of Political and Social Science*, 435 (January 1978), pp. 277–285. For a description of a regional social indicator program that focuses directly on social work concerns, *see*, for example, *Minnesota Youth Poll* (St. Paul, Minn.: Center for Youth Development and Research, 1976).

67. Panel on Youth of the President's Science Advisory Committee, *Youth: Transition to Adulthood* (Chicago: University of Chicago Press, 1974).

68. For an exception to the general lack of research on youths from minority groups, *see* Taylor, op. cit.

69. Denise B. Kandel, Ronald C. Kessler, and Rebecca Z. Margulies, "Antecedents of Adolescent Initiation into Stages of Drug Use: A Developmental Analysis," *Journal of Youth and Adolescence*, 7 (March 1978), pp. 13–40; Johnston and Bachman, op. cit.; and Radosevich et al., op. cit.

70. Neal E. Cutler, "Generational Approaches to Political Socialization," *Youth and Society*, 8 (December 1976), pp. 175–202; Denise Kandel and Gerald S. Lesser, "Parental and Peer Influence on Educational Plans of Adolescents," *American Sociological Review*, 34 (April 1969), pp. 213–223.

71. Kurt W. Back, *Beyond Words: The Story of Sensitivity Training and the Encounter Movement* (New York: Russell Sage Foundation, 1972).

72. Lipsitz, op. cit.

73. *See*, for example, Feldman et al., op. cit.; Feldman et al., "Treating Delinquents in 'Traditional' Agencies," *Social Work*, 17 (September 1972), pp. 72–78; and Genevieve Burch and Carol Davis, "Status Offenders and Non-Profit Youth Service and Advocacy Organizations," *Review of Applied Urban Research*, 6 (June 1978), pp. 1–6.

74. Panel on Youth of the President's Science Advisory Committee, op. cit.; McClosky, op. cit., chaps. 1 and 3; and Lipsitz, op. cit., p. 177.

75. Department of Economic and Social Affairs, *Service by Youth: A Survey of Eight Country Experiences* (New York: United Nations, 1975); and Central Office of Information, *The Youth Service in Britain*, and John Eggleston, *Adolescence and Community: The Youth Service in Britain* (London, England: Edward Arnold Publishers, 1974 and 1976, respectively).

76. Kenneth Wooden, *Weeping in the Playtime of Others: America's Incarcerated Children* (New York: McGraw-Hill Book Co., 1976); and Vinter, Downs, and Hall, op. cit.

77. For a discussion of similarly broad questions that federal funding agencies have proposed for research on adolescent pregnancy and delinquency, *see* Sephen P. Heyneman and Arlene Harrell, *Transition to Adulthood: Subjects of Research and Development Interest to the Federal Government with Respect to Youth* (Washington, D.C.: George Washington University Social Research Group, Spring 1975) (mimeographed), pp. 19 and 20. For proposals from social scientists for broad-scale youth research, *see* Hill, op. cit.; Hill and Frans J. Monks, *Adoles-*

Social Work Research on Minorities: Impediments and Opportunities

ROBERT B. HILL

ALTHOUGH THE TREATMENT of racial minorities in social work research has improved somewhat in recent years, it still suffers from several major deficiencies. It is important to identify these deficiencies and to develop strategies that effectively overcome them. It is equally important to take advantage of the increasing opportunities for enhancing the sensitivity of social work research on minorities.

The basic impediment to effective social work research on minorities is the failure to obtain adequate involvement of social scientists and community representatives from minority groups in all stages of the research, from issue formulation to the analysis of findings. A second major flaw in such research is its uncritical acceptance of conventional notions from social service practice about widespread deficits among blacks and other minorities. A third key defect is the use of traditional methodological techniques that are not appropriate for adequately understanding racial minorities.

Unfortunately, the focus of most social work studies of minorities reflects many of the shortcomings cited by Billingsley in his classic indictment of social science research on black families a decade ago.[1] The research issues still tend to fall into a few predictable categories: a focus on negative attributes of minorities or their most disadvantaged subgroups, a greater concern with the internal constraints of minorities than with the external or institutional impediments they face, and an emphasis on how attributes of minorities deviate from those of whites. Correspondingly, fewer such studies focus on (1) positive attributes of minorities, such as their assets, resources, strengths, and self-help and coping efforts, (2) external constraints to minorities, such as institutional racism, insensitive agency policies and regulations, inflation, and a recessionary economy, and (3) comparisons of cence and Youth in Prospect (Atlantic Highlands, N.J.: Humanities Press, 1977); Urie Bronfenbrenner, "The Next Generation of Americans," paper presented at the annual meeting of the American Association of Advertising Agencies, Dorado, Puerto Rico, March 1975; Bettye M. Caldwell, "Child Development and Social Policy," unpublished speech, Center for Early Development and Education, Little Rock, Ark., 1975; Adolescence in the Year 2000; Betty J. Sowder and Jerome B. Lazar, Research Problems and Issues in the Area of Socialization (Washington, D.C.: George Washington University Social Research Group, 1972); Heyneman, Toward Interagency Coordination: FY 1975 Federal Research and Development Activities Pertaining to Adolescence (Washington, D.C.: George Washington University Social Research Group, 1975); Heyneman and William Daniels, Adolescence Research Opinion and National Youth Policy: What We Know and What We Don't Know (Washington, D.C.: U.S. Department of Health, Education & Welfare and George Washington University Social Research Group, 1976); Lipsitz, op. cit.; and Assembly of Behavioral and Social Sciences, National Research Council, Advisory Committee on Child Development, Toward a National Policy for Children and Families (Washington, D.C.: National Academy of Sciences, 1976). For one of the few agendas for youth research proposed by a social worker, see Konopka, op. cit.

78. Gisela Konopka, Robert Teeter Frank Berdie, Youthwork Bibliograph Paul, Minn.: Center for Youth Develo and Research, 1973).

79. For an example of such a se research linkage in psychology, see R H. Price and Cary Cherniss, "Training New Profession: Research as Social Ac Professional Psychology, 8 (May 1977 222–231.

80. Carol H. Weiss, Using Social Re in Public Policy Making (Lexington, M D. C. Heath & Co., 1977) and "Improvi Linkage between Social Research and Policy," in Lawrence E. Lynn, ed., K edge and Policy: The Uncertain Conn (Washington, D.C.: National Academy ences, 1978), pp. 23–81.

81. For examples of social workers' p a major role in efforts to bring knowledg the social sciences to bear on policy fo tion for children, youth, and families, Sidney Johnson, Family Impact Se (Washington, D.C.: George Washingto versity, 1978). and Kamerman, op. ci evidence of the federal government's interest in sponsoring efforts to use soci ence research on youth to help shape see Request for Proposals: Youth Studies.

subgroups within the minority community on such issues as differences in income, religious affiliation, and cultural strata.

Since the social work profession is primarily concerned with providing adequate social services to families and individuals in need, it is understandable that research in this field would be heavily oriented toward problems. It is, however, a serious error to infer that because one's target groups for services are economically or socially disadvantaged, social services and research directed toward them must be organized on the premise that such groups lack positive value orientations and vital self-help and coping capabilities.

This presumption of deficits among low-income and minority client groups is the fundamental obstacle to effective social service delivery for these groups and, correspondingly, to effective social services research on them. It is widely believed that only individuals and families who are divested of virtually all their resources, assets, and self-help opportunities deserve assistance. Individuals and families who attempt to help themselves, such as through extended family ties, are not perceived as deserving assistance. This attitude is vividly reflected in welfare regulations that require potential clients to divest themselves of their economic assets and kin resources, such as by moving away from relations. Such policies often bind clients to longer-term assistance than they would have needed had they been able to retain some of those resources. Consequently, most welfare programs today are not directed toward helping those in need of short-term assistance.[2]

Although most social services are directed to groups presumed to need long-term assistance, most individuals in need do not require long-term support. Ten-year longitudinal studies conducted by the University of Michigan reveal that the economic status of most families in need is not static, but dynamic. Such families tend to remain in poverty for much shorter periods than is commonly believed and to move above and below the poverty level at various times in their life cycles. Thus, social welfare and income maintenance programs and services should be redesigned to reflect the changing economic status of most families in need as well as the static status of membership in a minority.[3]

Unfortunately, most social work research reflects the undue emphasis of social services on groups presumed to need long-term support. Little research has been conducted on groups in need of short-term assistance or on families that move out of poverty. What resources or coping strategies have both groups used?

Similarly, little is known about families that are economically eligible to receive public assistance, but do not. For example, there are about one million black families below the official poverty level who do not receive any public assistance. Few research studies have been conducted to determine what these families are doing to cope and survive. Such investigations could reveal coping strategies that might be transferred to other families in need to reduce their dependence on welfare.[4]

In fact, social services should be specifically designed to reinforce existing assets, strengths, resources, and self-help efforts among minorities and low-income groups. Social work research, consequently, should play a major role in identifying existing strengths, assets, and resources among these groups and in evaluating the programs and services that most effectively reinforce and build on those strengths and coping efforts.

The perennial credo of the social work profession is that families need to be strengthened, but then it proceeds to stress only the weaknesses of low-income and minority families. Since the only way to overcome weakness is through strength, a strategy of strengthening families should be one that reinforces and builds on their existing strengths.

This was the primary motivation in the preparation of the National Urban League's study *The Strengths of Black Families*.[5] That study identified five strengths among black families: strong kinship bonds, strong work orientation, flexibility of family roles, strong achievement orientation, and strong religious orientation. It held that most social policies, programs, and services directed toward blacks and other low-income groups fail to enhance their quality of life because such programs are based on the false presumption of a lack of strengths, assets, resources, and self-help capabilities in such groups. Most social research on blacks uncritically accepts this presumption of deficits. What is needed is research that identifies existing resources and recommends policies, programs, and services that reinforce existing strengths.

Although most social work research on minorities still tends to give greater emphasis to internal constraints than to external impediments, there has been a significant increase in research that focuses on agency policies and regulations as barriers to effective functioning of blacks and other low-income groups. Some excellent work has been conducted in this area on a variety of issues—welfare, adoption, foster care, child abuse, and so on.[6]

There remains, however, a serious dearth of social work research focusing on the impact of the economic environment on the functioning of racial minorities and low-income groups. For example, one could hardly tell from reading studies of low-income blacks conducted in recent years that the black community is still in the throes of a severe economic recession-depression and experiencing record-level inflation. Some commentators are puzzled as to why there has been an increase in the number of poor blacks in recent years without ever acknowledging that the most severe recession since the Great Depression of the 1930s is still taking its toll on the black community. Of course, social work researchers are not expected to emphasize the impact of the economic environment on the functioning of low-income groups; that is supposed to be left to the economists. But since economists are not trained to assess the social functioning of low-income groups and minorities, it is clear that some interdisciplinary modes of investigation are vitally needed. However, high-level economic training is not needed for one to conclude that if blacks are experiencing record-level unemployment, an increase in the number of blacks in need of social and economic services should be anticipated. At the least, such an increase should not be surprising.[7]

Furthermore, with this nation experiencing record-level inflation, there is a need for more studies that focus on the coping strategies of minorities and low-income families. It is vital that such studies examine especially the coping efforts of different subgroups of minorities, such as the elderly, families headed by working and nonworking women, families with two wage earners, and so on. Such analyses should also underscore the inadequacy of many consumer budget allowances established by the government for different types of low-income families and should lead to recommendations for improving those standards.[8]

Finally, there needs to be much more research on those attributes of minorities that are intrinsic to them alone. Since these patterns may vary widely within a particular minority group, it is important not to consider all minorities as monolithic. Moreover, one may merely wish to examine in depth particular behavioral patterns within one minority group without attempting to claim that such traits are unique to that group.

For example, this author conducted an in-depth analysis of informal adoption and foster care patterns within black families.[9] The primary objective of that study was to determine how such patterns varied within black families by such variables as type of family structure, size of family, age of head of household, region of residence, and economic status. Although some selected comparative data for whites were provided, the primary thrust of that investigation was to examine variations in patterns of child-rearing among subgroups of black extended families. The fact that the literature on adoption contains little research on informal adoption patterns is partly a result of the failure to focus on behavioral patterns within groups as opposed to those across groups.

Inadequate Research Design

The research designs of many social work research studies of minorities place undue emphasis on traditional experimental designs, use insensitive data collection procedures, and underutilize valuable secondary sources of data. These deficiencies, which are not unique to research on minorities, contribute significantly to the failure of social work research to obtain accurate and reliable information on racial minorities.

Imposing Experimental Designs. Although there has been a definite shift in recent years from traditional experimental designs to quasi-experimental and nonexperimental frameworks in research on minorities and low-income groups, social work research too often continues to impose experimental designs when they are not necessary or justified. Too many social work graduate students, both minority and white, are still being forced to incorporate experimental control groups in their master's or doctoral research even when such comparisons are not appropriate to achieving the primary objectives of their studies. A common complaint of many black graduate students who wish to conduct their research with a sample consisting only of blacks is that they are informed that such studies would be deficient if they did not have a control group of whites. In addition to imposing a gratuitous obstacle in the greater inaccessibility of white study populations to most minority students, such comparisons with whites often divert these students from their primary goal—to test hypotheses regarding attitudinal and behavioral patterns among subgroups within racial minorities. Moreover, these minority students contend that white students who wish to study white populations are not told that they must incorporate control groups of blacks.

The design of a research endeavor must be appropriate for the study objectives. Tripodi, Fellin, and Meyer have developed a useful system for classifying the major types of research—experimental, quantitative-descriptive, and exploratory studies:

> Experimental studies have the primary objective of verifying research hypotheses in the quest for empirical generalizations. . . . The distinguishing features of empirical methods used in experimentation include the experimental manipulation of one or more independent variables, the use of control groups and the employment of randomization procedures to assure that the experimental and control groups can be regarded as equivalent. . . . *Field experiments* involve the manipulation of independent variables in a natural setting. . . . *Laboratory experiments* include the crea-

tion of artificial situations in which independent variables are manipulated by the experimenter. . . .

The category of quantitative-descriptive studies is similar to that of experimental studies in that both seek quantitative-descriptions among specified variables. Quantitative-descriptions are obtained through the use of measuring devices to describe relationships among variables; hence, statistical concepts such as correlation, proportions, and so forth are employed. . . . Quantitative-descriptive studies differ from experimental studies in that they do not use randomization procedures in assigning subjects to experimental and control groups. In addition, they do not employ the experimental manipulation of independent variables. . . . Accordingly, we have classified these studies into four sub-types which form a hierarchy of research objectives within the major type: hypothesis-testing studies, program evaluation studies, studies describing characteristics of populations and studies seeking to identify relations among variables.

The category of exploratory studies is distinguishable from the category of quantitative-descriptive studies in that the major purpose is to refine concepts and to articulate questions and hypotheses for subsequent investigation. . . . Accordingly, representative sampling is of less importance than is the selection of a range of cases to stimulate ideas. In addition to quantitative data, researchers may use qualitative data in narrative form which may be derived from their observations of a particular phenomenon. . . . Exploratory studies typically include a great deal of information for a single case or for a small number of cases.[10]

Tripodi, Fellin, and Meyer proceed to classify exploratory studies into three subtypes—exploratory-descriptive research, research using specific procedures, and experimental manipulation research:

The sub-type of combined exploratory-descriptive studies is intended to serve as a transition between quantitative-descriptive and exploratory studies. The primary purpose of these studies is to refine and develop concepts and hypotheses. Both quantitative and qualitative-descriptions of the phenomenon being studied are included in the research. . . .

Studies which use specific data collection procedures to develop insights and ideas typically employ devices such as content analysis in an attempt to systematize qualitative material. Comparisons are made and then hypotheses are developed. . . .

Studies which experimentally manipulate independent variables to demonstrate ideas can be regarded as clinical studies or demonstrations of social action programs. Their essential purpose is to demonstrate the plausibility of using specified treatment methods or programs to accomplish some particular goal. These studies are distinguishable from experiments in that they do not use randomization procedures or experimental and control groups. They are different from quantitative-descriptive studies in that they typically involve the study of one case with little attention devoted to the problem of external validity.[11]

Although one may differ with Tripodi, Fellin, and Meyer about their classification of specific types of research studies, they have made an invaluable contribution to the field by identifying the wide range of research endeavors and relating the purposes of the research to the methods used to accomplish those purposes. Their classification system reminds the profession that research methods may vary considerably, depending on the research goals. This reminder is especially important when one is interested in enhancing the quality of knowledge about racial minorities.

Racial minorities in the United States are numerical minorities, and much of the research literature in the field of social work has historically been directed toward the majority white population. Consequently, most of the concepts, hypotheses, and generalizations about the needs and functioning of low-income families have been largely derived from study populations of whites.

Thus, there is a vital need for exploratory studies that are designed both to develop and refine concepts and hypotheses that more adequately reflect the circumstances of racial minorities. Such studies, in which representative sampling is less important than the selection of an appropriate range of cases, could serve as the basis for stimulating subsequent quantitative-descriptive investigations to determine the extent to which empirical generalizations may be derived for much larger populations of minorities. The state of knowledge about minorities in the social sciences is so fragmentary and unreliable that social work research could make a more significant contribution to this knowledge by placing greater emphasis on quantitative-descriptive and exploratory studies than on experimental studies.

The reality is that most of the so-called experimental studies of minorities often do not adhere to the rigors of experimental designs. This is especially the case with most field experiments or studies of groups in community settings. Most so-called control groups are only comparison groups. Although it is frequently possible for investigators to manipulate key variables and modes of intervention for treatment groups, it is extremely difficult to ensure that control groups do not receive similar treatment outside the investigator's control. Such frustrations in conducting traditional experiments in natural settings have contributed to the development of several modes of innovative quasi-experimental approaches, such as the single-subject design, that appear to be capable of attaining many of the objectives of traditional experiments. Thus, the quality of social work research on minorities would be enhanced more by quasi-experimental studies than by those that attempt to adhere to the conventional experimental designs.[12]

Insensitive Methods of Data Collection. A second inadequacy in the research design of many social science studies on minorities is the use of inadequate and insensitive procedures for data collection. Many of the interview schedules, questionnaires, and other instruments designed to elicit information from minority respondents are developed with little or no input or assessment from the minority community as to their comprehensibility, potential for minimizing rapport by unintentionally offending respondents, and ability to obtain accurate and reliable information on a variety of items. This insensitivity is compounded in many studies of minorities that incorporate attitude scales or behavioral indexes from past research conducted on whites. There is no reason to assume that scales and indexes which were validated on whites measure the same concepts, such as self-esteem, powerlessness, aggression, or socioeconomic status, among minorities. An independent validation of traditional scales and indexes is rarely conducted for specific minority groups. Instead, most investigators arbitrarily assume that these time-honored instruments measure the same concepts and dimensions in everyone and use them in studies as if they had been validated for minority groups.

Since the purpose of scientific endeavor is to accumulate knowledge and to build on positive contributions of the past, it is desirable to use scales and indexes with many different groups in many different circumstances. An initial step in such inquiries, however, should be to determine the validity and reliability of such instruments for specific populations, especially among minority groups. Too often investigators assume the adequacy of such measures without empirically validating them. There is clearly a need for exploratory studies to determine the validity of widely used concepts, scales, and indexes for minority groups.

Traditional procedures of data collection often make it exceedingly difficult to build a rapport with minority respondents. An initial impediment may be the race of the interviewer. Since most low-income blacks live in communities with few or no whites, whites who visit them are perceived as outsiders or as representatives of a white institution or agency that has some control over their lives. Thus their responses to interview schedules or questionnaires more often reflect political expedience than their actual situation. Although analyses of interviewer bias have shown that it is possible for white interviewers to obtain reliable information from black respondents on a wide range of items, the validity of some of that information is questionable. In general, minority respondents are more likely to be at ease with minority interviewers than with nonminority interviewers.

This is especially the case with regard to minority groups with special language considerations, such as Hispanics. The most desirable interviewer would be one of Hispanic origin. If this is not possible, the interviewer should be bilingual. The lack of facility of white interviewers with the language of their Hispanic respondents is a major obstacle to effective data collection on those groups.

Underutilization of Secondary Data.

Another common deficiency in most social work research, not just in studies of minorities, is the failure to make adequate use of valuable secondary sources of data. Too often investigators, especially graduate students, are pressured to spend an inordinate amount of time gathering data on relatively small numbers of people and then to make broad generalizations on the basis of that data. This practice is especially common in research on minority populations.

Social researchers, especially those seeking results with wide application to vital national policy issues, should take advantage of the rich secondary sources of data available. For example, there are two longitudinal studies, both with over-representations of minorities, that have been under way for more than a decade and that contain data of particular interest to researchers in the social work field: the University of Michigan's 5,000-family panel and the Ohio State University National Longitudinal Surveys conducted by Parnes.[13] Since each of these panel surveys has repeatedly interviewed the same cohorts of individuals and families, these studies offer social researchers a rare opportunity to analyze possible causes of changes in the composition and functioning of the same families at different stages. Cross-sectional data do not permit such rigorous causal analysis. The Parnes study in particular has tracked different age cohorts over a decade— young men and women, middle-aged men and women, and persons nearing retirement.

There are numerous other secondary sources of data available for social work researchers: the U.S. Census Bureau's 1960 and 1970 public use samples and its annual Current Population Survey data; the Health Interview Surveys of the National Center for Health Statistics and the center's data tapes on divorce and marriage; the longitudinal study of the high school class of 1972 by the National Center for Educational Statistics and its assessment of educational progress; the National Institute of Education's public use sample; and especially, the national surveys on Aid to Families with Dependent Children by the National Center for Social Statistics.[14] Unfortunately, neither graduate students nor faculty in social work are making as much use of these data as they should. The overrepresentation of minorities in many of these data sources would allow social work researchers to test generalizations that could significantly contribute to the national dialogue on policy issues relating to minority groups.

Inadequate Data Analysis

Major shortcomings in social researchers' analyses of data relating to minorities are an undue focus on proportions rather than absolute numbers, an emphasis on unrepresentative rather than representative proportions, and a tendency to understate differences between minorities and nonminorities.

Focus on Proportions. The widespread practice in the social sciences of giving greater attention to proportions than to absolute numbers has contributed to many popular misconceptions about the extent of deviant attitudes and behavior among racial minorities. This error of emphasis most often arises when researchers attempt to make sweeping generalizations about differences between persons and groups in different socioeconomic and racial groups. For example, if a study revealed that 60 percent of middle-income black high school graduates went on to college compared to 30 percent of low-income black high school graduates, researchers might be inclined to conclude that more middle-income than low-income blacks go to college. However, since there are about four times more low-income than middle-income black youth, the fact is that larger numbers of low-income than middle-income black high school graduates are going to college. Middle-income blacks are going in higher proportions, not higher numbers. Merton underscored the importance of absolute numbers over proportions:

> It has been repeatedly found that the upper social and educational strata have a relatively higher proportion of "geniuses" or

"talents." But since the numbers in these strata are small, the great bulk of geniuses or talents actually come from lower social strata. From the standpoint of the society, of course, it is the absolute numbers and not the proportion coming from any given social stratum which matters.[15]

Focus on Unrepresentative Proportions. It is also common for social researchers to base broad generalizations about "typical" class or racial patterns on unrepresentative proportions. Investigators often focus on the significance of the difference between two unrepresentative proportions and interpret these minority proportions as representing the majority of a group or class. For example, research on black families invariably gives greatest attention to the differences between the proportion of female-headed families among whites (11 percent) and the proportion among blacks (35 percent). Most generalizations about the "typical" black family as matriarchal have been based on the differences between these two unrepresentative minority proportions. That husband-wife families represent the overwhelming majority of black families (since this pattern is prevalent in about two-thirds of the black families) has not prevented numerous references to the matriarchy as the typical pattern among black families. Johnson and Leslie noted this methodological deficiency in their review of research on class differences in child-rearing practices:

> The understandable tendency of many researchers in this area to stress statistically significant class differences after having generally reported the overall similarities seemingly has aided in the development of what may be unwarranted class images. We contend that this results not only from over-reliance on statistical differences without representative proportions, but from the uncritical use in secondary sources of these more interesting differences to the relative exclusion of overall similarities and the researcher's qualifying statements. . . .

The uncritical acceptance by social scientists of current conceptions of class-linked child-rearing patterns may restrict and render sterile future studies of the variations that should exist in a complex society.[16]

It is important to underscore Johnson and Leslie's observations about social researchers' tendencies to overemphasize statistical differences between unrepresentative proportions and to understate the overall similarity between representative proportions. For example, suppose a research investigation found a statistically significant difference between the proportion of white (10 percent) and black (15 percent) parents who did not aspire for their children to go to college. The most common tendency for social researchers is to emphasize the differences in aspirations between these two groups by concluding that black parents are much less likely than whites to want their children to go to college. It is rare, however, for such researchers to focus on the overall similarities in the aspirations of black and white parents by emphasizing that the overwhelming majority of both white (90 percent) and black (85 percent) parents want their children to go to college. In short, the most relevant conclusion is that white and black parents have more similarities than differences in their educational aspirations for their children.

There is also a widespread tendency in social research to equate statistical significance with practical significance. A result may be highly significant statistically, but of little practical or substantive importance. Conversely, many findings may not be statistically significant, but may have much practical significance. Tripodi cited this shortcoming as one of the abuses of research in social work:

> Statistical significance depends considerably on the size of the sample that is used to make inferences to a population. The larger the sample size, the smaller is the difference between proportions that is required for statistical significance. A difference between proportions of 10 percent for a sample size of 200 is not statistically significant on a two-tailed test at the .05 level, but the same difference between [these] proportions is statistically significant for a sample size of 2,000.
>
> Practical significance depends on the nature and seriousness of the problem being investigated, and it is not necessarily equivalent to statistical significance. There may be a relationship between the incidence of deteriorated housing conditions and lead poisoning in children, but it may not be statistically significant because of the small number of cases contained in the sample. The finding is practically significant because of the potential health hazards for children, and it should not be ignored because statistical significance has not been obtained.[17]

The key point is that researchers should not arbitrarily assume that results that are not statistically significant have no practical or social significance. For example, because of the relatively smaller size of minorities in most representative samples, a lower incidence of statistically significant results is to be expected. Yet researchers may fail to uncover important attitudinal and behavioral patterns among minority groups if they arbitrarily dismiss those findings as having little practical or social significance.

Understating Differences. At the same time that many social researchers place unwarranted emphasis on differences between minorities and whites, there is also a tendency on the part of some researchers to understate differences between minorities and whites when they do exist. This occurs most frequently when researchers are attempting to minimize racial or ethnic differences in order to reduce justification for developing special social service delivery systems, programs, or policies targeted to specific minorities. Many examples of this practice can be found in research on the elderly that is intended to minimize differences between blacks and whites.

This practice of understating or obscuring minority differences can also be found in many policy-oriented studies. Since policymakers strongly resist making allowances in their legislation, programs, and services for differences between target groups, it is common for policy analysts to present their findings for an aggregate, even when there are fundamental differences between subgroups. Many social policies, programs, and services directed to low-income groups are ineffective with minority populations because little or no consideration has been given to the special needs of this population.

Minorities have many patterns in common with whites, and they have many different features from whites. To develop effective social policies, programs, and services for minorities, both the differences and similarities should be taken into consideration.

Opportunities for Future Research

Although barriers to effective social work research on minorities are numerous, it is important to underscore the opportunities available to improve the quality of such research. During the past two decades, there have been significant advances in the social and technological fields that have special implications for improving the quality of social work research on minorities.

There has been a sharp increase in the use of research techniques by social service agencies, and, most important, the appreciation of research has significantly increased in minority communities, especially among social action and social service organizations. Consequently, the number of minority persons and groups with research skills is steadily growing in communities throughout the nation.

This growing resource of minority persons and groups with research capabilities or an appreciation of the need for research provides unlimited opportunities for collaborative research efforts between whites and minorities. It is not "white research" that is opposed by minorities, but irrelevant and exploitative research, regardless of who conducts it. Research that attempts to be responsive to the actual needs and concerns of minorities will gain acceptance.

There must also be meaningful involvement of minorities. Researchers at universities are in advantageous positions to facilitate the development of collaborative research efforts with minorities by (1) providing research training for staffs of community-based agencies, (2) setting up research advisory committees with minority representatives from community agencies, (3) assisting community agencies in setting measurable program goals and in monitoring and evaluating their progress toward those goals, and (4) recruiting minority persons to key research projects as principal investigators, project directors, support staff, or consultants.

In the technological arena, the sharp increase in computerized data banks has made innumerable data tapes and files of various magnitudes readily accessible to social researchers. Such data sources contain much more information than any investigators could ever collect on their own. Of course, the accessibility of such data files makes considerations of confidentiality and ethics of paramount importance. Nevertheless, such an extensive amount of data affords researchers unprecedented opportunities to test generalizations about minorities that until now have been accepted uncritically.

Conclusions

The following measures, therefore, can be expected to enhance the quality of social work research on minorities:

1. Involve minority social scientists and community representatives in all stages of the research.

2. Provide technical assistance and training in research and program evaluation to minority persons and social service agencies.

3. Place greater emphasis on identifying existing strengths, assets, and resources among minority groups and on identifying and evaluating those programs and services that most effectively reinforce and build on those strengths and self-help efforts.

4. Place greater emphasis on exploratory and quantitative-descriptive studies of minorities than on experimental studies.

5. Among experimental studies, place greater emphasis on quasi-experimental than conventional experimental designs.

6. Use innovative exploratory studies to validate independently for specific minority groups attitude scales and behavioral indexes that have been derived from whites.

7. Increase the use of secondary sources of data on minorities.

NOTES AND REFERENCES

1. Andrew Billingsley, *Black Families in White America* (Englewood Cliffs, N.J.: Prentice-Hall, 1968).

2. *Black Families in the 1974–75 Depression* (Washington, D.C.: National Urban League Research Department, 1975).

3. Greg J. Duncan and James N. Morgan, *Five Thousand American Families: Patterns of Economic Progress* (Ann Arbor: Institute for Social Research, University of Michigan, 1976).

4. Robert B. Hill, "The Myth of Income Cushions during the 1974–75 Depression,"
Urban League Review, 2 (Winter 1976), pp. 43–53.

5. Robert B. Hill, *The Strengths of Black Families* (New York: National Urban League, 1971).

6. *See*, for example, Frank M. Loewenberg and Ralph Dolgoff, eds., *The Practice of Social Intervention: Goals, Roles and Strategies* (Itasca, Ill.: F. E. Peacock Publishers, 1972).

7. Robert B. Hill, *The Illusion of Black Progress* (Washington, D.C.: National Urban League Research Department, 1978).

8. Robert B. Hill, *Inflation and the Black Consumer* (Washington, D.C.: National Urban League Research Department, 1974).

9. Robert B. Hill, *Informal Adoption among Black Families* (Washington, D.C.: National Urban League Research Department, 1977).

10. Tony Tripodi, Phillip Fellin, and Henry J. Meyer, *The Assessment of Social Research* (Itasca, Ill.: F. E. Peacock Publishers, 1969), pp. 21–25.

11. Ibid., pp. 25–26.

12. Donald T. Campbell and Julian C. Stanley, *Experimental and Quasi-Experimental Designs for Research* (Chicago: Rand McNally College Publishing Co., 1963).

13. Duncan and Morgan, op. cit.; and Herbert S. Parnes et al., *The Pre-Retirement Years, Dual Careers, Years for Decision, and Career Thresholds* (Columbus: Ohio State University Research Foundation, 1974, 1975, 1977, and 1977, respectively).

14. U.S. Department of Health, Education, and Welfare, National Center for Education Statistics, *Directory of Federal Agency Education Data Tapes* (Washington, D.C.: U.S. Government Printing Office, 1976).

15. Robert K. Merton, *Social Theory and Social Structure* (Glencoe, Ill.: The Free Press, 1957), p. 411.

16. Kathryn R. Johnson and Gerald R. Leslie, "Methodological Notes in Research in Child-Rearing and Social Class," *Merrill-Palmer Quarterly*, 11 (October 1965), p. 357.

17. Tony Tripodi, *Uses and Abuses of Social Research in Social Work* (New York: Columbia University Press, 1974), pp. 161–162.